What others are saying about
Releasing the Power...

Looking for a one-stop shop in the arena of spiritual gifts? You've come to the right book. Dr. Stewart has done his homework, both personally and Biblically. He's examined his own life and given a template for discovering one's spiritual giftedness.

But more importantly, he's carefully examined the Scriptures and squeezed from them every ounce of information and insight into God's gifting of His followers to do His will "on earth as it is in heaven." You'll be enriched as you journey through this book, but the purpose won't be primarily for your enrichment. It will be for the building up of God's family. For when God blesses someone, He rarely has just that someone in mind.

George McGovern
Director of the NFL ministry, Athletes in Action

What a clear presentation of the spiritual gifts Mark Stewart has given in this helpful reference book. With his pastor's heart, he encourages all believers to find and use their gifts for God's kingdom and for what God designed the church to be. You can discover your own spiritual gifts and help the body of Christ be obedient to God's command to do each of the ministries of each gift. I will make use of this book as I continue in ministry.

Ruthie Almond Wiewiora
Cru staff member since 1976, ThM (Master in Theological Studies, 2010), Asbury Theological Seminary

Mark Stewart's new edition of *Releasing the Power of Your Spiritual Gifs* is a must read by every person interested in serious discovery, study, and application of their God-given spiritual gifts.

If you are a serious spiritual gifts enquirer or would like to grow in biblical knowledge of your spiritual gifts, READ THIS BOOK. After reading, you will know your spiritual gifts and the practical application of them from a scriptural standpoint.

Dr. Mark Stewart completed his doctoral dissertation on spiritual gifts while at seminary at Fuller Theological Seminary and has taught on the subject extensively both as a pastor and at Cru. His knowledge of this subject, in my experience, is unsurpassed.

Approach this book in a posture of prayerful inquiry, and you will find your GOD-giftedness in these pages.

Michelle Williamson
Editor and Project Manager
Foundress of Saint Mary Magdalene Young Adult Ministry
and Sacramental Catechist, Teen Bible Study Leader, and
VBS Coordinator at Good Shepherd Orlando

Releasing
the Power
of Your
Spiritual
Gifts

Releasing the Power of Your **Spiritual Gifts**

Dr. Mark A. Stewart

HIGHERLIFE
PUBLISHING & MARKETING
OVIEDO, FL

Releasing the Power of Your Spiritual Gifts — Revised and Expanded

Ordering Information: Quantity sales: special discounts are available on quantity purchases by corporations, associations, and others. For details, contact the Sales Department at the address below.

HigherLife Publishing & Marketing
P.O. Box 623307
Oviedo, FL 32762
AHigherLife.com

ISBN Paperback: 978-1-954533-32-5
ISBN Ebook: 979-8-9859212-2-9

Printed in the United States

10 9 8 7 6 5 4 3 2 1

Table of Contents

Preface

How to Best Use This Book

AS YOU MOST LIKELY noticed, this is an extensive book. It is intentionally so because it answers as many questions as possible about spiritual gifts.

My recomendation to you, if it is overwhelming to read the book all the way through, is to pick a chapter or gift you are interested in and start there, then go back and read whatever else is of interest to you. This is a book designed for you to reference the rest of your life.

Update

I spent five years studying and researching spiritual gifts and reading as many books written about spiritual gifts as possible before writing this one. In this new edition, I have added even more of my research which has continued over the years.

In composing another work on spiritual gifts, one might ask, "Why another work? Isn't there enough written on spiritual gifts already?" I believe the answer is no. There needs to be more, which is why I have written this book. While the subject of spiritual gifts has been partially covered in many books, this book is more comprehensive. Within you will find:

1. The twenty-two *charisma* gifts.
2. The difference between a *doran* gift (ministry gift) and a *charisma* gift (supernaturally empowered gift).
3. A thorough examination of each of the spiritual gifts and how to develop them.
4. What a spiritual gift is like being used when filled with the Holy Spirit and what it looks like when a person is not filled with the Spirit and is operating by the flesh.
5. A look at the gifts from an impartial, balanced, biblical viewpoint.
6. Addressing as many questions as possible about spiritual gifts.
7. Discovering your primary spiritual gift.

My desire and prayer is that this work will encourage and motivate you even more to use the supernatural power available to you every time you use your spiritual gifts and fulfill the ministry God has for you. I counsel many older Christians who struggle with burnout in ministry or have lost their passion to serve the Lord. My encouragement to them is to more fully center their life on their relationship with the Lord and their spiritual gifts. That way they will always be fruitful for the Lord. They will experience that which is life-giving and not life-draining.

May God bless you as you read this!

Introduction

CHRISTIANS ARE INCREASINGLY DISCOVERING the role spiritual gifts play in their lives. The Bible teaches us that without spiritual gifts we cannot serve God most effectively. You will never reach your full potential as a Christian without knowing and using your spiritual giftedness. In using your gift, the promise of God is activated, enabling you to receive supernatural power.

A very successful pastor at a community church in Chicago, who drew between ten to twenty thousand people into his church every week, spoke at a pastor's conference which I attended. He was asked this question. "If you were to tell a pastor one thing that would help him nurture his church and be satisfied in the ministry, what would it be?" Without hesitation he responded, "Know your spiritual gift and use it!"

His answer applies to each one of us today. If you want to see more spiritual power in your life, discover and use your God-giftedness: your spiritual gifts. If you want to be more effective in your ministry, learn to use your spiritual gifts! If you want to see God use you to change lives and build up other Christians, use your spiritual gifts! If you want to know who you are and what

God's will is for your life, discovery is waiting for you as you, yes, use your spiritual gifts!

God has a wonderful adventure and plan for your life. A plan that cannot be enjoyed and experienced apart from using your spiritual gifts. As mentioned earlier, God's plan for your life always includes the tools He has given you. Spiritual gifts are designed as God's means to use you through the empowerment of His Holy Spirit. Every time you use your spiritual gifts will be life-giving to you because you will see God using you to build up the lives of others.

Every Christian should fully know and use their spiritual gifts. *In fact, I believe no Christian can reach his or her full potential until he or she understands the purpose of spiritual gifts, what his or her own gift is, how to use it, and then serves God with it.* Without aquiring knowledge of their spiritual gifts and putting it into action, that person will miss out on God's reason for creating him or her. Christians seek God's direction and guidance for their lives. Very few fully understand what their giftedness is. Once their giftedness is discovered and placed into use, however, they experience great joy in ministry. Christians who know their gifts become excited about Jesus Christ, while those who do not know their God-given gifts encounter restlessness.

Do *you* know your primary spiritual gift, and are you using it? If not, you are not fully in God's will. Because you have chosen this book to read, I assume you either have not yet discovered your gifts or, like me, have discovered some of your gifts, but believe God has more for you.

Within, you will discover all about spiritual gifts—your spiritual gifts—the supernatural power available to you, and especially how you can discover the most exciting, joyful life Christ offers. You will discover His will for your life, because His will always includes the spiritual gift or gifts that He has given you.

The purpose of this book is to help you better understand spiritual gifts: what spiritual gifts are, which ones you have, how they differ from other gifts and talents, and how to best use them in the ministry God has designed for you.

One word of caution about this book: reading it means your life may never be the same! As you apply the scriptural truths in this book, your life and ministry will change!

CHAPTER 1

The Vital Importance of Knowing and Using Your Spiritual Gifts

H ERE I WAS, SITTING in class at a well-known seminary. After spending four years at a major theological seminary and five years as an associate pastor I was now back in school. This time, with two master's degrees behind me, I was in a doctoral program. My desire now was for practical ministries education. I was at a crossroads in my life, and as most people do, I was seeking God for some answers.

It was not that I wasn't being used by God — I was. It wasn't that I hadn't committed my life to Christ — I had. And it wasn't because there was some major sin in my life preventing God from giving direction to my life. I simply was not satisfied I was being used by God to the fullest capacity. Even though I was a Christian, a sense of incompleteness in my life remained. It stemmed from my belief that I was not being all and doing all I felt God wanted me to do. The problem was I just wasn't fully sure what exactly He wanted me to be doing. If I was serving Him the way He created me to serve Him, then I would learn to be content, but at this point I wasn't.

The doctoral level course I was in at that moment covered spiritual gifts. Spiritual gifts had always ignited my heart, and this course was no exception. As I sat in my seat, my heart was again ignited, ignited back to my early college days when I first trusted Christ. It was back then that I started looking to God, searching for answers to the questions, *How can He use me?* and *What are His plans for my life?* It was back then, as a young Christian, that I first wanted to learn what particular spiritual gifts God had given to me. Now, fast-forward many years, I knew fairly clearly what my main spiritual gifts were, and I was also using many of these gifts. But here I was again, with this feeling, with this interior searching, wondering if there was more to my Christian life than I had already experienced. Little did I realize it, but sitting in that class, I would find the answer.

The professor was enthusiastic as he talked about spiritual gifts. Although I had studied extensively regarding these gifts, I never felt I had learned all I could. As we studied some of the major passages, we approached chapter 12 of Romans. Here, the professor began to explain the whole context of the first eight verses of chapter 12 as knowing God's will for your life. He pointed out, in Romans 12:1 and 2, that in order to know God's will, Paul tells us that, we must offer up our lives. "Therefore I urge you, brothers and sisters, by the mercies of God, to present your bodies as a living and holy sacrifice, acceptable to God, which is your spiritual service of worship. And do not be conformed to this world, but be transformed by the renewing of your mind, so that you may prove what the will of God is, that which is good and acceptable and perfect." However, it is verses 3 through 8 where the understanding of God's will is found because Paul points out the necessity of spiritual gifts in our lives.

For through the grace given to me I say to everyone among you not to think more highly of himself than he ought to think; but to think so as to have sound judgment, as God has allotted to each a measure of faith. For just as we have many parts in one body and all the body's parts do not have the same function, so we, who are many, are one body in Christ, and individually parts of one another. However, since we have gifts that differ according to the grace given to us, each of us is to use them properly; if prophecy, in proportion to one's faith; if service, in the act of serving; or the one who teaches, in the act of teaching; or the one who exhorts, in the work of exhortation; the one who gives, with generosity; the one who is in leadership, with diligence; the one who shows mercy, with cheerfulness.

Here in these simple eight verses were the answers I sought. The will of God for my life—and for every believer—is clearly defined in the spiritual gifts He has given us.

It was like a light went on. One of the delights of knowing the Lord are times like these. Times when suddenly life makes sense and the Word of God opens up the answers. As I listened to what these verses taught, I realized I needed to have serious discussions with the Lord. I was asking Him for direction for my life, and here in these verses was the answer to how I could find that direction.

My answer would be found in the spiritual gifts which He had given me!

The End of a Long Journey

To gain an understanding of how God's will for my life became clear, I need to go back a couple of years. I knew God had gifted me in the areas of teaching and preaching. He had given me an ability to exegete Scripture, and I loved using this giftedness to watch the Word of God change other people's lives. The main reason I entered seminary was simply to learn more about the Bible and to be able to teach it more effectively. My intent was to remain in the college campus ministry, having been on staff of Cru (Campus Crusade for Christ) for several years. While in seminary, I seriously wrestled with the idea of teaching upon graduation either in a Bible college or in another seminary.

To be able to teach Scripture to teachable hearts was a deep love of mine. But I also wrestled with the desire to make disciples and to minister to God's flock as a whole. It was while in seminary that the Lord communicated to me that serving in His local church really was the most effective way I could serve Him. Upon graduation, I sought a position as an associate pastor in a church in San Bernardino, California. My feeling was that I still needed more time to determine if I wanted to be a senior pastor, and I wanted an opportunity to raise my family without major pressures. I also wanted to develop and refine the spiritual gifts God had given me.

It was during these five years that I had much opportunity to teach Scripture, occasionally preach, as well as disciple a number of individuals. So now I was asking myself the question, *Why am I still feeling that I am not being fully used the way God wants me to be used?* The conclusion that began to surface while serving was that there were particular gifts God had given me that I was not fully utilizing. If I remained an associate pastor, it would seem that I would not be using all my gifts to their fullest potential. Again, as I was working on my doctorate, the idea of teaching full-time surfaced, and I became excited about it all over again. I knew then I needed to spend time with the Lord to sort all this out.

Although I believed I knew what my gifts were, I thought it important to take a spiritual gifts inventory test simply to confirm them, and to see if I had, by some chance, missed any of them. The gifts I knew I had for sure were the gift of encouragement, gift of leading, gift of teaching, and the gift of prophecy (preaching). I wanted to know if there were gifts I was not using.

I went home and took two different types of tests. They both confirmed the same types of giftedness. There were several additional gifts other than those I already knew I had. What was interesting was that the gift of pastor surfaced on both of these tests. At that point, I needed to do some wrestling as to what to do with this gift. I looked at all my gifts and realized I was not using all of them to the fullest. I had somewhat of an aversion to being a senior pastor. In many ways I felt that being a pastor of a church would be limiting in terms of my ministry. My leaning had been toward teaching, but I realized that if I were in a full-time teaching position, my pastoral gift really would not be used as it would in a church. It was then, as if the Holy Spirit was speaking to me saying, *"Mark, how are you going to answer to God for this gift of pastor He has given you?* I knew that I would have to answer to the Lord some day for this gift.

I began to think through the goals I had set for my life and realized I had not seriously considered being a senior pastor. When a person comes to the realization that the goals he or she had set might not actually be God's goals for him or her, there follows a time of wrestling of who is in control. I eventually had to come to the point of saying, "All right God, I'm willing to lay aside my desires and go into the senior pastorate to spend full -time pastoring a church." At that point my heart was completely at peace. I realized that if I were a senior pastor, all the gifts God had given me would be in an environment in which they could be fully utilized. I went home rejoicing and told my wife, Jan. I had a new sense of destiny and direction for my life. It was not long before I heard from a church that needed a senior pastor, and through God's leading and direction, I finally ended up pastoring as a senior pastor.

When I became a Senior Pastor, I was able to use all my spiritual gifts. It was extremely satisfying. I knew I was being used by to maximum by God. When it became time to retire as a pastor (I was still young), I began other ministries but I made sure it enabled me to continue to use all my spiritual gifts. *I wake up every day knowing my job description because using my spiritual gifts is my job no matter what my occupation is!*

God is always free to change the direction of our lives. But one thing is for sure, He will always lead us to a place where we can use our gifts to the greatest degree!

Same Situation, Different Gifts and Responses

An illustration that might help you understand how gifts work and how people might respond to a situation based upon their particular gift follows. [1] As you read it the reason you respond to situations in a certain way might become clearer. You will also begin to understand why others respond as they do.

Imagine a large dinner party at Mary's house. The table is full with over twenty guests. Dinner is over, and Mary is in the kitchen preparing the dessert. She is finally finished and walks though the door carrying a large tray of little dishes of ice cream with toppings and whipped cream. Before she gets to the table, her arms give way and all the dessert crashes to the floor.

Here is how those with particular gifts might respond.

- *The one with the gift of **knowledge** would say: "That tray was way too heavy for her."*
- *The one with the gift of **helps** would say: "Mary, let me help you!"*
- *The one with the gift of **leadership** would say: "Let's all start to clean up!"*
- *The one with the gift of **administration** would say: "John, you pick up the glass. Bruce, go get a mop. Ellen, maybe you can get some rags…."*
- *The one with the gift of **service** would get up from the table and start moving chairs out of the way and cleaning up.*
- *The one with the gift of **wisdom** would say: "We all need to learn from this to ask help from others when the task is too big for us."*
- *The one with the gift of **teaching** would say: "We need to give thanks in situations like this. Remember, all things work together for good."*
- *The one with the gift of **evangelism** would say: "Our reaction to all this is a testimony to others as to how real Christ is in us."*
- *The one with the gift of **pastor** would say: "It is good that we all experienced this together. We can all grow from this whole incident."*

- *The one with the gift of **encouragement** would say: "Mary, that's OK. We all have done that. It is no big deal. We didn't need dessert anyway after that fantastic meal."*
- *The one with the gift of **prophecy** would say: "Everybody, we should have seen that she needed help sooner and gotten up to help her when she was in the kitchen."*
- *The one with the gift of **mercy** would say: "Mary, are you hurt? Let me give you a hug."*
- *The one with the gift of **discernment** would say: "Satan is trying to ruin this wonderful time. Let's not let him ruin it for us."*
- *The one with the gift of **faith** would say: "God has something better for us than even this great dessert."*
- *The one with the gift of **giving** would say: "What if I take everyone out for dessert or run to the store for another?"*
- *Mary, who has the gift of **hospitality**, would say: "Oh please, don't bother. I'll take care of it. You all just enjoy yourselves. I'll join you in a moment."*

As you can see, our giftedness causes us to perceive and respond to situations differently. Is one better than the other? Not necessarily. However, as you can see in this illustration, certain gifts are far better in particular situations than others. That is why different people have different gifts. Varied gifts ensure the most important need can be met for ministry to others.

Please note: If you would like to know your spiritual gifts right now, it is free on an app I produced for Apple and Google. Go to your app store and search for: *Spiritual Gifts* by Mark Stewart.[2]

Spiritual Gifts and the Local Church

Pastor John McArthur of Grace Community Church says, "No local congregation will be what it should be, what Jesus prayed that it should be, what the Holy Spirit gifted it and empowered it to be, until it understands the spiritual gifts."[3]

Leslie B. Flynn says, "Practice of the Biblical doctrine of gifts untaps reservoirs of godly manpower, thaws out frozen assets, roots out unemployment among saints, reflects the universal priesthood of believers, and edifies the church."[4]

Are spiritual gifts important in the local church? Absolutely. Spiritual gifts are the lifeblood by which the church functions. The church is made up of people using their spiritual gifts by listening to their Master to learn how best to use these gifts, and then by working together to build the church of Jesus Christ. For every church to be what God wants it to be, the people within the church must be all God wants them to be. That is why it is important that, first, each individual understands his or her spiritual gifts and how to use them with God's supernatural power. And second, that every church knows how to capitalize on the gifted individuals God has given to them. Ephesians 4:11 explicitly points out that God has given gifted individuals to the local church to build up the body of Christ. He knows what each church needs in each community in order to reach that community for Christ and build disciples and has equipped each church with gifted individuals. If particular gifts are absent in the church, we are told in 1 Corinthians 12:31 to pray and ask God for these gifted individuals.

Each Person and Their Local Church

I once read an analogy by David Hubbard, President of Fuller Seminary, that helped explain God's view of the spiritual gifts He has given us.[5] I want to elaborate on this. Imagine it is Christmas time and you are given a beautiful silver-wrapped gift. It is one of the most beautiful gifts you have ever seen. It is shiny with bright ribbons and an elaborate, perfect bow rests on top. You care a great deal about the friend who gave it to you. With great care, you place that gift underneath the tree waiting for Christmas to come, and every day as you walk by the room, you see that absolutely gorgeous gift and reflect on how nice it looks. Finally Christmas arrives, but as you look at that gift and again appreciate how beautifully wrapped it is, you think, *It would be a shame to ruin it by tearing open the box.* So you simply leave it wrapped up.

Would you ever do that? Of course not.

What is the purpose of a gift? A gift is to open and enjoy! God has given each Christian this wonderful spiritual gift, to enjoy, to explore, and to use, but some never open it up to discover what is inside.

When a new person walks into a church, all the members, including the pastor and staff, should look at that person as an unwrapped present waiting to be discovered and used. It should cause great excitement to realize another gifted individual has been given by God to the local body of Christ. The last thing that should happen to any person in the church is to be ignored.

Let me ask you, have you discovered, and are you fully enjoying, the spiritual gifts God has given you? If not, you are now on your way to fully unwrapping these gifts so you can begin using it the way the Giver intended. It will bring you incredible joy!

The Individual and the Local Body of Christ

Scriptural exegesis on the key passages relating to spiritual gifts will come, but one thing needs to be pointed out now. According to 1 Corinthians 14 and Ephesians 4, the main purpose of spiritual gifts is to build up the body of Christ. Does this mean we are not edified or built up as we use our gifts? No. Of course we will be. But we should remember that the gifts God has given to us are also for others. The fact that we receive benefit, grace, and blessing as a result is simply a matter of God's grace.

Why Is So Little Priority Placed on Spiritual Gifts in the Local Church Today?

Although there is a stronger movement today than ever before to emphasize spiritual gifts in churches, there are still few churches today utilizing them. There are several reasons for this.

To begin, the senior pastor may not fully understand his own giftedness and how gifts are used. Because of this, emphasizing spiritual gifts will not be a priority for him. I am convinced that any senior pastor who fully understands and is using his own giftedness will make it a priority to see that everyone in the congregation is also using his or her gifts.

Another reason spiritual gifts may not be a priority is because there is not enough understanding of what the Bible says about gifts. Because gifts are sometimes controversial, many pastors may want to avoid them so as not to create a controversy in the local church. However, Christ said in John 8:32, "You shall know the truth, and the truth will set you free." As a church discovers the biblical truth about spiritual gifts, it will be set completely free!

Too, Satan is avidly opposed to any church using its gifts because he knows that church will grow and have a serious impact for the kingdom of God. Therefore, he will try his best to keep spiritual gifts from being taught or emphasized in the church. Or if they are taught, he will try to bring some type of heresy into the church so as to destroy the effectiveness of spiritual gifts. If he can get a church or people on a tangent, away from the priority of Jesus Christ, then he has succeeded. Like any overemphasis, spiritual gifts, too, can become a tool by which Satan can confuse or misdirect a church.

Often times the local pastor is so overwhelmed with all the other various ministries of the church, that to oversee a gift-based church ministry is simply too much. There are so many other needs and pressures that seem to take precedence over this. Unfortunately, what the pastor doesn't realize is that this is exactly how God has chosen to free him and the church up. The intention is to get the ministry into the hands of the people. This truth is given to us in Ephesians 4:11–12 which states that the gifted individuals will equip the body to do the work of the ministry, not do the work themselves. The role of the pastor-teacher is not to do the work of the ministry, but to equip others to do the work.

> **"And He gave some as apostles, and some as prophets, and some as evangelists, and some as pastors and teachers, for the equipping of the saints for the work of service, to the building up of the body of Christ"** (Eph. 4:11–12).

All it takes is one person excited about his or her spiritual gift-edness, and that excitement will be contagious to others. Watch what happens to a church that begins giving the attention needed in teaching, leading, and directing the use of spiritual gifts. The church will grow, and the enthusiasm will increase. One thing I can assure you is this: once you finish reading this book and begin to apply its principles, you will never be the same. Your life will be changed in a dramatic way. You will love life, love serving Jesus Christ more than ever before. You will have a new sense of destiny and purpose for your life. Any confusion about God's will for your life will begin to fade away.

As you begin to use your spiritual gifts, you will find out that three things happen. First, you will benefit as you learn what God's will is for your life and how you can be better used by Him. Secondly, the kingdom of God will benefit. Your local church and the body of Christ will grow in their relationship with Christ as you use your gifts. And thirdly, Jesus Christ will glorify Himself through you using your gifts. The purpose of His creating gifts, and creating all things, is that He might be glorified. Is it worth it? Absolutely.

CHAPTER 2

Different Types of Gifts

I S WORKING WITH SMALL children a gift or a ministry? Is hospitality a gift or a ministry? Is the ability to sing or play a musical instrument a spiritual gift or talent? Or could it be a ministry? These questions are very significant. Does the Bible clarify these types of questions? Yes, it does!

The *Doron* Gift

Although, in the English language, there is only one major word for the word "gift," the Greek language has at least four that distinguish between spiritual gifts given only to Christians, and gifts given to people in general, whether or not they are Christians.

The normal, everyday word for "gift" in Greek is *doron, dorea,* and *doma.* I call these the "D" gifts because they all begin with "d." The word for the "supernatural gifts" God gives only to His children is "charisma." It is important in our study of spiritual gifts to understand the distinction between these different words. The main difference between *doron* and charisma is that with *doron,* the emphasis is on the gift and the free nature of the gift. With charisma gift, the emphasis is on the giver and the graciousness of the giver in giving the gift. In this case, the giver is God, and He is giving simply out of His grace.

As we will see ever more clearly, this distinction helps us understand that a person who is gifted in music, a star athlete or a whiz in math, does have a gift from God as a talent or skill, but it is not the supernatural charisma gift. It is a *doron* gift, which God gives to people simply out of His storehouse of blessing. As Christ said in Matthew 5:45, God "causes His sun to rise on the evil and the good, and sends rain on the righteous and the unrighteous." The sun and rain truly are wonderful gifts! But these are given to everyone. This is considered a *doron* gift. The skills and talents God gives to people are not conditional upon their spiritual state in life. These gifts can be used for the glory of God or the person's personal glory. The choice is up to them. Oftentimes in this case, the people notice the gift or talent more than the person or the source of the gift. This is especially true with highly-gifted athletes or musicians.

The first word in the Bible used for a generalized giving of a gift is *doron*. The other words derived from this word are *dorea* and *doma*. All three of these words have similar meanings with only slight variances. Again, the emphasis and focus is the gift more than the giver. *Doron* is used nineteen times in the New Testament, *dorea* is used fourteen, and *doma* four. What is fascinating is that the root word for these is the word *didomi*, which means "to give," in Greek and the word *dorean*, which means "freely, without cause or reason."[6] This makes sense in that any gift given that is not free or has conditions attached to it is not a gift. It becomes something earned, and the Bible calls that a wage.

The word used when one person gives a gift to another person is *doma* and is found in Matthew 7:11: "If you then, being evil, know how to give good gifts [*doma*] to your children, how much more will your Father who is in heaven give what is good to those who ask Him!"

The next word, *doron*, is used primarily for the gifts man gives to God. It is used this way seventeen of the nineteen times it is found in the New Testament. This is the word used for the gifts the Magi gave to Christ in Matthew 2:11 and for the gifts a person brings to God at the altar: "Therefore, if you are offering your gift at the altar…." This Scripture found in Matthew 5:23 is referring to gifts given to God by His children.

The last word, *dorea*, is used solely in reference to God's gift of salvation to mankind. Salvation is called the "gift [*dorea*] of God" (John 4:10). His gift of salvation and the gift of His Holy Spirit are all free gifts to the whole world but only those who believe receive this gift. This points out God's heart for everyone in the world! This gift of salvation is truly a free gift of God. It cannot be earned. It is a gift available to all of mankind without partiality or reservation.

The "Charisma" Gift

There is a particular supernatural gift, however, given only to God's children. It is a special privilege reserved only for His own. That gift is called a spiritual gift, or charisma. This gift is not available to unbelievers. It is a supernatural gift God has held out to give only to those who believe in Christ. This word is familiar to us because of the English word "charisma" and "charismatic." The use of the word "charismatic" means the emphasis is on the gift. However, the root word in Greek is *charis*, which means "grace." This gives us a clearer understanding of the word charisma (gift), in that it is a gift of God out of His grace, or a "grace gift." This kind of gift can only be given by God. One human being cannot give this gift to another. They can only give a *doron* gift. The reason for this is because a supernatural aspect accompanies this grace that God gives only to believers. In other words, God's power accompanies this gift to accomplish His purpose. The other gifts God gives to people do not necessarily have His power accompanying them.

The word "charisma" is found primarily in the New Testament. It is not even in the Septuagint (the Greek version of the Old Testament). It seems God had been holding this special gift only for New Testament believers, and it is to be an extension of His power through us today. Charisma is a very special word. It is referred to three times as "God's grace" in terms of the gift of salvation and eternal life. All the other times it is used to reference a supernatural spiritual gift or the implementation of this gift.

An interesting contrast is seen in the gift of salvation. Salvation is called both a *dorea* gift (Rom. 5:16–17) and a charisma gift (Rom. 6:23). As a *dorea* gift it means it is available to all people, but as a charisma gift, it will only be experienced and enjoyed by Christians.

When the spiritual gifts are talked about in terms of the body of Christ, it is always in reference to those gifts being used. In other words, we need to use our gifts. Paul exhorted Timothy in 1 Timothy 4:14 not to neglect the spiritual gift that was in him. He was to be sure to use it. He is told in 2 Timothy 1:6 to stir it up, to kindle it, to use it even more! Peter tells us in 1 Peter 4:10–11 to be sure to be good stewards of our gifts (charisma). The point being that God gave spiritual gifts to His children primarily so they would be used in the body of Christ.

All of this is outlined in reference to the gifts found in 1 Corinthians 12 and 14 and Ephesians 4. It clearly states that the purpose of gifts is not for our own edification, but for the building up of the body of Christ. It says in Ephesians 4:12–13 that the reason God has given gifted individuals to the church is to "equip the saints for the work of ministry, for building up of the body of Christ, until we all attain to the unity of the faith" (ESV).

How then should a spiritual gift be defined? I have many definitions, all of them similar, but with slight differences. As I have studied Scripture, the definition I feel best defines it is this:

> A spiritual gift is a supernaturally empowered ability given by God to each individual Christian for the building up of the Body of Christ and the furthering of the kingdom of God. When it is used, the supernatural power of God works through the person and the gift.

Notice a spiritual gift is a free gift given only to God's children and that His supernatural power accompanies this gift. You will experience this power as you use your spiritual gift; you will sense God's power at work through you. You will be overjoyed to discover this really does happen as God uses you in miraculous ways!

Notice too the purpose of these gifts. The gifts are not given to build ourselves up, although we definitely will be blessed and will grow spiritually as a result of using our gifts, they are to build up others and to further God's kingdom. **God will release His power through you every time you use your spiritual gift!**

CHAPTER 3

The Twenty-Two Spiritual (Charisma) Gifts

T HERE IS MUCH DISCUSSION today regarding the number of God-given spiritual gifts. Some believe there is an unlimited number of gifts and that the New Testament does not include them all. Others believe the New Testament includes some but not all; still others say the New Testament includes all the gifts, that no others exist. Because of the unique nature of the word charisma, and the distinction between the two types of gifts in the New Testament, it is always best to adhere strictly to what the Bible teaches.

If the view is taken that more gifts exist than those mentioned in the New Testament, there is no basis for determining which spiritual gift a person has. In this view, someone could say he has a spiritual gift, and who could argue with him? If someone says, I have the spiritual gift of "carpentry" or "perception" or "counseling," on what basis would we be able to say, "No, you don't"? A person would have no guidance or protection in using that so-called gift. I believe the Bible teaches clearly that all God-given spiritual gifts are listed. If the Bible does not call it a spiritual gift, then I think we should not call it a gift. If the Bible calls it a charisma gift, we need to consider it a spiritual gift. I believe what many people today consider spiritual gifts are, in actuality, ministries where spiritual gifts are exercised.

I don't believe the Bible restricts how gifts can be used. We will discover in 1 Corinthians 12 that there are a variety of gifts (and I believe these are all listed in the New Testament) and a variety of ministries. There is no listing of the different types of ministries anywhere, and I believe God leaves that up to each individual and their own personal calling and walk with Him. He states as well, that there are different effects, meaning different fruits (or results) from the use of the same gift will result, even in the same ministries.

The gifts defined as charisma gifts, I believe are spiritual gifts. The gifts considered *doron* gifts are not spiritual gifts but are ministries.

How many gifts, then, are attached to the word charisma? There are twenty-two. In addition to the spiritual gifts, there are five offices of spiritually gifted leaders of the church today: apostles, prophets, evangelists, pastor-teachers, teachers, elders and deacons. The office of apostle and prophet no longer exist (thought the ministries do). We will look at these offices and the difference between gifted people and spiritual gifts later on. There are five primary passages in which spiritual gifts are listed: 1 Peter 4:10–11, Romans 12, 1 Corinthians 12, Ephesians 4, and 1 Corinthians 7. Let's look at these passages and discover what the gifts are.

It's important to look at 1 Peter 4:10–11 first because Peter categorizes these gifts. He states:

"Each of you should use whatever gift you have
received to serve others, as faithful stewards of God's
grace in its various forms. If anyone <u>speaks</u>, they
should do so as one who speaks the very words of
God. If anyone <u>serves</u>, they should do so with the
strength God provides, so that in all things God
may be praised through Jesus Christ. To Him be the
glory and the power for ever and ever. Amen" (NIV
emphasis mine).

Peter identifies two categories of gifts: the serving gifts and the
speaking gifts. I believe each believer is given primarily a serving gift or a speaking gift. In other words, his or her primary gift
will be in the area of serving or in the area of speaking. This does
not mean the person who has serving gifts does not also have
speaking gifts, nor does it mean that a person who has speaking
gifts does not also have some serving gifts. It does mean that the
major emphasis of his or her ministry will be either in the area
of serving or speaking.

Although Peter does not mention specific gifts here, it is
highly important to know that he categorizes the gifts in the two
areas of service to the church. You will see that the majority of
all the other gifts fall within one of these two categories, serving
or speaking.

In Romans 12:6–8, we find seven spiritual gifts:

"However, since we have gifts that differ
according to the grace given to us, each of us is
to use them properly: if <u>prophecy</u>, in proportion
to one's faith; if <u>service</u>, in the act of serving; or
the one who <u>teaches</u>, in the act of teaching; or the
one who <u>exhorts</u>, in the work of exhortation; the
one who <u>gives</u>, with generosity; the one who is in

leadership, with diligence; the one who shows mercy, with cheerfulness" (emphasis mine).

1. Prophecy
2. Service
3. Teaching
4. Exhorting
5. Giving
6. Leading
7. Mercy

Some people call these gifts the motivational gifts.[7] All gifts, however, should motivate us to use them if we are to be good stewards. All gifts should also motivate the entire body of Christ to better serve God and motivate each person to use his or her own spiritual gifts.

We find eleven more gifts listed in 1 Corinthians 12 verses 1 through 31. Two gifts found in Romans chapter 8 are repeated here. The list is found in verses 8 through 10 and verse 28.

"For to one is given the word of wisdom through the Spirit, and to another the word of knowledge according to the same Spirit; to another faith by the same Spirit, and to another gifts of healing by the one Spirit, and to another the effecting of miracles, and to another prophecy, and to another the distinguishing of spirits, to another various kinds of tongues, and to another the interpretation of tongues. . . . And God has appointed in the church, first apostles, second prophets, third teachers, then miracles, then gifts of healings, helps, administrations, and various kinds of tongues" (emphasis mine).

These are the additional gifts that we find in 1 Corinthians 12, leaving out those already mentioned in Romans 12.

8. Word of Wisdom
9. Word of Knowledge
10. Faith
11. Healings
12. Miracles
13. Distinguishing of Spirits
14. Tongues
15. Interpretation of Tongues
16. Apostles
17. Helps
18. Administration

The gifts found in both 1 Corinthians 12 and Romans 12 are the gifts of prophecy and the office of prophets and teachers.

In Ephesians 4:11, four gifts are mentioned, two of which have already been mentioned: "And He gave some as apostles, some as prophets, some as evangelists, some as pastors and teachers" (emphasis mine). With the apostles and prophets, we discover also:

19. Evangelism
20. Pastor-Teacher (shepherd/teacher)

This is a unique passage in terms of spiritual gifts because it is not only listing spiritual gifts but gifted individuals God has given to the church.

The final biblical charisma gifts are found in 1 Corinthians 7. The entire chapter is focused on being either single or married. Paul says in 1 Corinthians 7:7, "But I wish that all of you were as I am. But each of you has your own gift from God; one has this gift, another has that" (NIV). The New Living Translation (2nd Ed.) translates it this way: "But I wish everyone were single, just as I am. But God gives to some the gift of marriage, and to others the gift of singleness."

Paul is talking about the gift of singleness, as he had, or the gift of marriage. Therefore, there are two more spiritual gifts listed:

21. Singleness
22. Marriage

Many wonder how these two are spiritual gifts. They are spiritual gifts because the purpose of a spiritual gift is to build up the body of Christ. The point of 1 Corinthians 7 is how to best serve the Lord. Apostle Paul is basically saying, "For some it may be better to remain single, for others, to be married." What he is pointing out is the importance of serving the Lord whether single or married. Each person should be in the position that best enables him or her to best serve the Lord.

A single person should be building up the body of Christ. Likewise, a married couple is to build up the body of Christ. In other words, God gives a person the gift of singleness so he or she can better build up the body of Christ. In like manner, He allows a person to be married, not to build himself or herself up, but that he or she would be better used of the Lord in building up the body of Christ.

Doron Gifts and Ministries

You may have heard of other gifts mentioned other than those mentioned above. Are these spiritual gifts? If not, what are they?

Other gifts people mention are in reality ministries. In other words, some people feel they are gifted in areas of working with children, youth, music, intercession (praying for others), exorcism, missionary, writing, hospitality, creative communication, etc. Are these really gifts? No, they are, in actuality, ministries by which particular spiritual gifts are exercised.

As stated in 1 Corinthians 12:5, there are a variety of ministries. Are these ministries gifts of God? Yes, they are. But they are not charisma gifts, they are the *doron* type of gift. In other words, the power for that ministry does not come from the ministry itself; it comes from the gifts God has given that person. Take for example, the apostle Paul when he talks about his gift of ministry to the Gentiles. In Ephesians 3:7 he states, "Of which I was made a minister, according to the gift [*dorea*] of God's grace which was given to me according to the working of His power" (insert mine). Some believe this was the gift of missionary, which the apostle Paul had. In reality, this is the ministry to which God had called the apostle Paul. His gifts were used in this ministry in reaching the Gentiles.

Consequently, a person who feels he or she has the gift of missionary really has the ministry of missionary which God has called him or her to. A Christian is given the gifts necessary to be effective in his or her ministry. Ministry calling is just as important as a person's spiritual gifts.

Your ministry calling is the area you will see the most effective use of your gifts. Just as Paul saw God's power in his ministry, so will you as you exercise your gifts in the ministry God wants you to be involved in!

Another example of ministry would be music. As you're aware, you do not need to be a Christian to be gifted in music.

However, can music be used for the building up of the body of Christ? Absolutely! Music is actually a ministry, not so much a spiritual gift. Several gifts can be used in the ministry of music. For example, have you, when you've heard a Christian sing, felt encouraged, comforted, or exhorted? If so, that is the gift of prophecy being exercised through the ministry of music. In a church I pastored, the worship leader had the gift of teaching. But he primarily used his gift of teaching through his music. He wrote music that was full of doctrinal teaching. As a matter of fact, he went to seminary primarily to be biblically accurate with his song lyrics! He was far more motivated to teach through his music than to teach in a Sunday school classroom or give a sermon!

The ministry of writing may use the gift of knowledge, teaching, or preaching (prophecy). Intercession, the ministry of praying for people, is most likely the use of the gift of faith and perhaps the discernment of spirits. It is still an important ministry that cannot be ignored if God has laid it on your heart. You will see God's power manifested through you as you fulfill this ministry.

Understanding a person's ministry also helps one understand where all the natural talents and gifts come in.

Please look at the following chart as to the difference between spiritual gifts, talents, and the fruit of the Spirit.

Spiritual Gifts Comparison Chart

SPIRITUAL GIFTS	NATURAL TALENTS
• Christians Only • Received at Conversion • Relies on Holy Spirit • Builds up Body of Christ • Purpose: To Glorify God • Can Be Used to Glorify Christ or Self	• Every Person • Received at Birth • Relies Mainly on Self • Entertains, Inspires, and Educates Mankind • Purpose: To Invoke Response to God as Creator • Can Be Used to Glorify God or Self
SPIRITUAL GIFTS	MINISTRY
• Supernatural Gift • Means of Ministry • Do Not Change • Edifies Christians • Cannot Reproduce Itself • Trains Others • Personal • Relies on Power of God	• Supernatural Calling • Sphere of Ministry • May Change • Edifies Christians and Non-Christians • Must Reproduce Itself • Trains Others • Public • Relies on Power of God

SPIRITUAL GIFTS	FRUIT OF THE SPIRIT
• Focus on What We Do • Matures the Body of Christ • Produces Many Disciples • Cannot Have All the Gifts • Relies on Filling of Holy Spirit • Manifested Power • Essential for Successful Ministry • Glorifies Christ • Empowers Others	• Focus on Who We Are • Matures Us Individually • Makes Us into a Disciple • Can Have All the Spiritual Fruit • Relies on Filling of Holy Spirit • Internal Power • Essential for Successful Life • Glorifies Christ • Empowers You

The Difference between Talents and Gifts

For example, can a superstar baseball pitcher who is a Christian use his baseball skills and talents for the glory of God? Of course. That may be his ministry, to evangelize. He can also use it to build up the body of Christ. If he has the gift of evangelism, he can use his giftedness in that capacity. Matthew 25 tells us we are to be good stewards of the talents, gifts, skills, and every resource God has given to us. Most people probably have some talent given to them by God that helps them perform better at something than other people. They need to use this also as a ministry.

In some cases talents and ministries may be somewhat confusing. For example, a person may be highly skilled at working with the junior high age group. He or she just seems to have a knack at holding their attention and helping them grow in their relationship with Jesus Christ. We stand in awe of these people.

Not only with those of junior high school age, but also with those who are able to work with small children more effectively than most. Is this a talent or a ministry? Probably both. It is a talent given to them by God, and it is their ministry. Their giftedness might be in the area of teaching, encouragement, prophecy, knowledge, etc.

Another common question pertaining to talents and spiritual gifts is this: **If a person has a particular talent in the world, does this talent become his or her spiritual gift when they become a Christian?** The reason this question is asked is because many people wonder that if a person is a good administrator, or a good teacher, or leader in the world, does that mean it will become his or her spiritual gift? The answer to that question is "no, not necessarily." When God gives a person a gift, it truly is a gift.

For example, I know of a man who is a school administrator. But as a Christian he does not have the gift of administration. He has absolutely no desire to help administrate the church. His gifts are in different areas. How do these two coincide? He simply does his job to provide for his family and uses his spiritual gifts God has given him in a different capacity for building the church.

Being a school teacher does not mean one has the spiritual gift of teaching. Sometimes churches will assume a school teacher would make a good Bible teacher for children or adults but that is not necessarily the case.

There are very talented Christians in the world who do use their talents alongside their spiritual gift. For example, a teacher in the world may be given the spiritual gift of teaching. In this case, the body of Christ would be blessed and so would the non-Christians who sense there's something different about their teacher. When I was a youth pastor and had the opportunity to teach in the public schools about abortion, it was amazing to watch the dynamic that took place as I taught. One of the students in my youth group happened to be in one of the classes I was teaching, and he came up to me afterward and said, "Boy, are you a good teacher. That was different." I knew what he was responding to. It was not so much my skills as it was the power of God behind my teaching, even in a non-Christian audience. I, however, had no desire or ability to teach before I was a Christian. Now that I am a Christian, I have great desire to teach, but only God's Word to people who want to learn.

Look at your own life. What are your talents and skills that you enjoy? Can you use these for God in some capacity? As you discover your spiritual gifts, think of more ways you can use them for furthering the kingdom of God.

Does God Have a Personal Ministry for Each Person?

This question has a quick answer: an emphatic yes! As you will see in 1 Corinthians 12, God has placed each person within the body of Christ for a particular reason. Our job is to determine what ministry God has called us to in the local church. Ask God to show you what particular ministry He's called you to so you can best use your gifts. Talk to your friends, talk to leaders, talk to your pastor about what you're interested in and where you can best be used. The role of each pastor is to help each person find his or her giftedness and begin to use it in his or her ministry. Once you discover and know your gifts, begin looking and asking God for the ministry He has for you. He does have one for you. He wants to bear much fruit through you. He wants His power to flow through you by means of the gifts He's given to you and the ministry He's called you to. Don't miss out on it. To use your gifts and fulfill the ministry to which God has called you is one of the most satisfying and rewarding experiences we have as believers.

Identifying All the Gifts

The purpose of this book is to not only identify each of the spiritual gifts and explain in detail what they are biblically, but to also help you learn to use your gift with specific areas of application. All twenty-two of the gifts will be looked at in detail. With each gift, certain goals will be sought.

1. What is the gift according to Scripture?
2. What examples are given in the Bible of using this gift?
3. How you can know you have this gift?
4. Practical ways this gift is used, and various ministries in which it can be used.
5. The positive and negative side of this gift when a person is filled or not filled with the Holy Spirit.

You will discover, as you study each of these gifts, what motivates you personally. You will also sense the Holy Spirit speaking to you, communicating to you what gifts He has specifically given you. Be on the lookout for that one primary gift the Holy Spirit has given to you. This is one gift that motivates you more than all the others. You will also come to understand why people respond to you the way they do and why some people might misunderstand you.

Breakdown of the Gifts

Some people have sought to divide the twenty-two gifts into separate categories. Some have tried to break them down between the speaking gifts, the serving gifts, and the sign gifts. There is much scriptural reason to do this. However, my goal is to simply divide them into two categories: speaking gifts and serving spiritual gifts. There is no list of either the speaking gifts or the serving gifts. In essence, if we are given a gift, we need to serve, or as the Greek word *diakonia* reveals, to minister. We minister with all of our gifts. However, to help, I will list them in the categories of speaking gifts and serving gifts.

Serving Gifts	Speaking Gifts
1. Helps	7. Administration
2. Service	8. Pastor-Teacher
3. Mercy	9. Teacher
4. Giving	10. Prophecy (Preaching)
5. Singleness	11. Exhortation
6. Marriage	12. Leadership
	13. Faith
	14. Wisdom
	15. Knowledge
	16. Miracles
	17. Healings
	18. Tongues
	19. Discernment
	20. Interpretation
	21. Evangelist
	22. Apostle

This list is not sacred, and some gifts can be changed in category, but it is helpful to identify and distinguish between the serving and speaking gifts. (Some spiritual gifts may be both: healings, miracles.)

None of these spiritual gifts are limited by gender. However, some of the positions or offices were limited. For example, only men were apostles but women can can have the spiritual gift of "apostleship," which is explained in the definition of the gift of apostleship.

CHAPTER 4

Knowing and Using Your Spiritual Gifts

F IRST CORINTHIANS 12:1 READS, "Now concerning spiritual gifts, brothers and sisters, I do not want you to be unaware." Paul's main concern is that he does not want us to be unaware of spiritual gifts or ignorant about them. This book's intent is to fulfill Paul's admonition in this verse.

Body of Christ

Before we begin studying about gifts, we need to gain a greater understanding of the body of Jesus Christ. Colossians 1:18 states, "He is also head of the body, the church; and He is the beginning, the firstborn from the dead, so that He Himself will come to have first place in everything." From this passage we learn the church is the body of Christ, and He is head of this body. In other words, Christ is in control. He directs and leads His body. He is the head so that He Himself might be first place. Not only first place in the world, but also and especially first place in His church. He is the beginning of the church and the end of the church, the beginning of the world and end of the world. For that reason it makes sense that we look to Christ for direction and leadership and allow Him to direct His church.

What is the "body of Christ"? I appreciate the work that Peter Wagner, author of several church growth books, has done on this.[8] I want to expound on his example.

- It is not a dictatorship in which one person rules. In other words, the church is not made up of a group of people with one person ruling over them.
- It is not a democracy in which everyone rules. The church is not to be run by consensus, or majority vote. The purpose of the leadership in the church is to determine the mind of Christ (1 Cor. 2:16). Once determined, the mind of Christ is then to be carried out.
- The body of Christ is an organized organism where Christ rules and every person has a part and functions within that body.

The body of Christ is described just as the human body (1 Cor. 12). Therefore, it is a highly organized organism. Because it is an organism, it is alive, it is growing, and it is dynamic.

Just as Scripture tells us what the spiritual gifts are, God's expectations for believers to whom He has given spiritual gifts are outlined. Your gifts are given to you for a purpose: to use. Here we examine the major Scriptures that teach about spiritual gifts. Keep a Bible nearby and read each of the suggested passages before reading the exegesis that follows.

The first major passage we want to look at is 1 Peter 4:10: "Each of you should use whatever gift you have received to serve others, as faithful stewards of God's grace in its various forms" (NIV).

We discover several things about spiritual gifts in these two verses: First, each believer has received a spiritual gift. (This is also confirmed in 1 Corinthians 12:7 which states, "But to each one is given the manifestation of the Spirit for the common good.") Peter tell us that this gift is to be used in serving one another, that we are to be good stewards of this grace which God has given to us (1 Pet. 4:10).

A steward, particularly in the Old Testament, is someone who managed someone else's belongings. This was the case for Joseph as he managed Pharaoh's belongings. Joseph was called a steward over Pharaoh's household (Gen. 39:4). This tells us volumes about special gifts in terms of our responsibility. Peter is emphasizing that we are to be good stewards of this gift that God has given to us because it is not really ours, but God's. It is simply on loan to us from God for His glory!

In verse 11, Peter speaks of the two types of gifts: speaking gifts and serving gifts. As mentioned in the last chapter, everyone has as their primary gift, either a speaking gift or a serving gift.

This is important to note, especially when selecting officers of the church.

In 1 Timothy 3 Paul lays out the qualifications for overseers and deacons. All the qualifications are the same except the elders are to teach and the deacons are to serve.

If a person does not have the speaking and teaching gifts, he should not be an elder but a deacon and vice versa. In selecting elders, it is very important to confirm the speaking type gifts of the candidate as they will need to teach and pastor at various times. The same is true for deacons. Their spiritual gifts must be known also.

If your church has deaconesses, you need to make sure the women on the board are servants. They may have teaching gifts but need to be gifted in serving and helps also.

We also see, in 1 Peter 4:11, that it is Christ who is glorified, not us, when He says "to whom belongs the glory and dominion forever and ever. Amen." If we are using our God-given gifts for our glory, then we are not being good stewards and are defeating the purpose for which God has given us the gifts.

The next major passage is the parable of the talents found in Matthew chapter 25 verses 14 through 30. This is a parable regarding the use of money. The main point of this parable, however, is not so much money as it is being good stewards of whatever God has given to us. It is important to look at this passage in light of the spiritual gifts entrusted to us. In other words, as you read through the parable, look at talents as spiritual gifts since we are told we are to be good stewards of our spiritual gifts. You will find interesting observations as you read this passage.

> **Matthew 25:14–29 (ESV, emphasis mine)**
> **The Parable of the Talents**
> **[14] For it will be like a man going on a journey, who called his servants and entrusted to them his property. [15] To one he gave five talents, to another two, to another one, to each according to his ability. Then he went away. [16] He who had received the five talents went at once and traded with them, and he made five talents more. [17] So also he who had the two talents made two talents more. [18] But he who had received the one talent went and dug in the ground and hid his master's money. [19] Now after a long time the master of those servants came and settled accounts with them. [20] And he who had received the**

> five talents came forward, bringing five talents more, saying, "Master, you delivered to me five talents; here, I have made five talents more." [21] His master said to him, "Well done, good and faithful servant. You have been faithful over a little; I will set you over much. <u>Enter into the joy of your master.</u>" [22] And he also who had the two talents came forward, saying, "Master, you delivered to me two talents; here, I have made two talents more." [23] His master said to him, "Well done, good and faithful servant. You have been faithful over a little; I will set you over much. <u>Enter into the joy of your master.</u>"

The servant given one talent did not invest it and the master said to him:

> [27] Then you ought to have invested my money with the bankers, and at my coming I should have received what was my own with interest. [28] So take the talent from him and give it to him who has the ten talents. [29] For to everyone who has will more be given, and he will have an abundance. But from the one who has not, even what he has will be taken away.

Many things can be learned from this Scripture passage.

- Notice in verse 14 that it was "his [the master's] possessions" that were entrusted to them. In verse 15 we then read he gave talents each according to "his own ability." It is important to see that God doesn't give us more than our ability or less than our ability. He never overwhelms us. He has not given us spiritual gifts that we cannot handle.

Then two of the three "immediately went" and began to trade and each of them gained as much as they had invested. The five gained five, the two gained two (vv. 16–17). The one who received the one talent obviously did nothing with his money and gained nothing.

- When the master returned (vv. 20–23), he was pleased and said to the one who gained five, "Well done, good and faithful servant. You have been faithful over a little; I will set you over much. Enter into the joy of your master." When the second one returned, **notice that the master gave him the exact reward for gaining two as the one who had gained five** (v. 23)! This points out that God rewards faithfulness, not quantity of work. The one who gained more did not receive a greater reward; they each received the exact same reward!

- It is important for us to realize that just because a person with the same gift is more fruitful than we are, does not mean he is more blessed. As a matter of fact, that person might not be quite as faithful to the gifts given to him as we are with our gifts. Again, it's wonderful to realize that God honors faithfulness.

- The one who received the one talent (vv. 24–27) may have been frustrated that he was given only one while the others were given more, and went away in disgust and did nothing with it. **Little did he realize that he could have received the same reward had he invested it just like the others. Notice here that he blamed the master for his inability to succeed.**

This servant's response is important here. We must realize that it is not God's fault if we are not successful; it is ours. He has done everything He can do to ensure our success in our Christian life and ministry.

Ultimately, the one with one talent (vv. 28–30) had it taken away from him and given to the one with ten talents. The Lord makes a promise, "For to everyone who has shall more be given, and he shall have an abundance but from the one who does not have, even what he does have shall be taken away" (v. 29). How does this verse relate to our spiritual gifts? **Does God take away our gifts? No, He simply stops using us and begins to use others who are more effective. The good news about being in the age of grace is that if we do decide we want to be used of God and use the gifts God has entrusted to us, then we can get right back on board.**

Verse 30 has been perplexing to many people because it seems like He is talking about a loss of salvation. However, a parable has only one main point. In other words, the details of a parable only support one main point. Jesus is not talking about loss of salvation but the importance of being good stewards of what God has entrusted to us. Jesus, however, has communicated to the disciples that this is serious and important to God.

Note: There was **no fourth servant** that invested his talents and did not see a return.

Because there was no fourth person, the major observation in regard to this parable is that we need to notice that **everyone who invested bore fruit!** This is a very significant fact and promise from the Lord.

- **If we are using our spiritual gifts, we will be successful!** We will see fruit! We will see God's power at work. The question comes, "What if I do not see any fruit?" The answer is: "That is not your gift." **If it were your gift, you would see fruit!** This brings great relief to people by helping them understand why they have ministered in certain areas and have not seen any fruit. They were obviously not using the spiritual gifts God had given them. Instead they were trying to use gifts God had not given them. God wants us to use our gifts, and He has promised to bless us when we do. This is a tremendously freeing truth from God's Word!

Each Believer's Role in the Church

The next major passage which mentions spiritual gifts is found in Ephesians 4 verses 11 through 16. In these verses we find an explanation of each person's role within the local body of the church. "So Christ himself gave the apostles, the prophets, the evangelists, the pastors and teachers, to equip his people for works of service, so that the body of Christ may be built.... From him the whole body, joined and held together by every supporting ligament, grows and builds itself up in love, as each part does its work" (Eph. 4:11–12, 16 NIV).

In 4:11 and 12, we learn that God gave gifted individuals to the church for a specific reason: to equip or prepare the saints for the work of service.

When I taught my new members class, I often joked with the people in it. As we read these verses, I ask them to share with me the role of the pastor. The class's reply is always the same, "To equip the saints for the work of service."

"Well, that's interesting," I reply. "Oftentimes churches hire the pastors to do the work of the ministry."

"Pastor, that's your job. That's why we hired you."

"Wait a minute; according to these verses, what is the pastor's responsibility?"

"To equip the saints for the work of service," they repeat.

"So whose responsibility is it, then, to do the work of ministry?"

"Ours."

At that point I wipe my forehead, "Whew. And all this time I thought it was mine! I'm so glad that it's yours! Now I can quit."

Then we all laugh.

The point here shouldn't be missed. The officers' job in the church is not so much to do the work of the ministry as it is to help, prepare, equip, and train others to do the work of the ministry. Even evangelists aren't so much to be doing the work of evangelism as they are to help the members of the body do the work of evangelism!

The purpose of equipping the body (vv. 13–16) is that the body builds itself up in Christ. The ultimate goal Christ has for us individually and collectively as a body is that we all grow to maturity in Christ. With all the gifts being utilized, we are no longer children easily persuaded to follow wrong teaching. By speaking the truth we all grow up; we grow into maturity in Christ. Note in verse 16 that everyone works together. We are all attached to each other, and we each have a part. It is at that point that the body causes itself to grow. This is called discipleship!

God's main tool for discipling people is through the local body of Christ. If everyone is doing his or her job, then anyone entering the church will immediately begin that discipling process. This is why it is very important that each person use his or her gifts and become deeply involved in the ministry of their church.

There is a sense of caution and warning in this passage. God's concern is for those who do not become involved in the local body of Christ. Those who are not involved become susceptible to wrong teaching and being tossed about in their faith. This is why it is very important that when we encounter "unattached

Christians" we encourage them to become involved in a church. It is not only for their protection, but for their spiritual growth. God never designed anyone to go it "solo" in the Christian life. He has designed all of us to be a part of one another. This leads us to the next major passage.

Spiritual Gifts as Found in 1 Corinthians 12–14

Chapter 12 of 1 Corinthians is one of the most extensive teaching on spiritual gifts. In actuality, chapters 12 through 14 encompass the greatest portion of teaching on spiritual gifts in the entire Bible. We have much to learn from this chapter. Take the time to read chapter 12, or even chapters 12 through 14 before continuing. To grow in our spiritual gifts, it is critical for us to be knowledgeable of Scripture that relates to their relevance and use.

At the beginning of 1 Corinthians 12, right off in verse 1, we learn that Paul does not want us to be ignorant about spiritual gifts and how they operate within a church. First Corinthians 12:1 says, "Now about the gifts of the Spirit, brothers and sisters, I do not want you to be uninformed" (NIV).

Then, Paul's main point in verse 3 is to ensure the Spirit of God is in control, not the spirit of Satan:

> **"Therefore I make known to you, that no one speaking by the Spirit of God says, 'Jesus is accursed'; and no one can say, 'Jesus is Lord,' except by the Holy Spirit" (NIV).**

Different Gifts, Ministries, and Results

Then verses 4 through 6 are absolutely crucial to understanding the differences between spiritual gifts, ministry, and fruitfulness. "Now there are **different gifts,** but the same Spirit. And there are **different ministries,** but the same Lord. And there are **different results,** but the same God who produces all of them in everyone" (1 Cor. 12:4–6 NET emphasis mine).

First notice there are different gifts, different ministries, and different results. Not every spiritual gift operates in the same sphere of ministry. In other words, just because a person has a particular gift does not mean it is always exercised the same way, as we learned in the previous chapter. For example, a person may have the gift of teaching, but his or her ministry may be to children or adults or to the poor or to the deaf. It may be just to women or just to men. It may be in a Christian organization; it may be in a church. It may also be through entirely different means. For example, a person's gift may be teaching, but his ministry is music. Others may use writing as the means to teach.

The point of all of this is that no matter what gift you have, you do not have to use it the same way others do. Someone with the gift of evangelism does not have to go out and become a Billy Graham. Likewise, others who have the gift of mercy may use that gift in a variety of ministries. The Holy Spirit is not limited in how He wants to use an individual with a particular gift.

In verse 6 Paul points out that there are different results, but the "same God who works all things in all persons." There are both different gifts and ministries and different amounts of fruitfulness. The word for "results" is the Greek word *energema*. It appears only two times in the New Testament, here and in

1 Corinthians 12:10. It is the noun form for *energeo*, (energy) which means "the effect produced by" something.[9] This word means that the energy source behind the gifts and ministry is the Holy Spirit. Paul is talking about the outworkings or supernatural energizing of the Holy Spirit, which means the result of the work of the Holy Spirit. This work of the Holy Spirit through our gifts and ministries is known as fruit or results.

The point is that there is not always the same amount or kind of fruit produced with the use of each gift or in each ministry. This makes a great deal of sense. If a person has the gift of evangelism, does it necessarily mean he or she will see the same fruit as Billy Graham? Obviously not. (Maybe more!) Not everyone who has the gift of helps or service will necessarily produce as much as another. A person with the gift of leadership who leads a few is just as effective as the one leading multitudes, provided they are both being faithful to the Lord and filled with the Holy Spirit. A pastor-teacher over a small congregation is just as fruitful in God's eyes as the one who is pastor-teacher over a large congregation! In other words, we are not to compare ourselves to each other or to someone else who has the same gift or are in the same ministry we are. This goes back to the parable of the talents. We will all have different results from the investment of our spiritual gifts, but we all will be rewarded the same!

This truth is freeing because it helps us keep our eyes on the Lord and not on others. We can simply be thankful that God is using us. Note in all three of these verses it is the Holy Spirit who is the power source behind using our gifts, fulfilling our ministry and producing fruit!

Each Is Given a Manifestation of the Holy Spirit

Verse 7 points out that each individual is given a visible "manifestation of the Spirit for the common good." The word "given" is in the passive tense, which means this was something given to us without our asking for it. In other words, we did not have anything to do with the gift given to us except that we became Christians and received it. The Holy Spirit has chosen to reveal and make Himself known to others through the spiritual gifts He has given to us. If you are a believer, it is amazing to realize the privilege you have, and that God has chosen you to manifest Himself! He has given you a gift, and every time you use that gift, God is revealing Himself through you. You are a chosen vessel! If that doesn't excite you, I don't know what will!

Notice also that the purpose of this gift is not just for our good, but even more for the good of others. Its purpose is to enhance others' walk with the Lord. The fact that we benefit is a side blessing. It really is a mark of maturity to be able to use your gift whether or not you derive some benefit from it.

The Holy Spirit as Gift Giver

Many of the gifts are listed in verses 8 through 10. Notice, however, that the gifts are distributed by the Spirit of God.

Verse 11 is an essential verse in understanding how a person receives a gift. It says, "But one in the same Spirit works all these things, distributing to each one individually just as He wills" (emphasis mine). Notice it is the Spirit who is at work and that He distributes to each one individually "just as He wills." He did not say they are distributed just as we will, or just as we ask Him to. We need to understand that this is God's world and God's kingdom that He is building. It is like a master chessboard. He determines where each piece is to be placed. We need to understand that God is in control. **He determines which gifts we are to receive and for what purpose.** For us to ask God for gifts He has not given us, not only contradicts this passage, but puts us in a position of determining how we want God to use us rather than His determining how He wants to use us.

Say theoretically we decided to ask for a gift He did not give us. If He gave us a gift He did not plan for us to have, then we would be using it the way we wanted to or thought best rather than the Holy Spirit determining how He wants to use it. This is why it is extremely misleading to encourage Christians to ask for a gift.

When I was a young Christian, I was in a group where another Christian brother kept insisting I ask God for a certain gift. However, assessing my situation in college, I realized I was not doing very well in my schoolwork. So I told him I really didn't want or need that gift, but I could really use the gift of knowledge. I thought if there were any gift I needed to get me through college, it was that gift. He, however, was insistent. So I kept responding by saying, "Well, I really don't want that gift. I want the gift of knowledge because I'm doing so poorly in school. And while God's at it, I wouldn't mind having the gift of wisdom either." This only frustrated him, and he eventually gave up trying to convince me I needed to ask for that one particular gift. Fortunately, I learned later that God had already given me all the gifts I needed.

The question may come up, "Does God give gifts later on?" or "What about the fact that I seem to pick up the gift at a later date?" We are admonished repeatedly to develop, practice, and work on our gifts. Most Christians don't realize that their gifts will lie dormant unless they are used.

The spiritual gifts we receive at conversion are with us our whole lives. Romans 11:29 says, "For the gifts and the calling of God are irrevocable." The word for gifts in this passage is charisma, meaning spiritual gifts. This also includes the gift of salvation. In other words, God does not give a gift then take it away again. Once you have the gift, you will always have it.

As we increasingly serve the Lord, the gifts God has given us rise to the surface. There is no way we will know whether or not we have a gift unless we go out and try to use it. As verse 11 clearly states it is the Holy Spirit who distributes the gifts as He chooses. Our responsibility is simply to go out, begin serving God, and allow those gifts to surface. I encourage you to try all spheres of ministry to find out what gifts you have and what ministries God has called you to.

We Are All Part of the Same Body

The point of verses 12 through 14 is that we are all attached to the same body, which is Christ. There is no discrimination as to background or gender because the body is not made up of one key person, but of many.

Verses 15 through 17 is where we find the analogy of the foot saying because it is not a hand, it's not a part of the body and doesn't seem to be as effective as the hand. It is not any less a part of the body. Paul points out in this passage that if we were all the same thing, how in the world would the body function? "If the whole body were an eye, where would the hearing be?" Every part is important, and we're not to seek after the most prominent gifted position.

God Knows Best

Then verse 18 emphasizes the point made in verse 11: "God has placed the members, each one of them, in the body, just as He desired." This is God's plan; He is in control. He's giving particular gifts to particular individuals, and He's placing those people in particular ministries for His purpose just as He desires. **It is not as we desire; it is as He desires.** What we find out is that when we let God put us in a ministry He wants us to be in, and use the gifts He's given to us, we will be entirely and fully satisfied and discover that His job choice for us is best.

Then reading verses 19 through 27, we find that we need to remember that there are many members to one body, but there is only one body. No member can say that he or she has no need of others. We all need each other. In verse 22 Paul is saying that the people in the body who seem to be weaker members, are, in actuality, very necessary. And to those that don't have much prominence in the body, God has actually given more honor.

God says in verse 24 that He gives more honor to those who are given less attention by people. He does this so there is no division (v. 25), and because everybody should care for one another exactly the same. His point in verse 26 is that we should suffer with those who suffer and rejoice with those who rejoice. A case in point: often in a Sunday school class when the teacher is sick, everybody says, "Oh, we need to pray for the teacher because he's not here today," but what about the quiet person in class who is sick? Does the class take the time to pray for that single mom who's not there that Sunday, or the new person who has stopped coming for awhile? Every person in the church is to be treated with the same honor.

Fortunately, God is saying that we are to show the same type of attention to every person, whether it's the very gifted person up front or the person who is gifted in ways that we don't yet know or who has gifts that are not as prominent. God wants no discrimination in His family! I am so afraid that many of the older, quiet people in our church do not receive the same attention as the younger prominent members of the church. God does not want any person slighted in His body. The point which Paul is making is that the supposedly weaker members are also central to the proper functioning of the body. In actuality, what people see as not that significant is extremely significant to God and the make up of the body of Christ.

Chances are, and this has been verified in my observations, that more people are gifted in the area of service and helps than in any other area. These gifts make up the backbone and structure of the church.

God Organizes the Church

In verse 28 it states that God determines how gifted people are placed. "And God has placed in the church...." Note that it is God who does the appointing or the putting the members in place within the congregation. He begins by listing three officers of the church: apostles, prophets, and teachers. Then he begins to list the gifts. In verse 29 Paul asks a rhetorical question. Are all apostles? The answer is obviously no. Are all prophets? Again the answer is no. He works through many of the gifts and then he concludes, "all do not speak with tongues, do they? All do not interpret, do they?" Again, Paul is expecting the answer, "no." It is not God's will that everybody have the same gift.

Should Christians Ask for Certain Gifts?

First Corinthians 12:31 (NIV) says, "Now eagerly desire the greater gifts," which has given rise to the question, "Aren't we to ask for particular gifts? Doesn't this verse teach that we are to ask for gifts we may not have or gifts we want?" On the surface it seems to say so since it states, "but earnestly desire the greater gifts." However, one must look at the Greek language to gain a clearer perspective of this verse. When Paul says, "but earnestly desire the greater gifts," it is not in the singular, but in the plural ("you all"). **In other words, he is not saying each individual should desire the greater gifts, but that the church as a whole should desire the greater gifts.** This makes perfect sense. How does this work?

It is always appropriate for churches to ask the Lord to send particularly gifted individuals to them. To give you an example, when I was an associate pastor in San Bernardino, California, our Elder Board was beginning to receive criticism from the congregation that it was very aloof, unconcerned, and uncaring toward the congregation. Now I knew the men on the board, being on the board myself, and I knew that wasn't true. I knew these men cared deeply about the congregation.

So what was the problem? I decided to have all the members of the Board of Elders take a spiritual gifts inventory test to determine what their gifts were. Interestingly, most of the men had gifts of leadership, teaching, and administration. Only one had the gift of pastor (not the Sr. Pastor). No one had the gift of mercy, service, or helps. And only the new worship leader had the ministry of hospitality. In other words, nobody had the gifts that would show a deep concern for the congregation. No wonder the people were disturbed! Their perception proved an accurate reading of the gifts the elders **did not have**. The church was running smoothly and the teaching was excellent; it was just that the spirit of pastoral caring and concern was not there.

It was not the fault of the elders. It was simply a matter of fact that none of the men had been gifted in these areas that would show concern and caring for the congregation. It was a great revelation for us! As a result, we began to ask God to bring men on the Elder Board who had the gifts of pastor, mercy, and even gifts of service and helps. It was not long before God provided these types of men, and the church became an even more caring and loving church as a whole! This is Paul's point here in verse 31. If a church is lacking teachers, it needs to pray for teachers. If a church is lacking pastoral care, it needs to pray for pastor-teachers. If it needs more people to serve and help, it needs to ask God to bring more people in to serve and to help. If it needs more evangelism, then ask for an evangelist.

Again, Paul's point is not for the individual to seek to edify himself or herself, but to build up the church. God's Word works, and it works well. His concluding statement in verse 31, "And I show you a still more excellent way," shows what to do when a church is lacking certain gifts and waiting for God to answer that prayer. His point in chapter 13 is that love covers the deficiency of all this, as well as showing that even if you had all of these gifted individuals, without love they would be nothing. Paul wants to make sure that no matter what kind of gifted individuals a church has, love permeates the congregation. It also points out that in our own lives, using our gifts without love have no eternal value.

Finding God's Will for One's Life through Spiritual Gifts: Romans 12:1–8

The final main passage is in Romans 12. It answer's the question: "How do we find God's will for our lives?" Romans 12 helps answer that question which most people want answered.

Offer ourselves up to God daily.

The first two verses of Romans chapter 12 are among the most significant verses in the entire New Testament, in regard to living out the Christian life. Here Paul is explaining that we as believers need to present our bodies as "living and holy" sacrifices. In other words, we need to give ourselves completely to God. It is interesting to note that Paul says we are to be a living sacrifice, not a dead sacrifice. A living sacrifice has the ability to crawl off the altar! This is why it is very important for us, when we have crawled off, to crawl back onto that altar of sacrifice and give ourselves to God daily! The way we stay on that altar of sacrifice is by not being conformed to the world, but by allowing God to transform our minds. In verse 2 Paul states that, at this point, you "may prove what the will of God is, that which is good and acceptable and perfect" to Him and to us.

Because these verses are so significant, you may have heard numerous messages on them. Oftentimes, the point of this is the importance of knowing God's will, and the only way to know God's will is to offer ourselves up to Him. The difficulty many encounter here is understanding how to offer him or herself up to God. Many people do give themselves to God, but God's will for them still isn't clear. Paul has just told us to prove what God's will is. These verses must be seen in their context.

Think of ourselves appropriately.

The next step to finding God's will is, as verse 3 points out, that we are to exercise appropriate faith: "Think of yourself with sober judgment, in accordance with the faith God has distributed to each of you." We are to step out in faith. We are not to think more highly of ourselves than we should. We are never indispensable, and no one person has all the gifts. Only Jesus did. Not even the apostle Paul had all the gifts.

This is not to say that you should think too little of yourself. You have spiritual gifts; you have a unique place in the body of Christ and people need you.

For this reason you need to step out in faith. God cannot steer a parked car. Start ministering to people. Get involved in different ministries. Get out of your comfort zone. God will use your availability. You already have God-given faith. Now you need to use it!

Now, in verses 4 and 5 it becomes clear that God's will for you involves the body of Christ: "For just as we have many members in one body and all the members do not have the same function." Notice that according to this verse, we are a member of the body of Christ, and, therefore, whatever God's will is for us, it involves other Christians. There is no such thing as "loner Christians." We don't all have the same role or function.

If you want to experience God's will for your life, you must be plugged into a local church or ministry where you can minister to people.

God's will for our lives includes the spiritual gifts He has given us.

Notice that the whole context of knowing God's will for your life is knowing and using your gifts. Spiritual gifts are crucial in understanding God's will for your life.

Don't miss the profound significance of this verse. **If you want to know what God's will is for your life, look at your gifts!** Doesn't it make sense that God's will for your life would include your spiritual gifts? Why would He give you gifts that He never intended you to use? Or a job without the tools? He has given you the equipment to fulfill His will for your life. **Therefore, for any person to understand and find God's will for their life, they must first know and understand the gifts God has given them.** Whenever someone comes to me and says they are struggling with God's will for their life, one of the first questions I ask is, "What gifts has God given you?" I look at not only their spiritual gifts, but also their talents and their desires for ministry. God combines our spiritual gifts, the ministry in which He wants us to exercise these gifts, and our personality and talents as part of His will. It is crucial, however, that we understand that to know God's will, we must have a clear understanding of our spiritual gifts. I have seen person after person live out the joy of Christ when they finally discover their gifts, because they know how God wants to use them. Then they are well on their way to experiencing God's will for their life!

Personally, I am not confused about God's will for my life. Because I know my primary spiritual gift, I know my job description. **When I get up every day, I know what God wants me to do. He wants you to know the same also!**

Gifts need to be developed.

Whatever gifts you have, they need to be developed so they can become even more effective.

> "We have different gifts, according to the grace
> given to each of us. If your gift is prophesying, then
> prophesy in accordance with your faith; 7 if it is
> serving, then serve; if it is teaching, then teach; 8
> if it is to encourage, then give encouragement; if it
> is giving, then give generously; if it is to lead, do it
> diligently; if it is to show mercy, do it cheerfully"
> (Romans 12:6–8 NIV).

Notice, if a person has the gift of prophecy (preaching) (v. 6), it becomes more effective as one's faith and convictions grow. This takes time and practice. If a person has the gift of service (v. 7), Paul says we need to become better in our service to others by serving. What we think might serve someone may really not. We learn by trial and error and seeking the Lord to become better in our serving.

It is the same with the gift of teaching; those with this gift need to be out teaching and learning and growing in our knowledge of the Word of God. We need to continually refine and improve our gift of teaching if we have this gift. That is why it is essential for someone who has the gift of teaching to continually study the Word of God to become a better teacher.

The same holds true for all the other gifts. One who has the gift of exhortation or encouragement must practice to find out how to best encourage and exhort others. The one who has the gift of giving must learn to give increasingly and strategically. The one who leads must continue to do so with diligence, and not give up or become discouraged. Finally, the one with the gift of mercy must learn to do so with increasing cheerfulness.

Again, Paul's main point is that our gifts need to be developed. They are not in their final form the moment we receive them. They are like a seed that requires water and sun to grow. This makes life exciting as it allows us to see God use us to greater degrees of effectiveness and fruitfulness in our lives.

In summary: Do you have any questions about God's will for your life? Do you know what your gifts are? Have you given yourself first to God and living a holy life? Are you part of a local body of Christ, or are you trying to go it solo? Are you more on the outskirts of your church or ministry organization, or are you right in the center helping other people grow to maturity in Christ? Where are you in the development of your gifts? Are you trying out different ministries? Are you stepping out in faith in serving God? Your answer to each of these questions is important in knowing and understanding how God wants to use you, and use you effectively. He wants your faith to continue to grow along with your confidence in Him and His ability to use you. Are you willing to let Him do that for you even now?

CHAPTER 5

How Each Gift Relates to Every Christian

How to Discover Your Gifts

TAKE A SPIRITUAL GIFTS inventory test. Even consider taking several. I took three or four different tests, and every one of them confirmed the same results. The process was a great assurance. The app I created, *Spiritual Gifts by Mark Stewart*, will also help you.

Refine your gifts. As we have seen in Romans 12, our gifts need developing and refining. It takes practice. Ask others for their help and evaluation. If you think you have the gift of teaching, but people do not show up to your class or Bible study, or they do not seem enthusiastic when you teach, chances are you do not have that gift. Look for people to give you feedback. As you practice the serving gifts, you will learn how to be more effective. As you develop the speaking gifts, you will learn how to be a better speaker. If you have the speaking gifts, you need to study all the more. If you have the serving gifts, you need to take leadership in serving. Be sure to evaluate yourself over and over and ask others to help evaluate you.

Remember, discovering your gifts takes time and the process involves prayer, being thankful to God for His gifts given to you, and trying out different gifts by serving in different ministries and in different capacities, from the usher ministry to Sunday school teacher, from leadership roles to the clean-up crew. Througout the process, be patient and continue to study spiritual gifts. Over time you will find that your God-given spiritual gifts are completely satisfying because through them you will experience God's supernatural power.

God has fully equipped you to serve Him by His gifts and the abilities and power and responsibility He has given to you. He is with you to help you discover, refine, and develop your giftedness. He will be with you as you venture out into different types of ministries to learn how best to serve Him. And as you do this, you will discover how God wants to use you for the rest of your life.

Relationships to All the Gifts

Knowing that God commands every believer to actually do every ministry of each gift, the only difference between participating in every ministry of each gift and being gifted with a particular gift is that God has gifted certain individuals with a supernatural ability with a particular gift to show the rest of us how we are to obey that command. For example, we are all commanded to be merciful. Fortunately, God has given certain individuals the spiritual gift of mercy to show us how to be merciful. We are all to give, but those God has given the gift of giving show us how to do it cheerfully and liberally.

The following will demonstrate that, even if we don't have certain spiritual gifts, we are still to exercise the ministries of those gifts.

Apostleship

Although the office of apostle is not in effect, we still must perform the ministry of the apostles. Remember that "apostle" means "sent one." We are ambassadors of Christ sent into the world (2 Cor. 5:20). The Word of God confirms this: "So Jesus said to them again, 'Peace be with you; as the Father has sent Me, **I also send you**'" (John 20:21 emphasis mine). We also know each of us are needed: "And He was saying to them, 'The harvest is plentiful, but the laborers are few; therefore beseech the Lord of the harvest to send out laborers into His harvest" (Luke 10:2). Finally, we are told, "**Go therefore and make disciples** of all the nations, baptizing them in the name of the Father and the Son and the Holy Spirit" (Matt. 28:19 emphasis mine).

As you can see, going out to reach the whole world was not the sole commissioning of the disciples, but for all believers.

Prophecy (Preaching)

Even though this gift means proclaiming God's Word to more than one person at a time, it is not reserved only for pastors or evangelists, or for men only, as nowhere in Scripture does it say that certain gifts are for men and certain gifts are for women. All the gifts are for men and women, with the exception of Apostle because Jesus chose only men.

There will be occasions when you will need to speak to more than one person at a time to exhort, encourage, or comfort them.

This may be in a small group or Bible study, a classroom, a dinner party, or even with your own family when they are gathered together. There will be times that God will give you a message that burns in your heart and you just have to share it with others. "'And it shall be in the last days,' God says, 'that I will pour forth of My Spirit on all mankind; and **your sons and your daughters shall prophesy,** and your young men shall see visions, and your old men shall dream dreams" (Acts 2:17emphasis mine). The Word of God also says, "**Preach the word;** be ready in season and out of season; reprove, rebuke, exhort, with great patience and instruction" (2 Tim. 4:2 emphasis mine).

Teaching

We know that parents are to teach their children the Word of God according to Deuteronomy 6:6–7 and Ephesians 6:4. We are also to teach other Christians when the opportunity avails itself.

> "**And what you heard me say in the presence of many witnesses entrust to faithful people who will be competent to teach others as well**" (2 Tim. 2:2 NET).

Service

Even though there are those with the special ability to **serve** others, we are all to serve one another. We were saved to serve God and others.

> "**For you were called to freedom, brethren; only do not turn your freedom into an opportunity for the flesh, but through love serve one another**" (Gal. 5:13).

> **"For even the Son of Man did not come to be served,**
> **but to serve, and to give His life a ransom for many"**
> **(Mark 10:45).**

If Christ became a servant for us, and we are to be like Christ, then how much more should we serve others?

Helps

It is important to be available to help anyone in need. The entire parable of the "Good Samaritan" is to point out that we should help those who are in need (Luke 10:30–35). Part of the gospel includes helping the weak.

> **"In everything I showed you that by working hard in**
> **this manner you must help the weak and remember**
> **the words of the Lord Jesus, that He Himself said, 'It**
> **is more blessed to give than to receive'" (Acts 20:35).**

> **"We urge you, brethren, admonish the unruly,**
> **encourage the fainthearted, help the weak, be patient**
> **with everyone" (1 Thess. 5:14).**

Knowledge

Proverbs 1:7 says, "The fear of the LORD is the beginning of knowledge."

Colossians 1:10 is part of Paul's prayer, and he prays "that you will walk in a manner worthy of the Lord, to please Him in all respects, bearing fruit in every good work and increasing in the **knowledge** of God" (emphasis mine).

It is crucial that we as believers grow in the knowledge of God and learn His will for our lives. The main way to grow in the knowledge of God is to study the Scriptures because that is where God has mostly chosen to reveal Himself.

Wisdom

Like knowledge, we are also to grow in wisdom. Proverbs 9:10 says, "The fear of the LORD is the beginning of wisdom, and the knowledge of the Holy One is understanding."

We are commanded to increase our wisdom as believers and to become wise. "**Acquire wisdom!** Acquire understanding! Do not forget nor turn away from the words of my mouth" (Prov. 4:5 emphasis mine). Wisdom comes from applying the knowledge we have. Who we are and what we become is the direct result of making wise decisions.

Encouragement

Scripture tells us that encouraging other believers is a ministry we are all to have toward each other. In this day and age, we need all the encouragement we can receive to keep living the Christian life.

> "**Therefore encourage one another and build up one another, just as you also are doing**" (1 Thess. 5:11).

> "**But encourage one another every day, as long as it is still called 'today,' so that none of you will be hardened by the deceitfulness of sin**" (Heb. 3:13).

Pastor-Teacher

Pastoring means to shepherd (spiritually feed, lead, care, and protect others). You may not be a pastor, but that doesn't mean that you don't help care for the spiritual condition of those around you and help to teach others the correct way to live their lives and how to grow in their faith.

> "So that there may be no division in the body,
> but that the parts may have the same care for one
> another" (1 Cor. 12:25).

> "Be shepherds of God's flock that is under your care,
> watching over them—not because you must, but
> because you are willing, as God wants you to be; not
> pursuing dishonest gain, but eager to serve" (1 Pet.
> 5:2 NIV).

> "We urge you, brothers and sisters, admonish the
> unruly, encourage the fainthearted, help the weak, be
> patient with everyone" (1 Thess. 5:14).

Ask any pastor. This is pastoring! It is a good thing that it isn't just up to one person in a church to do all of this! Urging, admonishing, encouraging, and helping is the work of every believer.

Faith

It is exciting to know that "faith" is not the sole possession of only certain gifted individuals. We all, as believers, must stretch, strengthen, apply, and grow our faith.

> "And Jesus answered and said to them, 'Truly I say to
> you, if you have faith and do not doubt, you will not
> only do what was done to the fig tree, but even if you
> say to this mountain, 'Be taken up and cast into the
> sea,' it will happen'" (Matt. 21:21).

Do you have this kind of faith? Don't be discouraged if you don't. God wants to help grow your faith to the point that there is nothing that you think is impossible with God and that He will honor this kind of faith!

> **"For in it the righteousness of God is revealed from faith to faith; as it is written, 'but the righteous man shall live by faith'" (Rom. 1:17).**

Living by faith is to be the hallmark of every Christian.

Leadership

Leading is something we all must do at some point in our lives. The word for leadership in Greek means to "go before" or "stand before" another.

We must lead others in the way that is right. "This statement is trustworthy; and concerning these things I want you to speak confidently, so that those who have believed God will be careful to **engage [lead]** in good deeds. These things are good and beneficial for people" (Tit. 3:8 emphasis mine).

Fathers must lead their families. 1 Timothy 3:5 asks us, "If a man does not know how to **manage [lead]** his own household, how will he take care of the church of God?" (emphasis mine).

Leading is often being an example and that we are all to be!

Administration

Administration (or the gift of organization) has the idea of doing things in an orderly way to achieve a goal. All leaders are to administrate. The overseers are elders who rule and administrate and all Christians are to do things properly and in an orderly way: "**But all things must be done properly and in an orderly manner**" (1 Cor. 14:40).

This is administration. In line with this, everything we do, should have the glory of God in mind. This ties in with doing things in a way that at least gives honor to God. Doing things in an organized fashion often honors God.

> "**Therefore, whether you eat or drink, or whatever you do, do all things for the glory of God**" (1 Cor. 10:31).

Mercy

There is no question that Christians are to be merciful to others. This is the point of the parable of the Good Samaritan (Luke 10:30). Mercy in this sense is defined as meeting the needs of someone who cannot meet their own needs or provide for themselves. It also carries with it the idea of extending forgiveness. Remember:

> "**But God, being rich in mercy, because of His great love with which He loved us**" (Eph. 2:4).

> "**Be merciful, just as your Father is merciful**" (Luke 6:36).

Discernment

Should Christians be discerning? Absolutely. We must be able to discern between right and wrong. We must be able to discern what is of Satan and what is of God. In Scripture, we are told to "test the spirits" as to whether something is of God or not.

> **"Beloved, do not believe every spirit, but test the spirits to see whether they are from God" (1 John 4:1).**

Concerning our relationship with God, we are told to learn discernment: "For the LORD gives wisdom; From His mouth come knowledge and understanding.... Then you will **discern** righteousness, justice, And integrity and every good path" (Prov. 2:6, 9 emphasis mine).

We are also told that our goal is to become mature in Christ which, among other things, means to discern between good and evil.

> **"But solid food is for the mature, who because of practice have their senses trained to discern between good and evil" (Heb. 5:14).**

Giving

All of us are to be giving people. Those with the gift of giving are to show us how much fun it is to give and how freeing it is to give away what God has given to us.

> **"Honor the LORD from your wealth, and from the first of all your produce; then your barns will be filled with plenty, and your vats will overflow with new wine" (Prov. 3:9–10).**

> **"Give, and it will be given to you. They will pour into your lap a good measure — pressed down, shaken together, and running over. For by your standard of measure it will be measured to you in return" (Luke 6:38).**

Evangelism

Even though there are those who have the gift of evangelism, everyone is to help spread the Good News. If the evangelization of the world were dependent only upon those who have this gift, the world would never hear the Good News. The work of someone with the gift of evangelism is actually to equip others to share their faith (Eph. 4:11–12).

Paul told Timothy that we are all to have a part of expanding the kingdom. Paul told this to Timothy: "But you, be sober in all things, endure hardship, **do the work of an evangelist**, fulfill your ministry" (2 Tim. 4:5 emphasis mine).

Even Christ, speaking to a person He just healed, said, "Go home to your people and report to them what great things the Lord has done for you, and how He had mercy on you" (Mark 5:19).

Tongues

The gift of tongues is the supernatural ability to speak in a foreign language for the purpose of declaring God's praises to others who do not speak your language, and in turn, they are witnessed to.

> **"And how is it that we each hear them in our own language to which we were born?... Cretans and Arabs—we hear them speaking in our own tongues of the mighty deeds of God" (Acts 2:8, 11).**

Although we are not commanded to speak in tongues, God's will is for us to declare His praises to the rest of the world.

> **"But you are a chosen race, a royal priesthood, a holy nation, a people for God's own possession, so that**

**you may proclaim the excellencies of Him who has
called you out of darkness into His marvelous light"
(1 Pet. 2:9).**

We can also make it a point to reach out to the internationals who come to our country and help them come to know how great God is, if they haven't discovered that already.

Interpretation

This was the gift given to certain Christians so that what was spoken in tongues could be interpreted and understood.

Again, this is a gift not commanded to all Christians, we do, however, have a responsibility to interpret and explain the Scriptures to others.

> **"Then Ezra blessed the LORD the great God. And
> ... explained the law to the people while the people
> remained in their place. Ezra read plainly from the
> book of the law of God, interpreting it so that all
> could understand what was read" (Neh. 8:6–8).**

Christ did this with the disciples (using the same word for the gift of interpretation). "Then beginning with Moses and with all the Prophets, He **explained** to them the things written about Himself in all the Scriptures" (Luke 24:27 emphasis mine).

This is our job with our children (Deut. 6:7) and to those who are our spiritual children (2 Tim. 2:2).

Healings

Although there was a special gift of healings, it does not mean that we shouldn't or can't pray for people to be healed. If God can heal through us, then we should seek to heal others through our prayers. We are told, "And the prayer offered in faith will restore the one who is sick, and the Lord will raise him up, and if he has committed sins, they will be forgiven him" (James 5:15).

This was a command given to the disciples: "**Heal** the sick, raise the dead, cleanse those with leprosy, cast out demons. Freely you received, freely give" (Matt. 10:8 emphasis mine).

The same Christ who healed the sick lives in us as believers and can perform the same work of mercy on others. All the power of the Holy Spirit is available to us today!

> **"And whatever you ask in prayer, believing, you will receive it" (Matt. 21:22).**

Miracles

This is similar to the gift of healing. Although, we are not commanded to perform works of miracles, our prayers can produce miracles. There is no reason not to pray for the supernatural if it will glorify God, expand the kingdom of God, and help others.

Christ told us as His followers: "Truly, truly, I say to you, the one who believes in Me, the works that I do, he will do also; and **greater works than these** he will do; because I go to the Father" (John 14:12 emphasis mine).

I see no limits put on what "than these" things are by Christ. Why not believe Him for the extraordinary?

Singleness and Marriage

The Bible is replete with passages about how to conduct our lives individually and as a married person (see Colossians 3, 1 Corinthians 7, and Ephesians 5). Little more needs to be said about this.

Summary

As you can see, the gifts are reflections of the ministries and characteristics that should be a part of all believers' lives. You have been given some spiritual gifts to show others how they too can serve the Lord!

CHAPTER 6

The Speaking Gifts

W E NOW BEGIN TO examine each of the gifts in detail to discover what the gifts are and how to use them. First, we encounter the gifts of apostle, prophecy, and teaching.

Apostleship: I am a pioneer

Definition: *The gift of apostleship is a supernatural position and empowerment to speak and exercise God's words and authority to others and whose mission is to plant and oversee churches and ministries in local and foreign regions.*

Like the office of prophet, the office of apostle is not necessary today. According to Ephesians 2:20, the apostles and prophets built the foundation of the church with Jesus Christ being the cornerstone. "His household, built on the foundation of the apostles and prophets, with Christ Jesus himself as the chief cornerstone" (Eph. 2:19–20 NIV). We are no longer laying the foundation of Christ's house but are now building upon it. However, the spiritual gifts of apostleship and prophecy/preaching are still necessary to expand the church.

The spiritual gift of apostleship is different than the office of apostle. One was a position of authority in the church, and this is the ministry which those who have this gift carry out. The meaning of the word "apostle" (*apostolos* in Greek) is literally "one sent forth." It is made up of two Greek words, "from" and "sent" meaning "sent from."

An apostle had:

- A calling,
- A mission field (i.e. To Jews, Gentiles, other parts of the world),
- The power of the Holy Spirit, and
- A commissioning to carry out this ministry.

Those with the spiritual gift of apostleship have the same ministry, and they are recognized as a "sent one" to go and establish churches or ministries in a different culture. (Some will call this the gift of missionary.) When selecting a replacement for Judas, the disciples were looking for a person "to take over this apostolic ministry" (Acts 1:25 NIV).

Goal: To plant new ministries and churches, go into places where the gospel is not preached, enter into other cultures to establish churches, and raise up and develop leaders and possibly elders for churches, and even pastor pastors and other key leaders of ministries.

> Those with the gift of apostleship often have many other gifts that allow them to fulfill their ministry. These are leaders of leaders and ministers of ministers. They are influencers. They are typically entrepreneurial and are able to take risks and perform difficult tasks. Missionaries, church planters, certain Christian scholars and institutional leaders, and those leading multiple ministries or churches often have the gift of apostleship.[10]

Characteristics of the Gift of Apostleship

Peter's ministry of apostleship was to reach the Jews. Paul's was to reach the Gentiles (non-Jews).

The person with this spiritual gift is excited to bring the gospel to unreached areas, either locally or in other parts of the world, or bring ministries where they are needed. For example starting churches, schools, seminaries, lead Christian organizations, start medical ministries, and help provide food, water, and other needs to places to spread the gospel. They also will venture into ministries in the area of sex trade, orphans, persecuted, ignored ministries, etc. They have God's hand on them to go where most people do not want to go or have not gone. They are able to gather those who want to form churches and people follow their leadership. Those with this gift also are able to start ministries that reach groups of people in other cultures. They often pastor pastors, develop leaders, and are influencers to encourage and inspire others to serve the Lord with their spiritual gifts.

Key Verses

> "And He went up to the mountain and summoned those whom He Himself wanted, and they came to Him. And He appointed twelve, that they would be with Him and that He could send them out to preach, and to have authority to cast out the demons" (Mark 3:13–15).

> "Go, therefore, and make disciples of all nations, baptizing them in the name of the Father and of the Son and of the Holy Spirit, teaching them to follow all

that I have commanded you; and behold, I am with you always, to the end of the age" (Matt. 28:19–20).

"My ambition has always been to preach the Good News where the name of Christ has never been heard, rather than where a church has already been started by someone else" (Rom. 15:20 NLT).

Apostleship When Filled with the Holy Spirit

Someone gifted with spiritual apostleship and filled with the Holy Spirit will exhibit the following characteristics. He or she:

- Exalts the Lord Jesus Christ. The words of John the Baptist characterize their attitude. "He must increase, but I must decrease" (John 3:30).
- Is able to speak and teach the Word of God with authority and accuracy.
- Exercises power over demonic forces (Matt. 10).
- Has a strong ministry of "strengthening the disciples."
- Has a passion for the lost and helps to plant churches and start new ministries.
- Has a very thorough knowledge of God's Word.
- Has a powerful ministry of prayer (Acts 6:4).
- Exudes the presence of God, Christ, and His power.
- He or she gives people the sense that God's hand is on them to lead and build the church or ministry.
- Looks for new opportunities to plant churches or start new ministries that reach those who are unreached.

Apostleship When Not Filled with the Holy Spirit

- Prideful
- Legalistic
- Demanding

- A ministry centered around him or herself.
- Will use his or her position to exalt themselves.
- Begins to lead people into false doctrine.
- Will control and dominate others and run the church or ministry their way.

Apostleship and Kingdom Building

Apostleship is a spiritual gift used to both reach the unreached and then to help establish leaders to equip those new believers.

If this is your spiritual gift, thank God that He has given you a passion to reach other cultures, either within your country or outside it. Look for opportunities to start churches or new ministries being neglected in your church, organization, or city. Get wise advice from others about how to start a new ministry to those whom God has laid on your heart. Step out in faith. God has most likely raised up those with the same passion, but they just need someone to take the lead. Know that you have the power of the Holy Spirit to fulfill this calling.

Prophecy/Preaching: I empower many

Definition: *The gift of prophecy (preaching) is the supernaturally empowered ability to speak words of exhortation, encouragement, and comfort to groups of people for the building up of the body of Christ to urge them to be obedient to the Word of God.*

The gift of prophecy is one of the better known gifts. It is the gift that is most widely evident in the body of Christ.

The gift of prophecy and the office of prophet are not the same gift, even though there are many similarities. In the Old and New Testaments, one who was a prophet was held in a position of honor and had authority and the ability to rule. For example, Samuel was both a prophet and also led Israel. In the New Testament, prophets were also in a positon of authority until the foundation of the church was established. Ephesians 2:20 says, "having been built on the foundation of the apostles and prophets, Christ Jesus Himself being the cornerstone." We are no longer laying a foundation, but we are building on that foundation. Here are more important details to know:

- Although some prophesying was predicting the future, the vast majority was urging the people of God to become obedient to the Word of God. All of the major and minor prophets exhort, encourage, and comfort the people of Israel. (See Isaiah 40:1.)
- This gift is identical to the gift of encouragement except the gift of prophecy is a gift that is used with large groups. This person is an encourager of many people at one time. The person with the gift of encouragement encourages one-on-one.
- There are three essential spiritual gifts necessary to pastoring a mega church (over a thousand). The three gifts are: leadership, faith, and prophecy (the ability to preach well with power and conviction). The pastor must have the gift of preaching. People are drawn to those who have this gift and use it with conviction! All mega and meta (over ten thousand) church pastors preach dynamically.

The Old and New Testaments' office of prophet was limited. The supernatural New Testament gift of prophecy is not limited at all! It includes both men and women and is distributed widely through the body of Christ.

Goal: To boldly proclaim God's Word to various groups of people to further motivate them on to godliness and ministry.

Uniqueness between Gifts of Prophecy, Knowledge, Teaching, and Wisdom

- Prophecy: seeks to <u>persuade</u> a person to apply and obey the Word of God (Rom. 12:1–2).
- Knowledge: <u>states</u> what the Bible says.
- Teaching: <u>explains</u> what the Bible says and how to apply it.
- Wisdom: seeks to specifically <u>apply</u> what the Bible says to a given situation.

A Description of Prophecy

- The supernatural New Testament gift of prophecy is not limited at all! It includes both men and women and is distributed widely through the body of Christ.
- The clearest definition of the gift of prophecy is found in 1 Corinthians 14:3: "But the one who prophesies speaks to people for their <u>strengthening</u>, <u>encouragement</u>, and <u>comfort</u>" (NIV emphasis mine).
- A similiar example is found in 1 Thessalonians 2:11–12: "For you know that we dealt with each of you as a father deals with his own children, **encouraging**, **comforting** and **urging** you to live lives worthy of God, who calls you into his kingdom and glory" (NIV emphasis mine).
- This is a three-fold ministry. What is fascinating about this description is that, in actuality, this is what pastors hope to do on Sunday mornings. **On any given Sunday, there are some people who need to be exhorted to stop destructive behavior in their lives. Others are doing well, and they just need to be encouraged to stay strong. Others have experienced loss in their lives and need to be comforted.** The pastor's sermom ideally should address each of these areas every time he speaks.

- The gift of prophecy is often called the gift of preaching today. Oftentimes a person asks, "What did the pastor preach on today?" In reality, he's asking on what did he "prophesy." We don't speak that way today, because it is too difficult to understand. Instead, the words often used are "to preach."

- The gift of prophecy and the gift of encouragement is the same gift, but preaching is a gift that is used with large groups whereas the spiritual gift of encouragement is a one-on-one gift.

In its distilled essence, the gift of preaching is urging, persuading, and convincing people that it is in their best interest to obey the Word of God!

When a person who has this gift uses it, they will experience God's supernatural power and enablement flowing through them. They will sense that they are on a mission for God and have a message to proclaim. This person is by nature a very persuasive person and knows words mean things, and God's Word especially is what changes lives. The driving force, especially for a pastor who has this gift, is Romans 15:4 which states, **"For whatever was written in earlier times was written for our instruction, so that through perseverance and encouragement of the Scriptures, we might have hope."** What drives this person is that he or she wants to encourage, strengthen, and bring hope to large numbers of people by use of Scripture!

This is exactly what a person who has the gift of prophecy does; **they give messages of encouragement and strength.** When a person leaves church on a Sunday morning or having heard from someone giving a talk as a speaker, they should be moved in their spirit to either deal with sin in their life, become stronger in their faith, or walk away comforted and encouraged in the trials they are experiencing. If they are not moved in any of these capacities, then the person who has the gift of prophecy (preaching) has not done their job. This gift can be used in Bible studies, conferences, through media, or any group setting where Christians are gathered and God's Word is proclaimed.

Key Verses

"Until I come, devote yourself to the public reading of Scripture, to preaching and to teaching" (1 Tim. 4:13 NIV).

"But the one who prophesies speaks to people for their strengthening, encouragement, and comfort" (1 Cor. 14:3 NIV emphasis mine).

"Judas and Silas, also being prophets themselves, encouraged and strengthened the brethren with a lengthy message" (Acts 15:32 emphasis mine).

"And with many other words John exhorted the people and preached the good news to them" (Luke 3:18 NIV emphasis mine).

Prophecy/Preaching When Filled with the Holy Spirit

If you have the gift of prophecy (preaching) and are filled with the Holy Spirit, you will demonstrate many of the following characteristics:

- You will enjoy speaking words of exhortation, encouragement, and comfort to groups of people.

- You will be able to discern from the Holy Spirit when a group needs to be exhorted, encouraged, or comforted.
- You will have a sense of urgency that people need to trust God with their problems.
- You will have a great passion to know and study God's Word.
- Your messages will be very encouraging to those who hear.
- You will have a deep love and concern for people.
- You will rejoice at other people's obedience to God's Word.
- You will seek to always apply God's Word to your own life before preaching to others.
- You will live a holy and devoted life to God.
- You will pray for the people to whom you preach.

Prophecy/Preaching When Not Filled with the Holy Spirit

An individual who has the gift of prophecy but does not walk in the Spirit needs to be very cautious and understand the negative side of this gift. If they have this gift and do not walk in the Spirit, then the following may come to characterize their life.

- Since they see things as black and white, they could become very impatient and intolerant of others. They may appear to lack understanding, forgiveness, or compassion.
- If they are carnal and use this gift, oftentimes they may not be interested in listening to others. They may only be interested in telling them how they can fix their life.
- They may come across as harsh and critical.
- They may tend to become argumentative.
- They may mislead others for personal gain.
- They can easily become manipulative.

- They may tend to be fearful and insecure. They may be more concerned about what people think of them rather than what God has to say through His Word. In other words, it is easy to become self-focused, not God-focused, and more concerned about what people think about you rather than what they think about God.
- They may tend to come across to others as a 'know-it-all'.
- When frustrated they try to control a person through legalism and the fear of God rather than the grace and mercy of God.

If Prophecy Is Your Primary Spiritual Gift

- Become a student of God's Word so that when you speak from God, you will be speaking accurately.
- Be willing to lead Bible studies, preach to small and large groups when you have the chance, and even do evangelistic crusades.
- Learn to be a good speaker who can exhort, build up, encourage, and comfort everyone who hears you speak.
- Study those who are great preachers and speakers to learn from them.
- Read as many books on how to speak publicly as possible.
- Go to workshops and training seminars (Dale Carnegie, Toast Masters, Cru's Communication Workshop, etc.).
- Step out boldly and preach knowing God will use you to lead people to Christ and help His people to grow.

Teaching: Answers the question "So what?"

Definion: *The gift of teaching is the supernaturally empowered ability to explain clearly, and apply effectively, the truth of the Word of God in such a way that others will understand it and know how to apply it to their lives to grow to maturity.*

Goal: To help others learn, understand, and become excited about what God says in His Word so that they will seek to apply it to their lives.

The gift of teaching is found in Romans 12:7, 1 Corinthians 12:28 and 29, and Ephesians 4:11. Of all the gifts, only two are mentioned in all three passages related to gifts. One is prophecy; the other is teaching. Although this does not mean that prophecy and teaching are more important than any other gift, it does mean that they are most likely predominant gifts among churches. Not only is teaching a gift, but it was also a position in the New Testament. Along with apostle, prophet, evangelist, and pastor-teacher is also the office of teacher. Acts 13:1 states that there were **prophets** and **teachers** in the church at Antioch. Teachers obviously play a major role in the growth of any church and in the lives of individuals. Those who have the gift of teaching have a very important role in terms of the discipleship of the body of Christ. It is definitely a gift that requires supernatural empowerment.

Characteristics of the Gift of Teaching

A person with the gift of teaching will always be asking themselves, "So what? What difference does it make in my life?" They ask this question because they want other people to know the answer. When they teach, it's like the light goes on for other people. They will hear comments such as, "Now I understand. I've looked at that passage so many times, but I never understood it until now!" If people are saying this to you, you know you have the gift of teaching. If you do not hear this from people, chances are you do not have this gift.

William McRae states,

> A person with the gift of teaching will be marked by two distinct characteristics. He will have a keen interest in a personal study of the Word, and in the disciplines involved in studying the Scriptures. These may include language study, principles of interpretation, methods of Bible study, history, geography, and theology. Also, he will have the capacity to communicate clearly the truths and applications of the Word so others may learn and profit.[11]

When a person sits under the teaching of someone who has this gift, he or she will not only understand what the Bible says, but also how it applies to his or her life. A person with this gift will crave to know more of God's Word. If you find yourself reading the Bible and wondering how you could communicate what you have just read to the lives of others, it may well indicate that you have the gift of teaching. A person with this gift will be excited about what he or she is learning, and not only want to apply it to his or her own life, but see it applied to others. This person has a strong desire to communicate God's truth to people. If you find yourself listening to a message, whether or not it is a sermon or conference or a Bible study, and you begin to think about how you might teach this same message to others, it is a good indicator that you most likely have the gift of teaching. Especially, if you can't wait for the opportunity to happen!

The gift of teaching differs from the gift of prophecy. For example, if after you opened the Bible and explained a passage to a group and how they could apply it to their lives, that would be using the gift of teaching. If, on the other hand, you get a group together for the purpose of encouraging them, open the Bible, and use a verse for their encouragement and urge them to take action, that would be the gift of prophecy. There are times when the Bible must be explained, and there are times when people must be encouraged through the Word of God. Sometimes, the gift of teaching can accomplish both.

It is very important that people know the Bible and how to become more Christ-like. **The person with this gift will do everything he or she can to make the Bible more understandable, relevant, and applicable to a person's life.** This can be done through a variety of ministries, not only teaching on Sunday mornings or in a Sunday school room, but also in Bible studies, one-on-one, and even through music. Colossians 3:16 states, "Let the word of Christ richly dwell within you, with all wisdom, teaching and admonishing one another with psalms, hymns, and spiritual songs, singing with thankfulness in your hearts to God." Another way of using the gift of teaching is through writing, as obviously the apostle Paul did. Drama is still another means of communicating spiritual truths.

Those who have this gift must communicate God's Word so others can understand it and apply it to their lives. Simply teaching the Bible so people know what it says is not the gift of teaching. That is more the gift of knowledge. It is very important that a teacher work hard to ensure that people understand what difference God's Word makes in their lives and how to apply.

Because this is a strong gift of mine personally, I have to work particularly hard finding illustrations for my sermons that explain the truths I teach from God's Word. This sometimes takes the bulk of my preparation time although it is only between three and five minutes of the actual sermon. I work hard to understand what the original languages say so hearers have a clear picture of what God is saying specifically. A teacher will work hard to find ways to make the Word of God more understandable to others.

Uniqueness between Gifts

- Knowledge: <u>states</u> what the Bible says.
- Teaching: <u>explains</u> what the Bible says and how to apply it.
- Wisdom: seeks to specifically <u>apply</u> what the Bible says to a given situation.
- Prophecy: seeks to <u>persuade</u> and <u>urge</u> a person to obey the Word of God.

Biblical Examples

The importance of the use of this gift is found in Acts 2:42. It states, "They were continually devoting themselves to the apostles' <u>teaching</u> and to fellowship, to the breaking of bread and to prayer" (emphasis mine). It was vital for the early Christians to be taught the Word of God. The apostle Paul, who also had this gift, communicated to Timothy that the gift of teaching was more than just imparting knowledge. It was making disciples. He says in 2 Timothy 2:2, "And the things which you have heard from me in the presence of many witnesses, entrust these to faithful people who will be able to <u>teach</u> others also" (emphasis mine). He points out that the Word of God should be taught in such a way that it can be passed on to others.

The model that everyone who has the gift of teaching should follow is Ezra. It states in Ezra 7:10, "For Ezra had firmly resolved to study the Law of the Lord and to **practice** it, and to **teach** His statutes and ordinances in Israel" (emphasis mine).

This clearly expresses the heart of the one who has the gift of teaching. His or her desire is not only to study the Word of God, but also to practice it. The only way a teacher can be the most effective is by learning the Word of God, applying it to his or her own life, then teaching others how to do the same. This keeps one who has the gift of teaching very genuine and sincere as well as understanding of his or her audience. Their primary motivation is not so much to teach others as it is to teach themselves. Once they have taught themselves, then their hearts are ignited to teach others how God's Word can work in their lives.

Luke is another excellent example of understanding the gift of teaching. Luke demonstrated very clearly that his primary gift was the gift of teaching. It is explained in Luke 1:1–4: "Since many have undertaken to compile an account of the things accomplished among us, just as they were handed down to us by those who from the beginning were eyewitnesses and servants of the Word, it seemed fitting to me as well, having **investigated** everything **carefully** from the beginning, to write it out for you in **consecutive order**, most excellent Theophilus, so that you may **know** the **exact truth** about the things you have been taught" (emphasis mine). If you read the book of Acts, you will see that Luke was very thorough. He added much detail, history, and precision in chronology. We learn from this passage five descriptors that tell us what is involved in the gift of teaching.

1. Notice the word "investigated" (v. 3). The word in Greek has the idea, "to know all about" (Strong's NIV). It means that Luke needed to know all about the truth until he understood what he was about to explain. This is essential for the one with the gift of teaching. Luke investigated everything!

2. Notice the word "carefully" (v. 3). The word in Greek means "perfectly, carefully, exactly, and diligently" (Strong's). Luke was very careful that what he was about to communicate was the exact truth. He wanted to make sure his investigation was accurate. It is important that teachers be accurate if they're going to teach what God says.

3. Notice the phrase "consecutive order." The word in Greek has the idea of order and succession (Strong's). Luke had a methodical way of presenting the material. He had a purpose for how and why he presented what he did. A teacher is not haphazard in how he or she presents information. A teacher of God's Word will work very hard to present things in an orderly fashion to make them more understandable.

4. Notice the word "know" (v. 4). This is not the Greek word for gaining knowledge for knowledge's sake. The word Luke uses here in Greek is the word *epiginosko*. This word has the idea "to more fully perceive with a greater participation by the knower in the object known."[12] The result is that this truth more powerfully influences the person learning so he or she will actually do something with the truth, not just walk away with their curiosity satisfied. It is the goal for the teacher to communicate knowledge in such a way that people will respond by changing their lives.

5. Notice that his goal was "the exact truth." It is "God's truth," not our opinion; that is important.

Key Verses

"The teaching of the wise is a fountain of life, that one may turn away from the snares of death" (Prov. 13:14 NIV).

"When Jesus finished these words, the crowds were amazed at His teaching; for He was teaching them as one who had authority, and not as their scribes" (Matt. 7:28–29).

"Day after day, in the temple courts and from house to house, they never stopped teaching and proclaiming the good news that Jesus is the Messiah" (Acts 5:42 NIV).

"But Paul and Barnabas remained in Antioch, teaching and preaching with many others also, the word of the Lord" (Acts 15:35).

"So Paul stayed in Corinth for a year and a half, teaching them the word of God" (Acts 18:11 NIV).

"Do your best to present yourself to God as one approved, a worker who has no need to be ashamed, who correctly handles the word of truth" (2 Tim. 2:15 NIV).

Development of the Teaching Gift

It is important to recognize that just a person who has the gift of teaching cannot immediately start teaching. First he or she must have something to teach. Their teaching gift must be developed. The way to develop the gift of teaching is by:

- Studying the Word of God intensively. Find good commentaries to use, ask questions, do word studies and cross-references. Saturate yourself in the Bible. Buy all the Bible study tools you can. Use Bible study apps. I use Olive Tree and have almost all my seminary books now on my personal tablet.
- As stated earlier, apply the Word of God to your own life. Learn from your own life examples of how the Word of God works in your life.
- As the apostle Paul states in Romans 12:7, "He who teaches, in his teaching," a person must begin to teach. When the apostle Paul says "in his teaching," he means that a person takes the opportunity to teach, and through his teaching learns to communicate the Word of God better and better. As you teach the Word of God, you should learn all types of skills that will make you a better teacher. This is why it is important to find illustrations and work hard at giving personal examples. It is also important that you gain insights from those who also have the gift of teaching to pick up examples of how to communicate the Word of God better. Don't be afraid to allow people to critique your teaching.
- Be sure to study how Jesus taught.

Teaching When Filled with the Holy Spirit

Obviously it is important to be filled with the Holy Spirit while teaching, because it is God who is going to communicate through you. Remember that we are not talking about the natural talent of teaching as school teachers might have. We are talking about imparting the supernatural, life-changing Word of God.

Remember that just because a person is a teacher by profession does not mean that he or she has the gift of teaching. The whole objective of the gift of teaching is different than secular teaching because it is more than imparting knowledge — it is changing lives. When a person attends school, it is not for the purpose of changing their lives, but for preparing them to make a living. Because teaching is a supernatural gift, and with it comes a supernatural power of God, if you are a person filled with the Holy Spirit in your teaching you will:

- See changes in your own life.
- Begin to see changes in the lives of others through your teaching.
- Have a strong devotional life so you will have something to pass on.
- Be very thorough in your study because of deep reverence and respect for the Word of God and your desire to teach it accurately.
- Be patient and joyful in teaching, not becoming easily discouraged knowing that it takes time for people to learn and change their lives.
- Speak the truth in love (Eph. 4:15).

Teaching When Not Filled with the Holy Spirit

What happens when a person is not relying on the supernatural power of the Holy Spirit? Certain traits become evident.

- There will be no application in his or her teaching. Only facts will be taught.
- Application to his or her own life will cease. He or she begin to appear as a hypocrite. A case in point are the Pharisees who would add burdens to people that they themselves would not carry.

- Compassion appears to be absent. There is little concern for others.
- He or she becomes very dictatorial in teaching.
- A superior attitude develops.
- Criticalness of other Christian teachers, especially other pastors, arises. He or she becomes a faultfinder.
- This person does not balance out grace and truth. John 1:14 states that Jesus Christ was "full of grace and truth." Notice that grace comes before truth. A carnal teacher will not have the grace and will only seek to speak truth.
- He or she will speak truth without love (Eph. 4:15). While a carnal teacher may be speaking truth, it cannot enter into the hearts of the hearers because it is not accompanied with love. People are turned off, not by the person's words, but by his or her attitude.
- He or she becomes unteachable. This is so sad, because this person has now lost the power of the Holy Spirit in his or her own life.

If Teaching Is Your Primary Spiritual Gift

- Sharpen your teaching skills.
- Learn to how to teach one-on-one, small groups, and large groups.
- Step out and teach.

Knowledge: Answers the question "What?"

Definition: *The gift of knowledge is the supernaturally empowered ability to search, systematize, and summarize the Word of God and relevant information, which helps clarify the Word of God and make it available to others for their growth and edification.*

It is important to look at the gift of knowledge (*gnosis*), especially after looking at the gift of teaching. Although these two are different, they complement each other. The third gift, which ties into these two as well, is the gift of wisdom, which will be looked at next. It is important to understand the distinction between these four gifts so they can be used most effectively.

The gift of knowledge is found in 1 Corinthians 12:8 where it states, **"And to another the word of knowledge according to the same Spirit."** It is not just the gift of knowledge; it is the gift of the "word of knowledge." The phrase "the word of knowledge" can also be translated the "utterance of knowledge." In other words, the main emphasis of this is that it is a knowledge that is not to be withheld. It is a knowledge to be shared with others. Not to puff one up with pride, but to build up the body of Christ.

Goal: To be able to know what God's Word says concerning any and every topic.

Uniqueness between Gifts
- Knowledge: <u>states</u> what the Bible says.
- Teaching: <u>explains</u> what the Bible says and how to apply it.
- Wisdom: seeks to specifically <u>apply</u> what the Bible says to a given situation.
- Prophecy: seeks to <u>persuade</u> a person to do what wisdom determines is right.

Characteristics of a Person Gifted with Knowledge

A person with the gift of knowledge loves to acquire information. This person enjoys searching out the Word of God to find out all that it teaches concerning specific topics. It involves investigation, analyzing, comparing, and clarifying Scripture. This person loves to learn, and he or she is very analytical. They have a hunger for the truth. They will often appear scholarly. Many, if not all, biblical commentaries are written by those who have the spiritual gift of knowledge.

Knowledge is an attribute of God. He knows all things. Job 36:4 states, "One who is perfect in knowledge is with you." To know God is to have knowledge and understanding. "The fear of the LORD is the beginning of knowledge..." (Prov. 1:7).

Knowledge from God, however, includes more than knowing information and facts. It encompasses insight (understanding) as well—both knowing information and being able to apply it correctly. So, to have the gift of knowledge is to also have insight into the present and to know what to do with the knowledge given. One example of having God-given knowledge that encompasses insight is found in 1 Chronicles 12:32: "From the sons of Issachar, men who understood the times, with knowledge of what Israel should do, their chiefs were two hundred; and all their kinsmen were at their command." **Scripture also tells us that to have the knowledge of God is to live a successful life.** "He will be the sure foundation for your times, a rich store of salvation and wisdom and knowledge; the fear of the LORD is the key to this treasure" (Isa. 33:6 NIV).

It is very difficult to talk about knowledge without speaking about wisdom. It is important to note that while knowledge and wisdom are similar, they have distinctions. Scripture tells us that God wants us to have both.

> **"Oh, the depth of the riches, both of the wisdom**
> **and knowledge of God! How unsearchable are His**

judgments and unfathomable His ways!" (Rom. 11:33).

"That the God of our Lord Jesus Christ, the Father of glory, may give to you a spirit of wisdom and of revelation in the knowledge of Him" (Eph. 1:17).

"In whom are hidden all the treasures of wisdom and knowledge" (Col. 2:3).

Even though God wants us to have both, He has given the gift of knowledge and wisdom as separate gifts for a reason. Both play an intricate part in the building up of the body of Christ.

A person with the gift of knowledge will seek to know what God's Word says concerning any and every circumstance. Some examples of applying the gift of knowledge include:

- My teenager is hanging around the wrong crowd. What does God's Word say? Answer: 1 Corinthians 15:33 says, "Do not be deceived: 'Bad company corrupts good morals.'"
- What does the Bible say about drugs, sex, dating, work, marriage, money, dancing, or the kind of music I listen to?
- Someone comes to you and asks: "What is God's will for my life?"

What are your answers to these common issues?

Oftentimes a person who has the gift of knowledge seems to be more excited about studying the Word of God than ministering to people. However, one characteristic that would always seem to apply to a person with the gift of knowledge is that he or she loves the Word of God.

A person with the gift of knowledge is an invaluable resource to the body of Christ. This is the individual you can go to and ask, "What does the Bible say about this particular topic?" This person will then be able to tell you where to look and may give you the information as well. Pastors can utilize a person with this gift by having him or her do research on a certain topic. This person is greatly motivated to do so.

A person with the gift of knowledge is also a great team player. This person may seem intimidating, but this is simply a misunderstanding of this person's nature. They are not trying to usurp a position or prove how smart they are; they are simply excited about communicating what they know about God's Word.

The ministry this person has is oftentimes involved in translating Bibles, helping in interpretation, writing commentaries, providing research, and supplying information.

Once, when I was teaching on spiritual gifts, I met a woman who had been in full-time Christian work with a Bible translating organization. When she took the spiritual gifts analysis test, one of her predominant gifts was the gift of knowledge. When I asked her about her job as a missionary, it had nothing to do with her giftedness! She had not been using her gift of knowledge. It was so sad to discover that her gift was not being used. She had become so discouraged as a full-time missionary that she left her overseas mission team which was understandable. When a person is not fully utilizing his or her gifts, they can easily become discouraged or restless in their ministry.

There are some misunderstandings that accompany those who have this gift. One is that oftentimes a person with the gift of knowledge is assumed to be a good teacher. This, however, is a tragic mistake if a person with the gift of knowledge does not also have the gift of teaching. I saw this happen several times in our Sunday school department. Someone with the gift of knowledge was asked to teach a class. It seemed logical because he knew the Bible so well. What was not determined was whether or not he had the gift of teaching. It was just assumed that because he was so knowledgeable of the Bible, he could teach it. Unfortunately, the class was not excited, and the people did not respond well to his teaching. It wasn't that the information wasn't significant, it was simply that there was no supernatural power that accompanied this person when he spoke. That was because he did not have the gift of teaching. The people became disinterested in the class, and the class quickly shrunk in size. Fortunately we found someone who did have the gift of teaching and the class grew again.

A similar incident took place while I was in seminary. In seminary, we were required to attend chapel. Chapels were the times set aside to keep our spiritual relationship strengthened and to encourage the students in their walk with the Lord. Many of the faculty were on a rotation basis in terms of speaking during the chapel time. I remember well one incident when one of our Old Testament professors, a brilliant man, particularly in the area of archaeology, was given the assignment of giving a devotion. I remember sitting there as he began to explain the archaeological finds of Daniel and their significance. His voice had little emotion, and there was not much enthusiasm in his presentation. Not only that, but as students with deep needs and personal struggles, this chapel message had no relevance to where we were in life. It wasn't long before I noticed a restlessness in the chapel, and it became apparent that many of the students were not even paying attention. I heard later that when the professor sat down at the end of the chapel service, he turned to one of the other faculty members and said, "I sure blew that, didn't I?" The seminary professor, known for his ability to speak directly, said with a smile, "You sure did." I felt sorry for this professor because he was placed in a position where he was not using his giftedness. If he had the gift of preaching, or even teaching, he would have been able to minister to the students. This does not negate the significance of his ministry in the seminary as his insights and knowledge were greatly needed in the body of Christ.

Another misconception of those who have this gift is that they don't seem to care much about people. This is not the case. In fact it can actually be their love of people that motivates them to want to offer their knowledge of the Word of God.

How to Respond to "Words of Knowledge" or "Words of Wisdom"

What should we do when a person states that they have a "word from the Lord for you"? Some will call this a "word of knowledge" or a "word of wisdom". Some might even view this as a form of prophecy. The Word of God must be the final and sole authority in our lives. I want to give you an example from my own life that drove this point home to me.

Some time ago, in a church I was pastoring, there came a point where a problem surfaced between another elder and myself. I was troubled with something he had done but was reticent to go to him about it. Would I be making a big deal out of nothing? Would it make our relationship more difficult? Would it start a wedge between us? I always viewed our relationship as a good one. I did not want to jeopardize our relationship.

I was struggling with what to do. Should I confront him or not?

Fortunately, there was our usual all citywide prayer meeting for pastors that day at noon. I was still struggling with this when I sat down to pray with the other pastors.

It was not long before another pastor of a different denomination sat down next to me. After a minute, he leaned over to me and said, "Don't do it!" He had said nothing to me prior to this time, and this was all he said. I was shocked! How did he know I was struggling with an issue in my life and that I really needed to hear from the Lord?

After the prayer meeting, I kept thinking about this incident. I had difficulty with receiving this as a word or sign from God. I went over in my mind what God's Word says about confronting someone when I have a problem with them or what they have done. God's Word says repeatedly that I must be the one to go to that person (Matt. 18:15, Gal. 6:1). So I said to the Lord, "Lord, I don't understand why this person was able to know this and why he gave that word. Your written Word tells me to go to this elder, so I reject what this pastor said and I am going to follow the Bible."

Later that day I called my friend who was an elder and told him what was bothering me. He humbly apologized, and the issue was dead. It even brought us closer as friends! I thanked God that our authority is His written Word and that I don't need some other person to give me a "sign" when what to do is already in God's Word. This is why it is so important to know what the Bible says and rely on it. Any advice someone gives you must first be checked out by the Bible, and it is always the Bible that must be followed first. The advice the pastor gave me was not from God. It might have been a coincidence, but it was not the supernatural work of God's Spirit. *God's Spirit would never lead us in a way that would contradict the Bible!*

What is a "word of knowledge"? It is having an appropriate verse that would give a person insight and encouragement to their particular situation. It biblically answers the question that is being struggled with. When someone shares a problem or difficulty with you, don't be surprised if the Holy Spirit gives you a verse for that person to encourage them!

Key Verses

"Of the sons of Issachar, men who understood the times, with knowledge of what Israel should do..." (1 Chron. 12:32).

"Give me wisdom and knowledge, that I may lead this people, for who is able to govern this great people of yours?" (2 Chron. 1:10 NIV).

"'Select only strong, healthy, and good-looking young men,' he said. 'Make sure they are well versed in every branch of learning, are gifted with knowledge and good judgment, and are suited to serve in the royal palace. Train these young men in the language and literature of Babylon'" (Dan. 1:4 NLT).

"And it is my prayer that your love may abound more and more, with knowledge and all discernment" (Phil. 1:9 ESV).

Four Ways to Grow in the Gift of Knowledge

1. Grow deep in your relationship with God: "You there-fore, beloved… grow in the grace and knowledge of our Lord and Savior Jesus Christ" (2 Pet. 3:17–18 ESV).

2. Become a student of God's Word: "For Ezra had set his heart to study the law of the LORD, and to practice it, and to teach His statutes and ordinances in Israel" (Ezra 7:10).

3. Study about God's Word. Learn also about church history and archeology.

4. Apply God's Word to your life: "If you **know** these things, you are blessed if you **do** them" (John 13:17 emphasis mine).

How to Develop Your Gift of Knowledge

To develop your gift of knowledge, you need to spend much time studying Scripture and doing topical Word studies. In other words, keep a notebook of words or topics you have studied. Also, read commentaries and books that help you to understand portions of the Bible better. Seek to develop your skills in interpreting Scripture. Bounce your findings off others and seek creative ways to get your findings out to the rest of the body of Christ. Download a Bible app like "Olive Tree," "Logos," or "You Bible" and purchase many commentaries and tools to assist your study. I have replaced almost all my study books from seminary onto my iPad.

Holy Spirit-Filled Knowledge

If you are a person who has the gift of knowledge and are filled with the Spirit, you will demonstrate many of the following characteristics:

- Your life will be in balance. Proverbs 1:7 states, **"The fear of the Lord is the beginning of knowledge."** This person has his or her priorities in line because his or her devotion is to the Lord. He or she understands it is God who gives knowledge.
- God will use you to give insights into His Word to the believers around you.
- You will desire the Lord more than you desire knowledge.
- You will despise false teaching.
- You will be humble about your gift.
- You will receive supernatural insight into the Word of God.
- You will have a strong devotional life.
- You will have a disciplined study of the Word of God.
- You will be very teachable.
- You will patiently look for areas to use this gift.

Knowledge When Not Filled with the Holy Spirit

What happens when a person who has the gift of knowledge is not filled with the Holy Spirit? There are certain characteristics that manifest themselves. He or she:

- Will become arrogant and puffed up (1 Cor. 8:1). He or she becomes prideful in their knowledge and feels superior to others.
- Will worship the Word of God more than the Author of the Word of God. This is a very subtle distinction. God is our God. The Bible helps us worship and know God. A

person needs to be careful that he or she doesn't zealously desire the Word of God more than God Himself.

- Will become analytical to the point of being critical of others. He or she concentrates more on identifying where a person is wrong rather than where a person is right.
- Will begin to have little to do with people and will simply want to hide away and study. He or she has forgotten the purpose of the gift.
- May have a tendency to form little cliques, which can become a point of division in a church.
- May become caught up in hunting down heresy rather than communicating solidly what the Word of God teaches.
- Will become impatient with others who do not know the Bible or facts as well as they do.
- Will not receive or respond positively to his or her communication of knowledge because it is not communicated in love or in the power of the Holy Spirit.
- Will begin to drift away from devotional study of God's Word and begin to have a poor prayer life.

If Knowledge Is Your Primary Spiritual Gift

Continue to develop it. Look for opportunities in Bible studies and other Christian events to bring what the Bible says in a tactful and meaningful way. Let your church leaders with whom you spend time with know how much you enjoy studying the Bible. Develop when to share a "word of knowledge" to groups and other people's lives in a way that they will be very receptive to. Step out in confidence with this gift knowing that others need to know what God's Word says about life. Consider writing commentary on Bible passages. Write devotions. Mayby even start a blog commenting on Scripture.

Look for God to bring people, Christians, and non-Christians into your life who are seeking Him and need to know intellectual answers to help them in their faith.

Wisdom: Answers the question "What now?"

The gift "word of wisdom" (*sophia*) (1 Cor. 12:8), is tied in closely to the gift of knowledge and teaching. The main difference between the gift of knowledge and the gift of wisdom is that the gift of knowledge is the <u>accumulation</u> of facts, whereas the gift of wisdom is the <u>application</u> of facts. It is the supernatural ability to see how Scripture and the Spirit of God directs in a particular situation. "Word" denotes not only expression, but time and place, beginning and end. The gift operates in a particular setting and time.[13]

Definition: *The gift of wisdom is the supernaturally empowered ability to know the mind of the Holy Spirit in such a way as to receive insight into how Scripture and given knowledge may best be applied to specific situations arising in the body of Christ.*

Goal: To apply the Word of God to one's own life and explain how it is applied to specific life situations.

I like what Peter Wagner says about someone who possesses the gift of wisdom: "When a person with the gift of wisdom speaks, other members of the body recognize the truth that has been spoken and the right course of action recommended."[14]

Here is one example of applying wisdom. If someone comes to you with a specific problem in their life you will know from Scripture what they should do in that given situation. They explain, "I am having trouble with this person at work (or school) who constantly drains me by sharing all their problems. I want to be nice, but it is exhausting me and bringing me down. What do I do?" The gift of wisdom will enable you to know how to answer that question. Speak the truth in love (Eph. 4:15.)

Characteristics of the Gift of Wisdom

A person with the gift of wisdom does not necessarily need to be a very scholarly person. A person with the gift of wisdom is able to take all the facts of a given situation and determine what the mind of the Lord is in this situation.

I remember well a board meeting where a particular situation arose, and the board of elders was seeking to determine the best course of action. Because the gift of knowledge is one of my stronger gifts, I began to explain what the Bible had to say concerning this matter. However, at that point I was not confident in saying what we should do. On the other hand, my friend Larry Huber, who has the gift of wisdom, immediately said, "Men, it's clear what we need to do. Here's what we need to do...." And then he proceeded to tell us all which of the options laid out by the Word of God was the right choice. At that point, all the men realized that God had spoken. It was confirmed in all our hearts. It seemed the obvious and right thing to do for our church, and we were all relieved. We felt great about the decision we made, thanks to Larry using his gift of wisdom and having examined Scripture. As it turned out, it was the right answer for the church. This is how the gifts work in conjunction with each other.

The person with the gift of wisdom has the keen ability to discern what the Spirit of God is saying in particular situations. The Bible does not always address every person's specific situation in life. That is why it is necessary to have those in the body of Christ with the gift of wisdom. People with the gift of wisdom can help supernaturally discern the mind of the Spirit concerning specific situations. This is one of the reasons this gift is called a "word of wisdom." It is the right "word" (advice) inspired by the Holy Spirit for a particular situation. It is the Word of God (Bible) applied to a specific, given situation.

Some people may well ask, "Doesn't God give wisdom to each individual?" The answer is obviously yes. He gives aspects of all the gifts to everyone. As a matter of fact, we have all the wisdom we need when we have Jesus Christ (1 Cor. 1:30), especially when it pertains to our own life. However, when it comes to discerning God's specific will for the body of Christ at large, or for other people, we need those with the gift of wisdom to help give us insight and direction.

Key Verses

A verse in the Bible which characterizes a person with the gift of wisdom is 1 Chronicles 12:32: "Of the sons of Issachar, men who **understood** the times, with knowledge of **what Israel should do**...." A person with the gift of wisdom has understanding and knowledge of what God wants done in a particular time and situation.

> **"Now Joshua son of Nun was filled with the spirit of wisdom because Moses had laid his hands on him. So the Israelites listened to him and did what the LORD had commanded Moses" (Deut. 34:9 NIV).**

> **"Give me the wisdom and knowledge to lead them properly, for who could possibly govern this great people of yours?" (2 Chron. 1:10 NLT).**

"For my words are wise, and my thoughts are filled with insight" (Ps. 49:3 NLT).

"And Jesus kept increasing in wisdom and stature, and in favor with God and men" (Luke 2:52).

"And He will be the stability of your times, a wealth of salvation, wisdom and knowledge; the fear of the LORD is his treasure" (Isa. 33:6).

Misperceptions about Those with the Gift of Wisdom

Sometimes a person with the gift of wisdom mistakenly appears to know more about what God is saying than other people do. This is not so; it is just that he or she has an ability to accumulate and analyze information and apply it. He or she may be misunderstood by being perceived as thinking only they have the answers or that they are speaking on behalf of God. All of us must use the Word of God as our authority and not simply rely on another person. Therefore, we should always take what someone says and analyze it according to the Word of God. Confirmation of a person's insight should not be based on only one person's opinion. It should be determined by more than one person so there is protection in terms of confirming what God's will is. That is why, when my friend Larry spoke, there wasn't just one person agreeing with him, but the whole board, and they perceived his suggestion as God's best choice for us as a church.

A person with the gift of wisdom is not a "know it all," but simply a person who seeks to be spiritually attuned to the Lord who wants His will done in every situation.

An effective counselor would need the spiritual gifts of wisdom, discernment, and encouragement.

Three Steps to Grow Wise

1. Study thoroughly God's Word.
2. Grow deep in your relationship with God, "In whom are hidden all the treasures of wisdom and knowledge" (Col. 2:3).
3. Apply God's Word to your life. "Yet wisdom is proven right by her deeds" (Matt. 11:19). Wisdom is an action word. It is who you are. A person is considered wise not by what they know but how they live their lives.

How to Develop the Gift of Wisdom

If you have the gift of wisdom and want to develop it, continue to study the Word of God. Study how certain challenges were solved by the Lord and keep your prayer life strong. Continue to seek the presence of the Holy Spirit in your life so you can keep spiritually in tune with Him. Have consistent devotional times where you spend time listening to God. When someone seeks wisdom from you, pray first, and if necessary, pray with that person and examine Scripture together concerning the situation. Learn to ask good questions of people.

Wisdom When Filled with the Holy Spirit

If you are a person with the gift of wisdom who is filled with the Holy Spirit, you will experience many of the following characteristics in your life:

- A strong desire to know the Lord. Proverbs 9:10 says, "The fear of the Lord is the beginning of wisdom, and knowledge of the Holy One is understanding." Not only does the fear of the Lord give knowledge, but it also gives wisdom.

- A sensitivity to the leading of the Holy Spirit in your own life.
- A strong hunger for the Word of God in order to know God better.
- A consistent devotional life.
- A strong prayer life so as to be in constant communication with the Lord regarding every situation.
- A humility about you. Jeremiah 9:23–24 states, "Let not a wise man boast of his wisdom ...but let him who boasts boast of this, that he understands and knows Me."
- A desire to bring much glory to the Lord Jesus Christ. Chapter 1 verse 30 in 1 Corinthians tells us, "But by His doing, you are in Christ Jesus, who became to us wisdom from God...."
- A desire to live a holy life by applying the Word of God regularly to your life.

Wisdom When Not Filled with the Holy Spirit

A person with the gift of wisdom who is not filled with the Holy Spirit must be careful about certain characteristics cropping up in his or her life.

- They can become dominating by telling others how they should live, whether asked or not.
- They can lead people astray. This person may use words like "God told me this is His will for you," then proceed to explain what God's will is for their life. This is a serious caution, as entire churches have been led astray by people who said they were speaking for the Lord when, in actuality, they were not. Any time a person speaks beyond his

or her authority or beyond the teaching the Word of God, this is not of God.

- They can become more concerned about how others live their lives than how they live their own.
- They may neglect to spend regular, consistent time in the Word of God.
- They can become boastful (Jer. 9:23). This person may feel superior to others because he or she thinks they have insight into God's will that other people do not have.
- They may not have a meaningful prayer life. Prayer is not that high a priority in this person's life.
- They can take on the characteristics of a busybody, gossip, or a meddler in other people's lives.
- They can become very opinionated, oftentimes giving their opinion even when it is not asked for.

If Wisdom Is Your Primary Spiritual Gift

Learn to use this in people's lives who are looking for answers for their particular situation. Know that God wants you to continue to direct them to Scripture and to Himself. Be a diligent student of God's Word so He can use you more. Look for God to bring even non-Christians into your life that need guidance. This is a wonderful gift to lead people to Christ. This is also a much needed gift for counseling.

Encouragement: I empower individuals

Definition: *The gift of encouragement, exhortation, comfort is the supernaturally empowered ability to come alongside of someone with words of comfort, encouragement, or exhortation in such a way that they feel hopeful, helped, healed, strengthened, and inspired to live by greater faith in the Lord.*

The gift of encouragement, as found in Romans 12:8, is a very significant gift in terms of its type of ministry. This gift is also referred to as the gift of exhortation. However, as you look at the New Testament, the word is translated one of three ways. To *exhort*, to *encourage*, or to *comfort*. Many times it simply depends on the context in which the word is being used. For example, *paraklesis* is translated differently in each of these passages.

> ***Comfort*:** "Blessed be the God and Father of our Lord Jesus Christ, the Father of mercies and God of all <u>comfort,</u> who <u>comforts</u> us in all our affliction so that we may be able to <u>comfort</u> those who are in any affliction with the <u>comfort</u> with which we ourselves are <u>comforted</u> by God" (2 Cor. 1:3–4 emphasis mine).

> ***Encourage*:** "Therefore <u>encourage</u> one another, build up one another, just as you also are doing" (1 Thess. 5:11 emphasis mine).

> ***Exhort*:** "Preach the Word; be ready in season and out of season; reprove, rebuke, <u>exhort,</u> with great patience and instruction" (2 Tim. 4:2 emphasis mine).

Often the word exhort is also translated urge. For example, in Ephesians 4:1 Paul states, "As a prisoner for the Lord, then, I <u>urge</u> you to live a life worthy of the calling you have received" (NIV emphasis mine).

A wonderful example is found in 1 Thessalonians 2:11–12, "For you know that we dealt with each of you as a father deals with his own children, **encouraging, comforting** and **urging** you to live lives worthy of God, who calls you into his kingdom and glory" (NIV emphasis mine).

To gain a better understanding of the word "encouragement", it is important to look at its definition. The word *paraklesis* is made up of two words. Both have a significant meaning.

1. *Para-* where we receive our word parallel. It means to "come alongside."

2. *Klesis-* the word "to call." The idea then, is to "call alongside" or to "come alongside" for a specific purpose. What is fascinating is that the Holy Spirit Himself is called the *Paraklete*. This word is often translated "helper" or "comforter." To fully understand the gift of exhortation or encouragement, all we need to do is look at who the Holy Spirit is and what He does. He is our comforter, our encourager, and our exhorter (John 14:16). This word is also used to describe the ministry that Jesus Christ has in our lives as the advocate, First John 2:1 says, **"And if anyone sins, we have an <u>Advocate</u> [one who comes alongside of us] with the Father, Jesus Christ the righteous"** (insert mine). This is significant because we see that the Holy Spirit and the Lord Jesus Christ are the Ones who exhort us, encourage us, and comfort us in our times of trials or discouragement. When we have sin in our life, the Holy Spirit and the Lord Jesus Christ convicts us concerning our sin so that we will repent of it.

As the Holy Spirit has come alongside us to comfort and encourage and exhort us, so also the person with the gift of encouragement comes alongside another person to exhort or encourage or comfort him or her, whichever the person has need of at that point.

The gift of encouragement and the gift of preaching are virtually identical gifts except for one major point. The gift of preaching (prophecy) is the gift of encouragement but is used on a large-scale, public basis. (See the gift of prophecy.) *The gift of encouragement, or exhortation, is used primarily on a one-on-one basis, whereas preaching is a public gift. One ministers to the body of Christ at large; the other ministers to the body of Christ individually.*

The word "encouragement" is a very significant word as it is used over 100 times in a verb form and over 30 times in its noun form. It is a good idea to study it to learn of its use and the ministry which we all have. Although we are told to encourage one another (Heb. 10:25), there are particular individuals in the body of Christ who have this as their primary gift and ministry.

Goal: To speak words that bring a person to the point that they are energized to trust the Lord more and get back to using his or her gifts to a greater degree.

Leslie Flynn says, "The gift of exhortation involves a supernatural ability to come alongside to help, to strengthen the weak, reassure the wavering, buttress the buffeted, steady the faltering, console the troubled, encourage the halting. Just as the Holy Spirit is an instrument of help, so the Spirit uses the gift to make us instruments of encouragement to fellow saints."[15] Dr. John Wex says this is the ability "to encourage specific steps to apply God's solutions to life's problems."[16] Dr. Wagner states that it is the ability to "minister words of comfort, consolation, encouragement and counsel to other members of the body in such a way that they feel helped and healed."[17]

If the gift of encouragement could be summed up in one phrase, it would be **"to strengthen another person in the Lord."** Whatever a person needs to be strengthened, the person with this gift will apply it.

Characteristics

How can a person know whether or not he or she has the gift of encouragement? There are major characteristics found in those who have this gift:

- The ability to see potential in others.
- Believing in the power of God in a person's life.
- The ability to inspire and strengthen others to press on in the Lord. They bring hope in God.
- They enjoy counseling and giving advice to a person who is in spiritual need.
- They can sense when someone needs to be encouraged.
- They are very positive and inspiring to others.
- They will not hesitate to confront sin in a person's life but will do it in such a way that a person is not bitter, resentful, or discouraged.
- They constantly use Scripture to help a person put their eyes on the Lord not on themselves, their sin, or their circumstances.
- They have a compelling desire to urge people on to greater heights in their walk with God and their ministry for God.
- Their greatest joy is seeing someone fall in love with the Lord and place their hope and trust in God.

A key verse for this person is the emulation of the apostle Paul's ministry in Colossians 1:28–29, "We proclaim Him, admonishing every person and teaching every person with all wisdom, so that we may present every person complete in Christ. For this purpose I also labor, striving according to His power which works mightily within me." A person with the gift of encouragement has the desire to see everyone become a fully devoted follower of the Lord Jesus Christ. He or she seeks to have a ministry of discipleship. They want to see every person reach his or her potential in Christ!

Note: To be a good counselor, a person would need the spiritual gifts of encouragement, wisdom, and discernment.

Biblical Examples

Those who have the gift of encouragement especially need to study the Bible thoroughly to learn more about this gift.

Old Testament

One of the major examples in the Old Testament of how to encourage another person can be found in the relationship between Jonathan and David. All three of the main aspects of the gift of encouragement are found in Jonathan's ministry to David. A clear example of this is found in 1 Samuel 23:16–17:

> **"Jonathan went to find David and encouraged him to stay strong in his faith in God. 'Don't be afraid,' Jonathan reassured him. 'My father will never find you! You are going to be the king of Israel, and I will be next to you, as my father, Saul, is well aware'"** (NLT).

Jonathan was a godsend to David at this time. David had known that he was to be king over Israel. The problem was, many years had passed and David was becoming discouraged. As a matter of fact, it seemed like he would lose his life at the hands of Saul.

Jonathan entered David's life to encourage him. Notice the three aspects here.

1. Jonathan had the ability *to see the potential* in David. In verse 17 he stated, "And you will be king over Israel." Jonathan was helping David see his future and potential.

2. He helped David *believe in the power of God.* This is seen when he said, "My father will never find you!" This inspired great hope in God and inspired David's ability to believe in the power of God to protect him.

3. Jonathan was able *to inspire and strengthen David to press on in the Lord.* This is seen in verse 16 which states that Jonathan "encouraged him in his faith in God." The word in Hebrew for encouraged literally means to strengthen. This is the very purpose of encouragement. To strengthen someone in God, he or she must be able to put his or her hope in God and nothing else. David left Jonathan inspired, believing in the power of God and strengthened to press on in the Lord. This is exactly what happened as you examine the rest of David's life. He did become king, and he continued to keep his faith and strength in God. In other words, he reached the goal and potential God had for him. Jonathan's main joy was not that he, himself, be exalted, but that David be exalted in the Lord. Jonathan was more concerned about David's growth than about whether or not he himself received the kingship over Israel. That's true encouragement.

New Testament

There are many examples of encouragement in the New Testament.

Paul: Of the multitude of gifts that the apostle Paul had, one of his major ones was the gift of encouragement. This is seen throughout his ministry. In Acts 14:22 he went throughout the churches "strengthening the disciples and encouraging them to remain true to the faith saying, 'We must go through many hardships to enter the kingdom of God' (NIV emphasis mine). He is comforting, inspiring, and strengthening in that passage. He continually did this throughout the churches (Acts 16:40).

Others: Judas and Silas encouraged the believers (Acts 15:31–32). The apostle Peter did this (1 Pet. 5:1–2), and the writer of the book of Hebrews did this as well (Heb. 13:22). Some say that the whole book of Hebrews was written to encourage the brethren.

Barnabas: He is perhaps the best known individual with the gift of encouragement. His name was actually called Joseph (Acts 1:23, 4:36) but was changed to Barnabas by the apostles, which means "son of encouragement." His ability to see the potential in others, believe in the power of God, inspire, and strengthen others is seen throughout the book of Acts and in the lives of two individuals in particular. He was the one, when all the others forsook Paul, who came alongside Paul and helped to disciple him (Acts 9:27). He was the one, as well, who continued to encourage and stand by the side of John Mark, even when the apostle Paul had given up on him (Acts 15:39). He also journeyed with Paul around the various churches strengthening and encouraging them. What a tremendous ministry Barnabas had! Who knows how history would have been rewritten had Barnabas not stepped into the life of the apostle Paul and encouraged, strengthened, and inspired him in the Lord. Anyone who wants to learn how to encourage others would do well to study the life of Barnabas throughout the book of Acts. Some even believe that Barnabas may well be the author of the book of Hebrews, which is an entire book of encouragement!

Development

In my observation, those who have the gift of encouragement, have a tendency to be stronger in one of the three areas of *exhortation, encouragement,* or *comfort.* In other words, a person who has this gift may do more exhorting than encouraging or comforting. Whereas another person who has this gift may be more of a comforter than an exhorter.

However, the person who has this gift <u>must learn to utilize all three aspects of this gift</u> if he or she is going to be most effective. A person who just simply exhorts all the time will eventually weary others. If you only exhort, people will eventually avoid being around you because that's not always what they need.

A person who has the gift of encouragement must discern when a person needs to be comforted, encouraged, or exhorted. A person cannot be continually comforted and press on in the Lord. Nor can he or she continually be encouraged or exhorted without being comforted.

The apostle Paul says in Romans 12:8, "He who exhorts in his exhortation." This means that, as you exhort, you learn how to be more effective exhorting when to use Scripture and when not to use Scripture. This verse could also be translated, "he who encourages, in his encouraging," or "he who comforts in his comforting." A person who is strong in exhorting needs to learn how to better encourage and comfort and vice versa. You learn how to better encourage by encouraging others to find out what works and what does not. I have had to learn skills in comforting because my tendency is to quote Scripture when someone is hurting, instead of simply listening and praying with him or her.

If you have the gift of encouragement (exhortation), do a word study to learn ways in which you can encourage others. Study the life of Paul and Barnabas to learn how they were able to persuade, exhort, and encourage others. Study the life of Christ and find out when He was comforting, when He was encouraging, and when He had to exhort.

For example, Jesus would <u>comfort</u> those who had fallen into deep sin and wanted to be rescued, as with the woman caught in adultery (John 8). There were times when the disciples needed to be <u>encouraged</u>, and He did that frequently. There were times when He had to <u>exhort</u> others, as in the case of the Pharisees, scribes, and lawyers who needed to be confronted with sin in their life (Matt. 23). The disciples needed, at times, to be rebuked for their unbelief. You will definitely need to depend upon the leading of the Holy Spirit to determine the needs of people in each situation. The more you exercise this gift, the easier it will be to discern what a person needs in a given situation. There will be times when you will need to use the authority of Scripture to confront sin in a person's life. There will be times when you can refer to Scripture to encourage a person to "hang in there," and there will be times when it is best or not best to use Scripture in comforting someone. Remember this, your overall objective is to get a person back on his or her feet living for the Lord not for himself or herself.

Not only is it important to know *how* best to use this gift but also *when* to use it. The apostle Paul brought this point out. He states in 1 Thessalonians 5:14, "And we urge you, brethren, admonish the unruly, encourage the fainthearted, help the weak, be patient with all men." A person who has this gift will need to learn when to admonish the unruly, encourage those who are fainthearted, and help those (comfort those) who are weak. In every situation, however, we obviously need to be patient.

Misunderstandings

A person who has the gift of encouragement can often be misunderstood. They see things very clearly and are most often positive. In a coaching or counseling situation, their advice may seem too simplistic to others when in reality it is exactly what is needed.

Sometimes they can be misunderstood as being insensitive or living an unrealistic life. This person simply knows that he or she gets great joy helping others regardless of whether or not they are having problems themselves.

One thing I have discovered is that those who have the gift of encouragement, often times need the most encouragement themselves. If you have this gift, you understand what I am saying. If you know those who have this gift, then please go out of your way to encourage that person. They will then be energized to go on and use their gift to encourage many others!

Key Verses

> **"If your gift is to encourage others, be encouraging"**
> **(Rom. 12:8 NLT).**

> **"But commission Joshua, and encourage and**
> **strengthen him, for he will lead this people across**
> **and will cause them to inherit the land that you will**
> **see" (Deut. 3:28 NIV).**

"Jonathan went to find David and encouraged him to stay strong in his faith in God" (1 Sam. 23:16 NLT).

"Hezekiah spoke encouragingly to all the Levites who showed good skill in the service of the LORD" (2 Chron. 30:22 ESV).

"Encourage the exhausted, and strengthen the feeble" (Isa. 35:3).

"So with many other exhortations he preached good news to the people" (Luke 3:18).

"When he (Barnabus) arrived and saw what the grace of God had done, he was glad and encouraged them all to remain true to the Lord with all their hearts" (Acts 11:23 NIV).

"For you know that we dealt with each of you as a father deals with his own children, encouraging, comforting and urging you to live lives worthy of God, who calls you into his kingdom and glory" (1 Thess. 2:11–12 NIV).

Encouragement When Filled with the Holy Spirit

If you have the gift of encouragement and walk in the power of the Holy Spirit, then you will see many of these characteristics manifested in your life:

- Discernment. You will have discernment from the Lord as to what a person needs for encouragement.
- Vision. You will have a vision for the potential in a person's life: what God can do in him or her.

- Wisdom. You will know Scripture so as how to best apply it in a person's life.
- Faith. You will have great faith in God in a given situation, and in God's work in the other person.
- Love. You will have a genuine love for the person. You will communicate a spirit of caring for the person and especially for his or her walk with God.
- Sensitivity. You will be able to show discretion in how to handle a situation.
- Enthusiasm. A person who is an encourager has great enthusiasm. You will be encouraged yourself by encouraging others.
- A deep devotional life. As you walk with the Lord, you will be strengthened yourself so you can, in turn, strengthen others. It is said of David in 1 Samuel 30:6 that "David strengthened himself in the Lord his God."
- A strong prayer life. You will not only pray for yourself, but for others and their walk with the Lord.

Encouragement When Not Filled with the Holy Spirit

Those who are not walking in the Spirit of God, and who have the gift of encouragement, will find certain characteristics begin to develop in their lives:

- Worldliness. Instead of depending on the wisdom of God, they will depend on their own wisdom. They may try to encourage people with wisdom of the world, not wisdom from God's Word.
- Judgmentalism. They will become critical of how others live their lives instead of helping them. Criticalness is the opposite of encouragement. You can tell if you are filled with the Spirit or not by noticing how critical you are of others.

- Insensitive. They will tend to use God's Word as a club rather than a means of encouragement. They will use it to point out people's faults continually, rather than to use it to bring hope and inspiration.
- Selfish motives. Instead of having godly motives and encouraging a person to turn to the Lord, they may try to encourage others so that they themselves receive the glory, not God.
- Discouragement and bitterness. Because a person with the gift of encouragement needs much encouragement themselves, they may become discouraged and bitter if they don't receive encouragement.
- Apathy. Discouragement and bitterness lead to apathy and instead of showing enthusiasm for others who are growing in the Lord, they will tend to be apathetic about a person's condition or plight in life.
- Laziness. They will slack off on their study of God's Word and time in prayer. They begin to lose their love for God and others.

If Encouragement Is Your Primary Spiritual Gift

Your job description every day is to encourage, exhort, or comfort those with whom you interact. God has people in your life that need encouragement and to be strengthened in their relationship with God. Learn when to comfort, when to encourage, and when to exhort. Be good at all three. Urge people to persevere in their walk and service to the Lord and not give up or be discouraged. You have a lifetime of ministry before you. God may lead non-Christians to you who need encouragement whom you can lead to the Lord. Know that God wants to use you everyday.

Pastor-Teacher: I care for each person in the group

Definition: *The gift of pastor-teacher is the supernaturally empowered ability to assume a long-term, personal responsibility for the spiritual wellbeing of a group of believers by leading, teaching, and spiritually protecting them.*

Goal: To care for a group of believers so that they are spiritually nourished and growing in their faith.

The gift of pastor-teacher (Eph. 4:11) is the only hyphenated gift. It is a two-fold gift, and the reasons for this will become clear. The word "pastor" (*poimen*), literally means "shepherd." A pastor is a shepherd of God's people. Because it appears in Ephesians 4:11, it is not only a gift, but also an office in the church. However, it needs to be noted, that it is not an office of authority, but of ministry. The authority of a church resides in the overseeing elders. Among the elders however, there are pastor-teachers. Paul refers to elders who **"work hard at preaching and teaching"** (1 Tim. 5:17).

The Lord Jesus Christ Himself is called the "Chief Shepherd" (1 Pet. 5:4). He oftentimes refers to Himself as the "Good Shepherd" (John 10). In Psalm 23, the Lord is spoken of as our Shepherd.

The analogy of a literal shepherd over sheep implies that a shepherd had a particular responsibility toward sheep.

1. He would **lead** the sheep to other pastures.
2. He would be responsible to **feed** the sheep.
3. He was responsible to **protect** the sheep.

As you look at Psalm 23, you will see that this is what the Lord Jesus does for each one of His children. The two main passages which refer to the responsibilities of one who shepherds, is found in Acts 20:28–31: "Be on guard for yourselves and for all the flock, among which the Holy Spirit has made you overseers, <u>to shepherd</u> the church of God which He purchased with His own blood. I know that after my departure savage wolves will come in among you, not sparing the flock and from among your own selves men will arise, speaking perverse things, to draw away the disciples after them. Therefore be on the alert, remembering that night and day for a period of three years I did not cease to admonish each one with tears" (emphasis mine).

The second passage is found in 1 Peter 5:1–4 as Peter addresses the overseers of the churches in that region: "Therefore, I exhort the elders among you, as your fellow-elder and witness of the sufferings of Christ, and a partaker also of the glory that is to be revealed, <u>shepherd the flock</u> of God among you, not under compulsion, but voluntarily, according to the will of God and not for sordid gain, but with eagerness nor yet as lording it over those allotted to your charge, but proving to be examples to the flock. And when the Chief Shepherd appears, you will receive the unfading crown of glory" (emphasis mine).

Notice in each of these passages, there is the underlying theme of **leading, teaching,** and **protecting** the flock.

It is also very interesting that Christ Himself told Peter in John 21:16 that if he truly loved Him he was to **"shepherd My sheep."** Part of Peter's doing that is teaching doctrine through his two epistles.

One can have the gift of teaching without the gift of pastor. However, it is not possible to have the gift of pastor without the gift of teaching. This makes sense when one realizes that to truly care and minister to another person in the sense of shepherding, one has to teach them the Word of God. To simply care for a person and help meet his or her physical and emotional needs is more the gift of mercy than it is the gift of pastor-teacher. One of the primary ways in which a person who has the gift of pastor helps another person is by feeding them the Word of God.

It is interesting to note also, that as shepherds would lead their sheep onto various grazing lands, they would come to areas where bushes were too high for the sheep to reach. The shepherd would then often bend down the branches so the sheep could feed on the tasty berries and leaves. Likewise, a pastor-teacher must also "bend down the Word of God" to feed people what truly nourishes the soul, and that is the Word of God!

As it was noted earlier, a person in the position of pastor who does not have the gift of teaching ends up having a weak and anemic flock. People will care for each other but are not grounded in their faith.

It is exciting to know also, that it is not only men who have this gift, but women as well. There are many women "pastor-teachers" in the body of Christ. Although they do not have the same ministry, their gifts are equally important and effective.

Characteristics

A person with the gift of pastor-teacher obviously cares about people. This person has a special ability to nurture the spiritual wellbeing of other believers with a deep sense of love for them and for God. They do not necessarily need to be leading a group or team to use this gift. They have a great desire to protect the people who are under their care or part of the group they are in. Remember, a person who has the gift of encouragement is concerned about an individual; the person with the gift of pastor-teacher cares about a group as a whole. He or she cannot stand it if one person in the group is not doing well in their relationship with God.

For example, if a woman has a Bible study, and she has the gift of pastor-teacher, she will care about how every person in the group is doing, so that the group as a whole will do well. If one person in the group is not doing well, she will then not only reach out to that person, but try to encourage others to help bring that person back into the group. This person has the heart of the Lord Jesus Christ when He stated how He wished He could wrap His arms around the people of Jerusalem as a mother hen does with her wings to her chicks.

Another characteristic of a person who has this gift is that he or she is an example to others (1 Pet. 5:3). He does not mind using himself as an example. The apostle Paul, who was a pastor-teacher, had no problem with this as he stated, "Be imitators of me, just as I also am of Christ" (1 Cor. 11:1).

A person with this gift will also be willing to make sacrifices to nurture and care for people under his or her designation (1 Thess. 2).

Misunderstandings

There are some misunderstandings that may take place. For example, because the pastor-teacher desires to be involved in a person's life, this may be interpreted by others as intruding. As a result, you may experience rejection. Your motives may be questioned because you have a deep love for those who are hurting. This is especially difficult with individuals with this gift who are caring for members of the opposite sex. You may also be misunderstood when you seem very concerned about a loss of a member from a group. You will seem to have the feeling of being incomplete. You may also become very emotional when you see that a group is being attacked spiritually.

For example, someone in a Bible study may have picked up an article or book that has heresy in it. This person may not understand that its teaching contradicts the Bible. Oftentimes the person with the gift of pastor-teacher becomes very concerned about the other person being exposed to this material. The young Christian may not understand what the "big deal" is. However, the one with this gift definitely understands why it is such a "big deal."

Some people feel that this is an essential gift in order to have a mega-chuch (over 1,000 in attendance on a given Sunday). This is not so. Pastors of mega and meta-churches need the gifts of preaching, faith, and leadership.

A pastor who has pastor-teacher as his primary gift will find that this gift often keeps his congregation from growing much over 200–300. The reason for this is that he will want to be able to keep watch over every member of his flock. If the church grows very large, then he tends to be frustrated that he cannot watch over all his sheep in a personal manner. That family feeling is lost, and he struggles with thinking he is doing a good job because of the loss of contact. In actuality, if the Sr. Pastor's primary gift is pastor-teacher, then it can be a hindrance to the largeness of a church.

With all this said, most churches will not become mega-churches (due to location, culture, tradition, building limitations, etc.), and, therefore, men with this gift are needed to pastor the majority of churches.

Development

The person with the gift of pastor-teacher must work hard to be a student of the Word of God. If this is your gift, you must also learn skills in how to shepherd a flock whether you are the leader or not. This may mean making phone calls or coming up with ways to determine how a people are doing. You must learn how to monitor without coming across as a meddler. Much can be learned from the life of Christ, since He is the ideal Shepherd, and He shepherded His disciples through difficult trials and on to spiritual maturity. You must learn how to confront false teachings that crop up in churches and groups. You must develop your skills as a teacher and how to work with people. You must learn to utilize those things which keep the ministry personal.

Key Verses

> "Then Jesus told them this parable: 'Suppose one of you has a hundred sheep and loses one of them. Does he not leave the ninety-nine in the open country and go after the lost sheep until he finds it? And when he finds it, he joyfully puts it on his shoulders and goes home. Then he calls his friends and neighbors together and says, 'Rejoice with me; I have found my lost sheep'" (Luke 15:3–6 NIV).

> "Be shepherds of God's flock that is under your care, serving as overseers — not because you must, but because you are willing, as God wants you to be; not greedy for money, but eager to serve; not lording it over those entrusted to you, but being examples to the flock" (1 Pet. 5:2–3 NIV).

"May the LORD, the God who gives breath to all living things, appoint someone over this community to go out and come in before them, one who will lead them out and bring them in, so the LORD'S people will not be like sheep without a shepherd" (Num. 27:16–17 NIV).

"He chose David his servant and took him from the sheep pens; from tending the sheep he brought him to be the shepherd of his people Jacob, of Israel his inheritance. And David shepherded them with integrity of heart; with skillful hands he led them" (Ps. 78:70–72 NIV).

"When Jesus went ashore, He saw a large crowd, and He felt compassion for them because they were like sheep without a shepherd; and He began to teach them many things" (Mark 6:34).

"Brothers and sisters, we urge you to warn those who are lazy. Encourage those who are timid. Take tender care of those who are weak. Be patient with everyone" (1 Thess. 5:14 NLT).

"Beware of the false prophets, who come to you in sheep's clothing, but inwardly are ravenous wolves" (Matt. 7:15).

Pastor-Teacher When Filled with the Holy Spirit

A person who is spirit-filled and has the gift of pastor-teacher will see many of the following characteristics:

- A genuine love and concern for people.

- An ability to discern how individuals in a group are do-ing spiritually.
- An intolerance for false teaching or any intrusion of "wolves" into his flock.
- A willingness to exercise discipline when necessary for the protection of the entire flock.
- A clear direction on where the group should be going.
- A desire to see men, women, and children discipled.
- A patience in nurturing younger Christians.
- A warmth and friendliness to people.
- A deep, personal walk with the Lord and strong prayer life.
- A very deep knowledge of the Word of God with good study habits.

Pastor-Teacher When Not Filled with the Holy Spirit

Those who are carnal (not walking in the power of the Holy Spirit), and have this gift, may manifest many, if not all, of these characteristics. They:

- May become too involved in the lives of other people and too controlling.
- May create a dependency on himself or herself for spiri-tual growth and not on the Lord.
- May exalt themselves over the Lord Jesus Christ.
- May become controlling and dominating in the life of a person.
- May become very possessive of a person, not willing to let him or her go to another church or have other relationships.
- May misuse authority. Remember this is not a position of authority, but a position of ministry. There is no God-giv-en authority to the pastor-teacher.

- May think they have all the answers.
- May neglect to teach the Word of God. Instead, they will appeal to emotions and feelings, not to the solid teaching of God's Word for nourishment.
- Should be cautious about taking over a Bible study when they are not the leader. Start your own Bible study if you want a group to teach and shepherd.

If Pastor-Teacher Is Your Primary Spiritual Gift

You have a significant gift in terms of caring for people. God wants to use you to care for people who are in groups whether it is a Bible study, a staff team, office personnel, your family, or even a group of friends. You know that your job is to help people grow spiritually, and you have a role of teaching the Word of God to groups. Know that God has you in a group to help them bond spiritually. Become a good student and teacher of God's Word.

Faith: I instill vision

Definition: *The gift of faith is the supernaturally empowered ability to discern the will and purpose of God for the future of His work and to act on the power and promises of God with extraordinary confidence which inspires others to do the same.*

This is an unusual and exciting gift. Found in 1 Corinthians 12:9, it is unusual in the sense that faith is so common to us in the Christian life, that everyone must exercise faith. That is why it is surprising that there is a gift of faith, when everyone already needs to live by faith. It is exciting in the sense that faith is what accomplishes miracles. It is faith which releases the power of God. It is faith that rests in the promises of God. Even if you do not have this gift of faith, a study of this gift will do much to enhance and challenge you to increase the level of faith that you currently have. It will stretch you to greater heights in your own personal faith.

Goal: To have an unconquerable faith in the greatness of God and to help others increase their faith.

Description

This is an inspiring gift to define. Paul Hamar states, "Faith is infinite trust and belief in God and often appears in times of great crisis or opportunity. It is divine certainty!"[18] William McRae states, "This person has the capacity to see something that needs to be done and to believe God will do it through him even though it looks impossible. He is a man of vision with firm conviction that God will bring it to pass. Such a man dreams great dreams and tackles great tasks for God. He establishes great movements or great schools. He is called a 'man of faith' by his close friends."[19] Peter Wagner says of this gift, "People with the gift of faith are usually more interested in the future than in history. They are goal centered, possibility thinkers, undaunted by circumstances of suffering or obstacles. They can trust God to remove mountains as 1 Corinthians 13:2 indicates. They, like Noah, can build an ark on dry ground in the face of ridicule and criticism, with no doubt at all that God is going to send a flood."[20]

Obviously the gift of faith is not just ordinary faith. It is extraordinary faith! And it is a gift that manifests itself in action. It is not a blind belief, but a faith that motivates and produces fruit. It accomplishes something!

Characteristics

A person with the gift of faith is also a person with vision. These are the people who are positive thinkers. Every church needs many of these individuals. They are the ones who say to all of us, "God can do it!" Sometimes they drive people within the church crazy, because they always seem upbeat and positive. Oftentimes they do not seem to be realistic. However, these are the individuals that have great confidence in the promises of God. Churches need these individuals if they are ever to move out and accomplish great works for God. These are the ones who believe that God can heal people. These are the ones who believe that God can perform miracles. These are the ones who believe that what God did in the past, in terms of His miracles in the Bible, He can still do today. These are the ones who believe that God can move mountains. These are the ones who want to start new ministries. They are men and women of action. They are men and women of confidence in the promises of God. God places these type of people in the body of Christ to inspire all of us in our faith. They are those who help the body of Christ keep their eyes on the Lord. They have an unquenchable optimism. They never seem to be daunted in their faith towards God. They have the ability to see God come through in the face of impossible obstacles.

Biblical Examples

Old Testament

The Old Testament is full of men and women who demonstrated extraordinary faith. Noah is one (Gen. 6) who, by faith, built the ark. Elijah was an individual of extraordinary faith (1 Kgs. 18:30–46). The writer of Hebrews, chapter 11, writes of individuals who also demonstrated extraordinary acts of faith. These were more acts of faith than they were the manifestation of the gift of faith. All believers are admonished to accomplish what the individuals of Hebrews 11 accomplished in terms of faith. However, a person with the gift of faith should at least be inspired to know that he or she can perform such feats and more. Cross-reference each of these to study on your own.

New Testament

Stephen, in Acts 6:5, is stated to be "a man full of faith and of the Holy Spirit." In 6:8, "Stephen, full of grace and power, was performing great wonders and signs among the people." Although Stephen may have had the gift of miracles, it is a reflection of his faith.

Other Examples

History is replete with individuals who did extraordinary works for God. McRae lists some of these individuals.

> Hudson Taylor saw the interior of China as an untouched mission field and believed God would evangelize those teaming millions through him. The China Inland Mission was founded. Taylor opened a door and led the way for hundreds into the interior. He was a man of faith. George Müller saw the need of thousands of orphans during those difficult days in England. He believed God would meet that need through him. Five great orphanages were established in Bristol, England. Over his seventy years he received seven million dollars to

carry on his work. The great work of God was done through the leadership of that man of faith.[21]

A story is told about George Müller in his later years:

A transatlantic sea captain, after twenty-two hours on the ship's bridge in a dense fog off the banks of Newfoundland, was startled by a tap on the shoulder. It was Müller, then in his seventies. 'Captain, I have come to tell you I must be in Quebec on Saturday afternoon.' This was Wednesday.

When the captain said it was impossible, Müller replied, 'If your boat can't take me, God will find some other way. I've never broken an engagement in 57 years.' 'I'd like to help,' responded the captain, 'but what can I do?' 'Let's go below and pray,' Müller suggested. 'But Mister Müller, don't you know how dense the fog is?'

'My eye is not on the fog, but on God who controls the fog and every circumstance of my life.'

Down on his knees, Müller prayed the simplest prayer the captain had ever heard. In his opinion it fitted a child of nine. 'O Lord, if Thou wilt, remove this fog in five minutes. Thou dost know the engagement made for me in Quebec for Saturday.'

Putting his hand on the captain's shoulder, Müller restrained him from praying. 'First, you don't believe God will do it, and second, I believe He has done it, so there's no need for you to pray. Open the door, captain, and you will find the fog gone.' And so it was. Müller kept his Saturday engagement in Quebec![22]

Another example of an individual of faith is Bill Bright. In 1951, he had the vision to reach the college campuses for Christ. It was then that Campus Crusade for Christ (Cru) was started. With just a few staff, it has now expanded to not only hundreds of campuses, but hundreds of countries around the world. It was by faith that Bill Bright launched Expo '72 where over 100 thousand people attended, in Dallas, Texas, the largest gathering of Christians anywhere at that time. I don't know how true this story is, but I have heard that in his planning this, those working with him kept saying, "But Bill, where will we park all the cars?" Bill, not worrying about where the cars would be parked, said, "We can park them on the highways!" This is a typical example of dealing with a person of faith. They do not see the details, they just see the grand picture. Two years later, Expo '74 was launched in Korea, and Bill Bright, because of his faith, was able to see a million people stand in response to his invitation to give their life to Christ on an airstrip. Hundreds of millions have come into the kingdom of God through Cru.

A man whom I had the privilege to be acquainted with was Calvin Chow and his wife, Faith. This couple, in their late seventies, decided to start a Chinese seminary here in the United States that would be able to teach the Bible and give a degree to Chinese speaking students. In their eighties they finally saw it come to pass. In their late eighties they saw God not only open the doors to the Chinese that are in America, but God opening the door from mainland China for students to come over to the United States specifically to receive a seminary education! God used Calvin and his wife Faith to change all of eternity.

These are examples of individuals who did works that became renown. However, people with the gift of faith do not necessarily need to perform works of faith that are heard around the world. They simply need to do acts of faith which touch people's lives for Jesus Christ. They can be the ones who start tape ministries within churches, begin summer camps, start schools or seminaries, start a new ministry within a church, start a Bible study for single moms, start an AWANA ministry within their church, a Vacation Bible School for the summer, a greeters ministry, a youth ministry, any type of ministry which requires trust in God for it to come to pass. Or, they may be used of God to encourage leaders to accomplish the vision given to them.

Misunderstandings

These people are very often misunderstood. Their exceptionally high confidence may cause others to think that they are not being realistic or are presumptuous. It may appear that they are not listening to reason, when, in reality, they don't understand why the other person does not see the greatness of God coming through in a particular situation. They may appear at times judgmental, because their faith is greater than others. They are often misunderstood as being naive to the real problems.

Development

If you have the gift of faith, it does need to be developed. There are several ways to expand your gift of faith:
- Increase your knowledge of the Word of God. Romans 10:17 says, **"Faith comes by hearing and hearing by the word of Christ."**
- Step out in greater degrees of faith. Trust God to use you in even greater capacities than He's already used you.
- Pray boldly. Pray out loud, pray frequently, and pray confidently.

- Take action. Get to work in believing what God wants you to do.
- Enlist others in your vision. If it is of God, others will follow you.
- Pray that your gift of faith will be unimpeded.
- By faith, maintain your optimism and enthusiasm.

Key Verses

"Then He touched their eyes, saying, 'It shall be done to you according to your faith'" (Matt. 9:29).

"And looking at them Jesus said to them, 'With people this is impossible, but with God all things are possible.'" (Matt. 19:26).

"Barnabas was a good man, full of the Holy Spirit and <u>strong in faith</u>. And many people were brought to the Lord" (Acts 11:24 emphasis mine).

"Abraham never wavered in believing God's promise. In fact, his faith grew stronger, and in this he brought glory to God" (Rom. 4:20).

"So faith comes from hearing, and hearing by the word of Christ" (Rom. 10:17).

"So that your <u>faith</u> would not be based on human wisdom but on the power of God" (1 Cor. 2:5 emphasis mine).

"And if I have prophetic powers, and understand all mysteries and all knowledge, and if I have all faith, so as to remove mountains, but have not love, I am nothing" (1 Cor. 13:2).

"To this end we always pray for you, that our God may make you worthy of his calling and may fulfill every resolve for good and <u>every work of faith</u> by His power" (2 Thess. 1:11 emphasis mine).

"<u>Who through faith conquered kingdoms</u>, enforced justice, obtained promises, stopped the mouths of lions, quenched the power of fire, escaped the edge of the sword, were made strong out of weakness, became mighty in war, put foreign armies to flight" (Heb. 11:33–34 emphasis mine).

Faith When Filled with the Holy Spirit

The person who is filled with the Holy Spirit will manifest many of these characteristics:

- You will inspire others to trust God.
- You will lead a bold and strong prayer life.
- You will be very familiar with the promises of God in the Bible. You will be studying the Bible regularly.
- You will see God use you consistently to accomplish great works.
- Without hesitation, you will pray for miracles and healings for people knowing that God can do it if it is His will.
- You will have a sense of joy, enthusiasm, and optimism about you.
- You will want to see your church or ministry grow.

Faith When Not Filled with the Holy Spirit

What are some of the characteristics of those who have the gift of faith and are living carnally?

- They will start claiming by faith things which have very little to do with the kingdom of God, i.e. cars, mansions, money, etc.
- They will presume that God has promised something which He has not.
- They will mislead others in how to exercise faith. For example, believing in their faith rather than believing in the Word of God.
- They will become critical of those who do not have faith like theirs. He or she will oftentimes chastise others for their lack of faith.
- They will become boastful in how great their faith is as opposed to others. Phrases such as, "If you only believed God..." will often frequent their conversation.
- They will attempt to generate faith on their own power.
- They will have a poor prayer life and neglect the study of the Word of God.

If Faith Is Your Primary Spiritual Gift

Know that God wants you to inspire people to live more by the promises of God. People need your enthusiasm and constant confidence in the power of God and His word. Every day will be an opportunity to lift someone's spirit. Your job will be to help people, groups, teams, and those around you to focus more on God than their circumstances. Let people know that God is greater than their circumstances and problems. Instill confidence in God to your family and co-workers. Keep reminding people that God can solve any problem. Step out in faith and start new ministries or build up existing ones. You are a breath of fresh air to people.

Leadership: I see ahead

Definition: *The gift of leadership is the supernaturally empowered ability to set biblical goals and direction in accordance with God's purpose for the future and to communicate these goals to others in such a visionary way that they voluntarily and harmoniously work together to accomplish those goals for the glory of God.*

Goal: To enthusiastically lead others to obey the Word of God and to accomplish more for his Kingdom.

The spiritual gift of leadership helps set direction and vision for what a church, ministry, or team must do to accomplish the goal. It is a position of motivating and inspiring others to follow in a particular direction. Those with this gift are constantly looked at to take action.

Leadership is sometimes doing those things others do not want to do. It is taking risks. It is casting a vision and encouraging others to pursue that vision.

The word which the apostle Paul uses in Romans 12:8 for leadership is the word *proistemi*. *Proistemi* is the combination of the words "before" and "stand" meaning "stand before" or "go before." Some books consider this the same gift as administration found in 1 Corinthians 12. However, they are not the same word. They are different words in Greek.

This word for leadership was used in classical Greek to mean those who "stood before" an army in order to lead or those who "stood over" the affairs of government.[23]

- In the Septuagint, Joseph and Azarias are ordered to "take charge" of the people in Jerusalem in order to defend the city against an attack (1 Macc. 5:19).

This same idea is found in the New Testament. *Proistemi* appears eight times, all in Paul's writings.

- To take charge and give instruction (1 Thess. 5:12).
- To manage. The qualifications of an overseer is one who "**manages** his own household well" (1 Tim. 3:4 5–12). This means going before them as an example and providing direction and guidance.
- To rule (1 Tim. 5:17) as in ruling a congregation.
- To lead the way in good deeds (engage) (Tit. 3:8).

All of these definitions give the idea of what Paul says is the gift of leadership. The gift of leadership means to take charge. To go before others as an example. To lead the way. To provide direction and vision.

A person with the gift of leadership is like the "captain" of the ship as opposed to the "navigator" of the ship. **The one who has the gift of leadership is like the captain; the one who has the gift of administration is like the navigator.** The gift of administration is the same word for the navigator of a ship (Acts 17:11). The captain determines where a ship should go. The navigator determines the best course to get the ship to its destination. When we look at the gift of administration, we will see the distinction. Those with the gift of administration do not <u>determine</u> the goal to be achieved, but <u>how</u> to achieve the goal. Leaders determine the goal and provide the enthusiasm and persuasion to convince others to follow. It is not so much a position of power and authority as it is more a position of influence.

Pastor Bill Yaeger states, "Those who are called upon to lead must not apologize for their calling, nor should they ever abandon their responsibility because of peer pressure."[24] He defines leadership as, "Leadership is guiding others, motivating and inspiring them when they are afraid to do (or do not want to do) what they *must* do."[25] He also goes on to point out, "...where no leadership exists, other leaders—good or bad—will arise. A leadership vacuum *never* remains."[26]

I have found that leadership is very lacking in the church. This may be because not that many have this gift, or it may be that those who do, are afraid to step out and lead because they might be criticized.

Characteristics

A key word to describe a person with the gift of leadership is "visionary." These people see the future. They see the end result. They know what the final outcome needs to be. A key characteristic about a leader is that leaders lead. If they don't have followers, they will get followers. They cannot be stopped. They keep going on whether or not anybody follows. They are enthusiastic and eager.

Peter Wagner states, "The best leaders are relaxed. They know what has to be done and they know they cannot do it themselves. So they develop skills in delegating and transferring responsibility to others."[27]

Leaders often do not like details and can easily become bogged down with them. In many cases they do not like administration, so they are very good at delegating responsibility to someone else who has different gifts. One aspect of this person is that they are able to give vision and direction with the ability to communicate that clearly. They are effective in persuading others to move toward achieving biblical objectives. They have a sense of direction in their own life that is contagious. Others seek to be around these individuals. They are good at motivating others. A person with the gift of leadership tends to arise to the occasion. I saw this in my own life in an unusual way when I was called to jury duty. At the conclusion of the trial, we all retired to the jury chamber. The first order was to select a jury foreman. When someone said, "Let's all point to the person we think should be the jury foreman." They all pointed to me. I was surprised because I had little to no contact with any of them during the trial. This tends to be the nature of those who have the gift of leadership. Others seem to notice.

Another characteristic of the gift of leadership is that a person with this gift tends to think much about long-range goals rather than short-range goals. The short-range goals he comes up with are all related to achieving a long-range goal.

Those with the gift of leadership make good leaders for adult Sunday school classes. They are not necessarily the teacher, or the one who organizes everything; they are often the M.C. They help keep the class focused and moving forward. They generally make good disciplers as well, because they like having people around them. The apostle Paul constantly had individuals around him: Timothy, Silas, Apaphroditus, Titus, and numbers of others. He was always being followed. This characteristic was obviously evident in Christ's life; wherever He went, He, too, was followed. A leader is generally a person who ultimately ends up in a position of authority. A man who fits the other qualifications for elder would make a good overseer. Any pastor who wants to have a large, growing church must have the gifts of preaching (prophecy), faith, and **leadership.**

Other characteristics of the gift of leadership are:

1. This person is able to detach himself or herself from details to keep the big picture in mind.

2. This person is not a people pleaser, but a God pleaser.

3. This person does not lead by consensus, but by conviction! When a person with the gift of leadership is concerned about what others think, he or she will never get there. Christ was a perfect example, that even though He loved people, He was not a people pleaser. He pleased only His Heavenly Father.

4. This person is able to endure criticism. Remember this word means to stand before or in front of others. Who is the one who is first shot at in the infantry? It is the one in front! Remember that the person in front will be the most criticized. The person with the gift of leadership will be able to press on despite the criticism of others. This person will, however, need the person with the gift of encouragement to come alongside to strengthen him or her. Those of you with the gift of encouragement have a tremendous ministry in the life of your leaders. People with the gift of leadership really cannot worry about hurting people's feelings, or they will end up hurting God's feelings. They know that ultimately these people will be blessed when the goal is reached.

5. This person is very loyal and wants loyalty in return.

Misunderstandings

Those with the gift of leadership can be misunderstood in several ways:

1. They may appear bossy. This is not actually so; they simply want to see something done. If a person with the gift of leadership is in a group, and nobody is taking charge, he or she will take charge.

2. Sometimes they appear overly authoritative. This is only because they want to see things done and are anxious for people to get moving.

3. They sometimes seem pushy or appear to be trying to get their own way. This is not so, but it is because they know where the group needs to be heading. If the gift is truly being manifested, the person will want God's way, not his or her own way.

Development

The apostle Paul states in Romans 12:8 that **"He who leads, with diligence."** The word translated "diligence" here is the Greek word *spoude*. This word has several meanings. It means with passion, enthusiasm, earnestness, and eagerness. Diligence has the idea of determination. In other words, Paul is saying that a person with the gift of leadership needs to be enthusiastic. He or she needs to be earnest and zealous in his leadership. It has the idea of perseverance with great enthusiasm. It is easy for leaders to become discouraged because people do not see the urgency of moving forward. Paul's admonition is to not get down because of the situation. Keep at it. *The Complete Biblical Library Dictionary* says this word "is often extended to the ideas of being eager about doing something, or applying oneself to a task with diligence.... of being serious about something, of being busy at doing something, of being zealous, and of being eager."[28] Another meaning of this word is to "do one's best" as in 2 Peter 1:10, and the idea to "work hard at something."

A leader needs to continue to work hard to fulfill God's vision and do it with enthusiasm. If you have this as a gift, don't stop leading. Surround yourself with those who feel the same way. If you are in a church, work with the leadership; do not go out on your own. If it is truly a vision of God to do something, then the leadership will be with you on that and will give you the designated responsibilities that go with it. Sharpen your persuasion and motivation skills. Be cautious about being a demanding person. The best way to develop this gift is to be an example yourself of someone who knows where they are going and how to get there. As people see you moving in a positive direction, they will want to go along with you. Jesus Christ is the perfect example of this. He continued pursuing a direction regardless of whether anybody followed Him. That is one of the reasons His life was so contagious. No opposition or fallout from His ranks kept Him from His desired objective. If you have the gift of leadership, then God wants you to be "captain" of a ship. Whether it is a large ship or small ship, He has a ship for you in which He wants you to be "captain" (supervisor, team leader, Sunday school class, Bible study, care ministry, outreach ministry, etc.)

Leadership When Filled with the Holy Spirit

If you have the gift of leadership, the following characteristics should be evidenced in your life:
- You have clear vision and direction for your own life from God.

- You have a sense of joy about you.
- Your life is inspiring and motivating to others. People tend to look to you for direction.
- You think in terms of building the kingdom of God.
- You have a supernatural enthusiasm about you. You will not be discouraged easily.
- Others will follow you. If others do not follow you, then you need to question if this is your gift.
- You have a dynamic prayer life constantly praying for God's direction and wisdom.
- You have an enthusiasm for God's Word. You know this is important, because it is ultimately God's Word that is the basis for your direction in life and all your goals.

Leadership When Not Filled with the Holy Spirit

A person with the gift of leadership, who is living a carnal life, will demonstrate many of these following characteristics. He or she:

- May be impatient, pushy, controlling, or demanding.
- May want to take over the leadership of someone who is not leading well without invitation.
- May become frustrated when others don't follow.
- May become critical of how others live their lives.
- May become shortsighted rather than far-sighted.
- May become manipulative of others.
- May begin to lead people in a wrong direction for his or her own benefit not the Lord's.
- May have very little interest in prayer or use of God's Word.
- May begin to be apathetic about building God's kingdom, but desirous of building their own.
- May begin to use people as objects for their own goals.

- May have a loss of direction. This makes sense, since this person is out of touch with the Holy Spirit, he or she no longer has direction in their own life.

If Leadership Is Your Primary Spiritual Gift

Take the intitiative to lead knowing that those around you need encouragement, vision, and someone with a passion to be an example. Be confident in the fact that God has established you as a leader. Learn how to lead without offending people and follow your leadership voluntarily. Continue to cast vision with your team or church ministry. Stay enthusiastic. Stay diligent to your calling. Pace yourself and get support when you are discouraged. Your leadership is needed in the kingdom of God today.

Look for God to use you.

Administration: I see how (Navigate)

Definition: *The gift of administration is the supernaturally empowered ability to understand clearly the immediate and long-range goals of a particular unit of the body of Christ and to devise, organize, and execute effective plans for the accomplishment of those goals.*

Goal: To help organize the necessary factors to accomplish the established goals of the God's kingdom.

The word for "administration" *(kubernesis)* is translated in other bibles as the gift of governing. In 1 Corinthians 12:28 where this gift is found, it is in the plural form which means that it is not just a single act, but multiple acts of administrating. The literal definition of this word means "to steer a ship." It has the idea of guiding a ship through its proper course. In the Septuagint, it is translated in Proverbs 1:5 as "wise counsel." A person with the gift of administration will guide whatever he or she is in charge of wisely. This is a person of much influence.

Because this is a nautical term, to gain full understanding of this word, it must be examined in terms of its usage in contrast to other uses. This word is used in Acts 27:11 as a steersman or pilot of a ship. It is not the word that is used for the captain or owner of a ship. This distinction is clear. **"But the centurion was more persuaded by the <u>pilot</u> [navigator] and the captain of the ship, than by what was being said by Paul"** emphasis mine). The pilot (navigator) is not the captain. Think how these two make sense. The captain determines the destination of the ship. *The navigator, or pilot, must determine the course that the ship must take, and navigate the ship through safely in order to reach its desired destination.* A captain may have no idea how to be the helmsman of a ship. He can determine the destination of the ship, but it is the responsibility of the pilot (navigator) to map out the proper course.

This tells us volumes in terms of how the gift of leadership and the gift of administration operate together. The one who has the gift of leadership is like the captain. He or she can determine where a group of people must go. A person with the gift of administration will determine how to achieve that goal. For example, the leader of a Sunday school class may determine that a retreat would be best for the class. The one with the gift of administration will know how to organize and put together the plans for the retreat.

Characteristics

- A person with the gift of administration is more motivated about reaching a goal than making goals.

- They are able to break long-range goals down into smaller, achievable goals.
- They are not discouraged by the size of the task.
- They are able to visualize how tasks are to be organized.
- They are able to organize others to accomplish the task.
- They are able to do things properly and in an orderly manner.
- They are able to make the complicated, simple.

An experience I had in my former church illustrates how well this works. I felt the need for my wife, Jan, and I to have a Bible study. I took the initiative and the leadership in terms of putting this study together. I chose what to study and what I wanted to see accomplished. Jan, who has the gift of administration, would often help me get organized. Toward the end of our Bible study, I determined that it would be better for us to have a potluck rather than another Bible study. This is the gift of leadership being used. When I suggested this to the group, everyone thought it was a wonderful idea. They all said, "Let's do it!" However, at that point, I immediately felt overwhelmed. I was trying to figure out how to put a potluck together! Immediately, Jan, using her gift of administration, said, "I have an idea," and then she began to point to each person and tell them what to bring, what she would provide, and within a minute and a half or less she had that entire potluck organized. My reaction was, "Whew!" All the others in the Bible study said, "Wow! That was easy. You did that so fast and so well!" I had to laugh, because I know how strong Jan's gift of administration is. That's what an administrator does. Once given the goal or the task, he or she will then determine the easiest, quickest, and best course to achieve those goals. I have also seen her use this gift as she teaches our children, organizes our household, and helps me to accomplish the goals of the church.

Another example of this was when I decided where and when our family was to vacation for the summer. Jan, upon hearing our course of direction, got on the internet and planned out how far we would drive and what camp sights we were to stay at. I was amazed at all this. Even though at first I was a little reluctant to be this structured (I tend to try and find a place at 10:00 p.m. when everyone is exhausted and tired), we followed her plans, and it was one of the best organized and fun trips we had in a long time! The gift of administration is a blessing to a family.

Those who have the gift of leadership are extremely dependent on those who have the gift of administration. Without this cooperation, it is like a captain that has no navigator, or helmsman, to steer his ship. They will find it very difficult to get to the desired destination.

Misunderstanding

There are some misunderstandings which come with the gift of administration. He or she:

- May be perceived as using people. This is common in that the one who is administrating everything is not the one necessarily explaining why it has to be done. They are simply trying to get the task done. The leader needs to communicate the vision and the motivation for why something needs to be done.
- May at times seem more concerned about details than people. This, however, is not true, because the person with the gift of administration knows that attention to the details will minister to the people.

- May become discouraged at the lack of enthusiasm shown by others. People at times may dread receiving a phone call from these individuals knowing that they are going to be asked to do something. The person with the gift of administration becomes discouraged when people do not volunteer their help. They become frustrated, because they know how important the task is, and don't understand why others do not.
- May appear to be avoiding work due to their ability to delegate responsibility.

Development

Learn skills to work with people. There are many good books on managing, organizing, and administrating. Study the life of Moses and Nehemiah. Pray for God to show you ways to better your gift of administration. Ask leaders how you can be of help. Learn to set goals. Communicate well with those in charge so they understand that you want to help and how you can help. Many leaders may misunderstand those who have the gift of administration and may feel threatened because of their personal inadequacies. Teach others how to become organized.

Key Verses

Moses and his father-in-law is an excellent example of how someone uses their ability to administrate to help a leader. Let's read Exodus 18:13–26:

> "The next day Moses took his seat to serve as judge
> for the people, and they stood around him from
> morning till evening. When his father-in-law saw all
> that Moses was doing for the people, he said, "What is
> this you are doing for the people? Why do you alone

sit as judge, while all these people stand around you from morning till evening?' Moses answered him, 'Because the people come to me to seek God's will. Whenever they have a dispute, it is brought to me, and I decide between the parties and inform them of God's decrees and laws.' Moses' father-in-law replied, "What you are doing is not good. You and these people who come to you will only wear yourselves out. The work is too heavy for you; you cannot handle it alone. Listen now to me and I will give you some advice, and may God be with you. You must be the people's representative before God and bring their disputes to him. Teach them the decrees and laws, and show them the way to live and the duties they are to perform. But select capable men from all the people — men who fear God, trustworthy men who hate dishonest gain — and appoint them as officials over thousands, hundreds, fifties and tens. Have them serve as judges for the people at all times, but have them bring every difficult case to you; the simple cases they can decide themselves. That will make your load lighter, because they will share it with you. If you do this and God so commands, you will be able to stand the strain, and all these people will go home satisfied.' Moses listened to his father-in-law and did everything he said. He chose capable men from all Israel and made them leaders of the people, officials over thousands, hundreds, fifties and tens" (NIV).

"In those days when the number of disciples was increasing, the Grecian Jews among them complained against the Hebraic Jews because their widows were being overlooked in the daily distribution of food.

So the Twelve gathered all the disciples together and said, 'It would not be right for us to neglect the ministry of the word of God in order to wait on tables. Brothers, choose seven men from among you who are known to be full of the Spirit and wisdom. We will turn this responsibility over to them and will give our attention to prayer and the ministry of the word.' This proposal pleased the whole group. They chose Stephen, a man full of faith and of the Holy Spirit" (Acts 6:1–7 NIV).

"So David reigned over all Israel; and David administered justice and righteousness for all his people" (2 Sam. 8:15 NIV).

"Where there is no guidance the people fall, but in abundance of counselors there is victory" (Prov. 11:14).

"For by wise guidance you will wage war, and in abundance of counselors there is victory" (Prov. 24:6).

"For God is not a God of disorder but of peace—as in all the congregations of the Lord's people" (1 Cor. 14:33 NIV).

"But all things must be done properly and in an orderly manner" (1 Cor. 14:40).

Administration When Filled with the Holy Spirit

The person who has the gift of administration and lives a Spirit-filled life will experience many of these characteristics. He or she:

- Will live an orderly life. This person has great difficulty with a disorganized life.
- Will have clear direction in life.
- Will enjoy setting goals.
- Will be responsible and handle responsibility well.
- Will be able to motivate others to a task.
- Will be patient with others. They understand others do not have the skill they have.
- Will be joyful about the task.
- Will not be easily discouraged.
- Will be decisive and able to make clear-cut decisions.
- Will have determination. The Captain has given the orders and he or she wants to see them carried out.
- Will be loyal. This person can be counted on to accomplish a task.
- Will have a strong prayer life and study of God's Word. They want to hear from their Captain (Jesus) the assignment for the day.

Administration When Not Filled with the Holy Spirit

The person who is not depending on the power of the Holy Spirit will evidence many of the following characteristics. He or she:

- May become pushy. Instead of depending on the strength and power of God to accomplish something, they try to do it in their own stgrength.
- May become critical of others when they do not see the importance of the task and don't volunteer.

- May become dictatorial. He or she often tries to intimidate, coerce, or use guilt as a means of motivation. Remember, Christ never used any of these methods to motivate.
- May use people to accomplish personal ambitions.
- May take over in areas where they were not asked to take over. Oftentimes, this person thinks they can do a better job.
- May be unresponsive to suggestions and appeals. They have to have things done their way.
- May fail to give proper appreciation and praise to the other workers. They want it all themselves or simply are not willing to give it at all to others.
- May have little interest in personal devotions. This is because they are often more interested in their own plans for their lives than God's plan for their lives and receiving direction from Him. They think they are better off being in control of their own lives themselves.

If Administration Is Your Primary Spiritual Gift

You have a wonderful gift to help build the kingdom. You can be of great service in your church or with your organizion. Speak out when your church leader, supervisor, or team leader wants to get a project done. Let them know that you have some good ideas as to how the goals might be accomplished. Don't take on more than you can handle and make sure the Lord is leading you. There are times you may have to say "no" to someone who asks for your help. Show others how to accomplish goals. God may want to use you to come along side others to help them accomplish their goals. He may even lead you to non-Christians and use this as an opportunity to lead them to the Lord.

Evangelism: I multiply

The gift of evangelism is an exciting gift. It is a front-line ministry. These are the individuals who are on the cutting edge.

Definition: *The gift of evangelism is the supernaturally empowered ability to share the gospel with unbelievers and to equip others to share the gospel with unbelievers, in such a way that men and women become Christ's disciples and responsible members of the body of Christ.*

Goal: To help other believers fulfill their role as a witness for Christ.

The gift of evangelist is found in **Ephesians 4:11: "And He gave some as apostles, and some as prophets, and some as evangelists, and some as pastors and teachers" (emphasise mine).**

This word "evangelist" *(euaggelistēs)* is made up of two words in Greek. The words are "good" and "messenger." Therefore, the words "good messenger" or "harbinger of good news" are derived. The term "evangelize" originally stood for proclaiming a military victory. This is significant in that Christ has given us a victory far more significant than any military victory. He has given to us a spiritual victory.

The verb form means to "preach the gospel," and the noun is translated "evangelist." In the gospels, Christ constantly "preached the gospel," meaning that He "proclaimed good news."

We are all told to "do the work of an evangelist" (2 Tim. 4:5). **2 Timothy 4:5 says, "But you, be sober in all things, endure hardship, do the work of an evangelist, fulfill your ministry" (emphasis mine).** However, God has gifted some individuals in that this is their primary ministry. Ephesians 4:11 speaks to this point. What is interesting, as I have mentioned before, is that this is not just a gift, but is also an office in the church. Most full-time evangelists unfortunately are not in the local church, but are out with mission organizations. Because of this, the local church suffers greatly in terms of their potential in evangelizing their community. As a church, we realize that to be a fully biblical church, we need to have a full-time evangelist. Every church needs an evangelist-pastor that is not only concerned with people coming to Christ, but seeks to involve them in the entire process of discipleship.

I have read many of the books on the gift of evangelism, and have found that, unfortunately, most of them have missed the point. Most of them address the evangelist doing the work of evangelism. The Bible makes it clear that the main role of an evangelist is not so much to do the evangelizing himself or herself, but to train and equip others to do the work of evangelism: "And He gave some as apostles, and some as prophets, and some as **evangelists**, and some as pastors and teachers, **for the equipping of the saints for the work of service,** to the building up of the body of Christ" (Eph. 4:11–12 emphasis mine).

These people are compelled to do the work and have a heart for the lost to such a degree that they seek to enlist others to be involved in evangelism. For any church to reach its full potential in terms of reaching its community for Christ, it would be well for them to have a full-time evangelist or at least someone able to mobilize all those with the gift of evangelism in the church. Dr. C. Peter Wagner of Fuller Theological Seminary surmises that in his professional opinion, ten percent of any local members of the body of Christ have the gift of evangelism. I hope this is true, because at this point I have not seen that statistic borne out in churches. Ten percent would be an exciting number of believers to have this gift.

Characteristics

How does a person know if he or she has the gift of evangelism? There are several distinct characteristics:

- They have a consuming passion for the lost. They are like the apostle Paul who states, "For the love of Christ controls us...." (2 Cor. 5:14).
- They have a clear understanding of the key points of the gospel message. In other words, they understand clearly how a person goes from a state of being unsaved to saved. There is no ambiguity in his or her mind.
- An ability to present the gospel message clearly. I saw this evidenced in a tremendous way by a man called Uncle Charlie. He was an older man who accompanied a group of college students and me to Florida one spring break. There was a joy about him that was unbelievable. The tool he used was the children's "wordless book." This was simply a little book of the colors black, red, white, green, and gold that a person could use to share the gospel. What was amazing was that when we were in Florida, and spent the night at a fraternity, many of us college students were having difficulty trying to understand how to approach these fraternity men. Several of us were praying about how to initiate conversation so that we could talk about Christ. What was interesting was that when several of us entered the men's room, there was Uncle Charlie using this wordless book with several of the fraternity students. One of the men was actually crying as he prayed to receive Christ. We all stared at each other in amazement at how God could use this man and the simplest form to present the gospel. Many others of the fraternity were

standing around listening intently as this simple man presented a simple, yet clear message. We all learned an invaluable lesson that day.

- They have great joy in seeing men and women come to a personal and saving knowledge of Jesus Christ.
- A special ability to turn any conversation into an opportunity to present the gospel.
- A desire to be around non-Christians more than Christians. A person with the gift of evangelism is often restless when he or she finds out that others already believe in Christ and are Christians.
- An ability to train and mobilize others to share Christ. This ability may be more a function of the office of evangelist than a person who has the gift of evangelism. However, a person with the gift of evangelism would at least seek to teach someone else how they can lead others to Christ.

Dwight L. Moody said,

I believe that if an angel were to wing his way from earth up to heaven, and were to say that there was one poor, ragged boy, without father or mother to care for him and teach him the way of life and if God were to ask who among them were willing to come down to earth and live here for fifty years and lead that one to Jesus Christ, every angel in heaven would volunteer to go. Even Gabriel, who stands in the presence of the Almighty, would say: 'Let me leave my high and lofty position, and let me have the luxury of leading one soul to Jesus Christ.' There is no greater honor than to be the instrument in God's hands of leading one person out of the kingdom of Satan into the glorious light of heaven.[29]

I had a professor in seminary who said that a person with the gift of evangelism is like the married person who never forgets what it's like to be single. A person with this gift never forgets what it is like to be a non-Christian. He or she has the unique ability to identify with non-Christians in their situation in life and then use that identification to share the gospel with them.

Biblical Examples

There are several examples in the New Testament. One is Philip, who is called the evangelist (Acts 21:8). He was the one whom God used to lead the Ethiopian eunuch to Christ (Acts 8:26–40). As you study his life, you realize that sharing Christ was the compelling motivation of his life.

Another wonderful example of an evangelist is the apostle Paul. What is amazing about his heart as an evangelist, is that he was willing to give up his salvation if there was some way that the Jews could be saved (Rom. 9:3). What an amazingly unselfish heart to be willing to be separated from God for all eternity so that others would not. Of course that is impossible, but it at least expresses the apostle Paul's heart. Another example is Peter. He demonstrates the principle that the one who has been forgiven much is much thankful. You see him at work in Acts chapters 2 and 3. He had the ability to take whatever situation he was involved in, and use it as an opportunity to draw people's attention to Jesus Christ. In the book of Acts, Peter led 3,000 and then 5,000 people to Christ.

Misunderstandings

There are several misunderstandings about a person who has the gift of evangelism:

- Their boldness may appear to be insensitivity to others. They may sometimes convey the message that the unsaved are more important than the saved. This, of course, is not true in God's eyes. It is simply a person realizing that it is far more important that a person come to Christ than anything else.

- A misunderstanding in teaching the Word of God. A pastor, especially, who has the gift, is often criticized that his messages are primarily evangelistic rather than teaching from the Word of God. A pastor needs to learn to balance the feeding of the flock as well as reaching the lost in his sermons. The purpose of coming to Christ is to grow into holiness, not simply be baptized or experience one recommitment after another. A person who has become a Christian wants to grow, and he or she needs to learn how to grow. Any pastor who is strong in evangelism should seek ways to express that gift other than just the pulpit on Sunday mornings.

- His or her association with non-Christians and being in the midst of their lifestyle is sometimes perceived as compromising one's own lifestyle. This often is far from the heart of one who has this gift. They simply are following the example of Jesus Christ of going where those who need the gospel are.

- Often viewed as excessive. Others view this person as having one track which is the gospel, and sometimes considers him or her off balance or overzealous.

- An emphasis on evangelism might be misinterpreted as shallowness in his or her faith. In many cases, just the opposite is true. For example, **Louis Sperry Chaffer**, founder of Dallas Theological Seminary, one of the most renowned seminaries for expositing the Scriptures, began his ministry as an evangelist. It was his work as an evangelist that prompted him to start a seminary. **Dwight L. Moody** was the same way. Although he never had a college education, he was a man excited for the Lord and ended up starting Moody Bible Institute. A person with the gift of evangelism is often very strong in the Scriptures. **Charles Fuller** was also an evangelist who started Fuller Theological Seminary. Even **Billy Graham** started a Bible School.

- A person with this gift may often find themselves frustrated by those who show no interest in witnessing to others. They are irritated by weak and watered-down presentations of the gospel which do not clarify the message or challenge the listener to accept Christ. They are extremely distraught at messages like, "The Gospel of Jesus Christ Is Love," or "Accept the Love of God." These types of messages do not make clear that a person is a sinner and in desperate need of a holy Savior. They are frustrated by training classes in evangelism that do not have actual evangelism as part of their curriculum. They often feel incomplete if they have not had the opportunity to share Christ for an extended period of time.

What Evangelism Is Not

- It is not yelling at a person to repent.
- It is not forcing someone into believing something they don't want to believe in.
- It is not promising someone that if they trust Christ they will have no more problems.
- It is not scaring people into a decision that will fade when the emotions fade.
- It is not shouting out a Bible verse at someone as you drive by.

- It is not simply telling someone God loves them or that they are a sinner.
- It is the responsibility of everyone to share the Good News not just those who have this spiritual gift.

What Evangelism Is

"It is simply taking the initiative to share Christ in the power of the Holy Spirit and leaving the results up to God." — Bill Bright, Cru

To me it is simply one beggar telling another beggar where to find food. Simply telling others what God has done for you.

Key Verses

"Now after John was arrested, Jesus came into Galilee, proclaiming the gospel of God, and saying, 'The time is fulfilled, and the kingdom of God is at hand; repent and believe in the gospel'" (Mark 1:14–15 ESV).

"And He said to them, 'Let us go on to the next towns, that I may preach there also, for that is what I came for'" (Mark 1:38).

"So they went out and proclaimed that people should repent" (Mark 6:12).

"Day after day, in the temple courts and from house to house, they never stopped teaching and proclaiming the good news that Jesus is the Christ" (Acts 5:42).

"But the believers who were scattered preached the
Good News about Jesus wherever they went" (Acts 8:4
NLT).

"Then Philip opened his mouth, and beginning with
this Scripture he told him the good news about Jesus"
(Acts 8:35 NIV).

"For Christ's love compels us, because we are
convinced that one died for all, and therefore all died.
And he died for all, that those who live should no
longer live for themselves but for him who died for
them and was raised again" (2 Cor. 5:14–15 NIV).

"All this is from God, who reconciled us to
himself through Christ and gave us the ministry
of reconciliation: that God was reconciling the
world to himself in Christ, not counting people's
sins against them. And he has committed to us the
message of reconciliation. We are therefore Christ's
ambassadors, as though God were making his appeal
through us. We implore you on Christ's behalf: Be
reconciled to God. God made him who had no sin
to be sin for us, so that in him we might become the
righteousness of God" (2 Cor. 5:18–21 NIV).

"For I delivered to you as of first importance what
I also received: that Christ died for our sins in
accordance with the Scriptures, that He was buried,
that He was raised on the third day in accordance
with the Scriptures, and that He appeared to Cephas,
then to the twelve. Then He appeared to more than

five hundred brothers at one time" (1 Cor. 15:3–6
ESV).

Development

If you have the gift of evangelism, there are several ways to develop this gift:

- Learn the multiple uses of Scripture. Peter and Stephen used many different illustrations and quotes from the Old Testament to speak directly to an audience. The apostle Paul in Acts 17 learned to use not only Scripture, but quoted from the modern poets of their day to speak to the hearts of men about their need for Christ.
- In like manner, learn to use current events to point people to the gospel.
- Learn sensitivity of when to plant, water, and harvest (1 Cor. 3:6).
- Learn several methods of sharing the gospel.
- Have your testimony summarized in a very brief, yet understandable and significant manner.
- Accompany those who are good at leading others to Christ to learn how they do it.
- Learn to take others with you so that you will be able to multiply your ministry.
- Develop a strong prayer life. More people are won to Christ by praying for them than any other way.
- Learn to be patient with those who do not immediately receive Christ. Learn also to be patient with those who do not have your zeal. Often this is more caught than taught.
- Keep your intake of the Word of God consistent. This will keep you motivated as you study God's Word on a daily basis.

- Learn to follow the leading of the Holy Spirit (Gal. 5:27). It is essential to follow the leading of the Holy Spirit as to whom He wants you to share Christ.

Evangelism When Filled with the Holy Spirit

The person with the gift of evangelism, who is walking in the Holy Spirit, will find several characteristics true about his or her life:

- You will have a consuming heart for the lost.
- You will clearly be able to discern "divine" appointments. You will see God continually leading you to those who are spiritually hungry.
- You will have clear thinking when it comes to sharing the gospel of Christ. You will know what to say because the Holy Spirit will give you the words.
- You will not compromise your life with sin. You will not rationalize sin in your own life as a means to reaching others for Christ.
- Your life will be demonstrated by joy.
- You will have a clear sense of direction and purpose to your life.
- You will see God use you regularly to lead others to Christ.
- You will seek to teach and train others to share Christ.
- You will have a strong prayer life, understanding that the battle is won in heaven before it is won on earth.
- You will have a strong devotion time in the Word of God. You will realize that you must depend on God and His Word for daily strength.

Evangelism When Not Filled with the Holy Spirit

It is so important for the person with this gift to be filled with the Holy Spirit. If not, the following characteristics can become evident:

- Loss of love for God and desire for others to come to know Christ.
- Loss of vision for one's life.
- Insensitivity to where a person is spiritually.
- Will simply share Christ by rote.
- Will have ulterior motives in wanting to lead someone to Christ, i.e., friendship, monetary gain, etc.
- After leading a person to Christ, allowing them to become dependent on him or her rather than God.
- Losing sight of the real issues. He or she loses sight of the fact that there truly is a hell that people will go to unless they become Christians.
- Rationalization of sin in his or her own life. Many evangelists, who have become involved in sin, rationalize their sin as okay because, "Look how God is using me, I am leading so many people to Christ, I must be okay." This is a major deception of the Enemy and leads ultimately to downfall and irrefutable damage, even to those who have been led to Christ by that person.
- A poor prayer life. This person simply quits praying for the lost.
- No desire for Bible study.

If Evangelism Is Your Primary Spiritual Gift

You have a very crucial gift for the expansion of the kingdom. Place yourself in a role that, not only where you can share Christ, but show others how simply it can be done. Let your church leaders know that you have this gift. Consider teaching a Bible study or a class on "how to share your faith." Know that the Holy Spirit will be leading you regularly to people who are hungry for the gospel. Take someone with you when you share Christ. Your job will be to help others come to Christ and teach others how to lead a person to Christ. Try different evangelistic tools so that you will have many ways to reach unbelievers for Christ. Be confident the Holy Spirit will lead you and that you do not need to do this in your own energy.

Discernment: I have insight

Definition: *The gift of discerning of spirits is the supernaturally empowered ability enabling a person to know with assurance whether certain circumstances, behaviors, or teachings claimed to be of God are in reality either divine, human, or satanic; and to distinguish between truth and error.*

The gift of discernment *(diakrisis)* is a gift which is needed as much today as in any other time of history. The intensity of the war between Christ and His forces and Satan and his forces continually mounts. As the world reaches its consummation, Satan is at work more than ever before, seeking to deceive as many people as he can. His ways are extremely subtle. He has been able to imitate and use forgery to deceive people. Christians are called on to discern not only the age which they are in, but to discern the type of spirits which are at work today.

The gift of discernment (1 Cor. 12:10) is technically the gift of "discerning of spirits." This speaks volumes as it is identifying the fact that behind good and evil is a spirit. It is either a spirit of God or an evil spirit of Satan.

The word "to discern" *(dia-krisis)* is a compound word. The two words which make it up are "through" and "judge," meaning "judge through." It has the idea of looking beyond the surface. To judge not just words or actions, but the spirit behind the actions as well. This is another one of those gifts which every Christian is told they must perform in some way. Every Christian is to be discerning.

> **"Beloved, do not believe every spirit, but test the spirits to see whether they are from God because many false prophets have gone out into the world" (1 John 4:3).**

> **"Let two or three prophets speak, and let the others pass judgment" (1 Cor. 14:29).**

> **"Do not quench the Spirit; do not despise prophetic utterances. But examine everything carefully hold fast to that which is good" (1 Thess. 5:19–21).**

This word is also used in Hebrews 5:14 which explains how a Christian moves from being a baby Christian to a mature Christian. "But solid food is for the mature, who because of practice have their senses trained to <u>discern</u> [diakrisis] good and evil" (emphasis mine). The mark of a mature Christian is that he or she is able to discern what is right and what is wrong: what is of God and what is not of God. To lead the way in this example of discerning the spirits, God has given to the body of Christ those individuals with the gift of discernment. *The Complete Biblical Library* defines the usage of this gift as that which "implies the supernatural power of spiritual insight to detect and expose Satanic strategies and demonic activities."[30]

The key aspect of this verse is to understand the spiritual realm which is taking place in this world.

The apostle Paul tells us in Ephesians 6:12 where true reality is found. It is not found in what we see and hear around us, but what is taking place in the spirit realm. "For our struggle is not against flesh and blood, but against the rulers, against the powers, against the world forces of this darkness, against the spiritual forces of wickedness in the heavenly places." He also states in 2 Corinthians 10:4, "For the weapons of our warfare are not of the flesh, but divinely powerful for the destruction of fortresses." We are in a spiritual battle, and we need to fight it with powerful, spiritual means. This is why the ability to discern is so important for each believer and why the person who has the gift of discernment needs to be in the front lines exercising this gift.

Goal: The goal of the gift of discernment is to evaluate everything by the truth of the Word of God.

Key Verses

> **"So give Your servant an understanding heart to judge Your people to discern between good and evil"**
> **(1 Kgs. 3:9).**

> **"Do not judge according to appearance, but judge with righteous judgment" (John 7:24).**

> **"Whoever is wise, let him understand these things; whoever is discerning, let him know them. For the ways of the LORD are right, and the righteous will walk in them, but transgressors will stumble in them"**
> **(Hos. 14:9).**

Biblical Examples

What I have found throughout my years in the ministry is that many people are deceived simply because they encounter something supernatural. They assume that if something is supernatural, it must be of God. This is a great deception of Satan. What people fail to realize is that there are supernatural forces, but they are not all of God. Just because something is supernatural, or deals with the spirit realm, does not mean that God is involved. In fact, the Bible acknowledges that there will be supernatural phenomena to which people will be exposed. God's warning is to stay away from these things.

Old Testament

Deuteronomy 18:10–11 states, "There shall not be found among you anyone who makes his son or his daughter pass through the fire, one who uses divination, one who practices witchcraft, one who interprets omens, or a sorcerer, or one who casts a spell, or a medium, or a spiritist, or one who calls up the dead." This covers the spectrum of what people are involved in today. Whether it is seances, reading one's horoscope, or involvement in occultism, God's people are to stay far away from all of these. Otherwise, they are playing with fire. They have no idea the powerful forces that are involved in this, and the incredible deception used to hook them into becoming increasingly involved so that God no longer directs their lives, but the other spiritual dimension does.

New Testament

A fascinating example of how quickly the spiritual forces are at work is found in Matthew 16:16–23. Peter made an amazing proclamation that Christ was "the Son of the living God."

Jesus answered and told him he was blessed because flesh and blood did not reveal this to him, but his Father who is in heaven. Within a short time after that, and a few verses following, Christ had to rebuke Peter for being an instrument of Satan. As soon as Peter heard that Christ had to go to Jerusalem to die, he claimed, "God forbid it, Lord! This shall never happen to You." Christ then turned to him and said, "Get behind Me, Satan! You are a stumbling block to Me for you are not setting your mind on God's interest, but man's." Here is an amazing example of how quickly Satan works even in the life of one who is a believer. One minute God is communicating to him who Christ is, and the next minute Satan is at work trying to deceive Peter. If this happened to Peter, an apostle, how much more should we as believers be concerned about what could happen to us? Later it becomes evident that Peter was given the gift of discernment as revealed in Acts 5:1–10. In this case, Peter was able to discern that Ananias and Saphira were lying to God. Without any questioning, Peter simply makes that statement, "Ananias, why has Satan filled your heart to lie to the Holy Spirit, and to keep back some of the price of the land?" He tells him he has not lied to man, but to God. The consequence to Ananias, was that he was immediately slain in the Spirit and died. Peter demonstrated this gift again in Acts 8:20–24 when he dealt with a man named Simon who tried to buy the power of the Holy Spirit. Peter immediately penetrated the man's heart when he said, "You have no part or portion in this matter, for your heart is not right before God.... For I see that you are in the gall of bitterness and in the bondage of iniquity" (Acts 8:21, 23 emphasis mine). Peter was able to discern that not only was the man's heart not right with God, but he was in bondage to the spirit of bitterness.

The apostle Paul demonstrated this gift in Acts 13:9–11. This is the incident when Paul ran into Elymas the magician, who was trying to lead people away from faith in Christ. It says that Paul, "filled with the Holy Spirit fixed his gaze upon him, and said, 'You are full of deceit and fraud, you son of the devil, you enemy of all righteousness, will you not cease to make crooked the straight ways of the Lord?'" (Acts 13:9–10). At that point, Paul struck him with blindness. What is interesting to observe is that Paul not only realized that he was not of God, but that he had a spirit of deceit and fraud about him. It is also very important to notice that the apostle Paul was filled with the Holy Spirit.

My wife Jan has this as her primary spiritual gift. I have learned the hard way to highy value her gift. As a pastor I wanted to hire a particular individual that I felt was highly qualified for the position. We took him and his wife out for dinner, and I was very happy with the time. I ask Jan how she felt about it, and she said, "I feel a strong warning about him, and I don't think you should hire him." I felt she just couldn't see how qualified he was, and I hired him anyway. Within weeks he became a nightmare to me and very divisive as time went on. I eventually had to fire him. Several other times Jan warned me about investing money in a Christian venture, and I ignored her discernment, and we lost all the money I invested. I have learned since then to honor her spiritual gift and not move forward with something when she recommends not.

Illustrations

People with this gift can sense in a church service if a church is a healthy church. A person's spirit may be vexed and not sure why only to discover later that the teaching of Scripture was not accurate or if there are serious issues in the church.

This also explains why when others seem very excited about a speaker's message, you don't feel the same way. You actually felt like something was not right. Later, when you examine it against Scripture, you find your spirit was right because false teaching was taking place. This is the gift of discernment at work. It helps protect the body of Christ.

Misunderstandings

The misunderstandings which are involved with these people is that they may seem judgmental. This is not the case; they are simply able to know what is happening behind the scenes spiritually.

People have a difficult time taking those with this gift seriously. They think they are just fanatics making too much out of nothing.

Another area of misunderstanding is that people think the person with the gift of discernment is seeing too many demons in the world. The truth is, this person is probably not seeing enough. There is probably far more at work going on than people realize.

Development

If this is your gift, then it is absolutely crucial that you be a thorough student of the Word of God. What will often happen is that you will sense that what somebody is saying is wrong, but do not know why. As you study the Word, God will show you where His Word was contradicted by this teaching. Even when others are saying how wonderful a person's teaching is, you will be able to discern why it was misleading. For that reason, it is of utmost importance that you have not just a devotion time, but that you become a student of God's Word.

You must live a holy life. Part of Satan's way to diminish the use of this gift, or to even deceive the one who has this gift, is to allow sin to make its home in your life.

Discernment When Filled with the Holy Spirit

As the apostle Paul was filled with the Holy Spirit (Acts 13:9), it is absolutely essential that you continue to walk in the Spirit. When walking in the Spirit:

- They will have the ability to sense the spiritual battle which is taking place in any situation (a team meeting, Bible study, or group setting).
- They will be able to listen to a teaching and perceive whether or not it is of God. This person's spirit will be uneasy when he or she hears false teaching.
- They will have an ability to discern immediately right from wrong.
- They may receive a warning about a person's motives.
- They will have the ability to tell whether or not a person has been deceived by Satan or not.
- They are able to perceive the difference between truth and error. They can listen to someone either teach the Bible or talk about some philosophy and immediately be able to perceive where the truth or the error is in this teaching.
- They have a boldness to engage in spiritual warfare.
- They have a deep compassion for those who are in bondage to Satan and his spiritual forces.
- They will have the ability to know what to pray for another person, which will help free them up from bondage.

- They will know how to pray for specific situations. When you are around a person or group, you will have a sense of what to pray for in that situation.
- They will have an ability to discern the spiritual battle that is being engaged in their own life. You will be able to sense what areas of weakness Satan is attacking in your life.
- A powerful prayer life. You will be used by God through prayer to free people from the bondage which they have been held in by Satan.
- A strong desire to know the Bible. This only sharpens the skills of discernment.

Discernment When Not Filled with the Holy Spirit

Those who have this gift and do not walk in the Spirit are on dangerous ground. Many of the following characteristics will become evident their lives:

- A critical spirit. What they discern in others will lead them not into feelings of compassion, but to become critical of others.
- A misreading of the Holy Spirit. They will not be able to discern what the Holy Spirit is saying. In reality, they will be deceived by a false spirit.
- A life controlled by emotions. They will tend to be very emotional and have their lives controlled by emotions not the Word of God.
- Domineering and authoritative. They tend to tell others how they should live their lives.
- Prideful. They feel they are superior in some way because they have spiritual insights.
- Judgmental and insensitive. They begin to question and judge everyone's motives.

- Poor prayer life. Criticizing people rather than praying for them.
- Very little reliance on the Word of God. This is a subtlety that happens when a person begins to trust his or her emotions. Their commitment to the Word of God decreases, and at this point, a person is in serious danger spiritually.

If Discernment Is Your Primary Spiritual Gift

You will be a great asset to your church, Bible study, and any team you are on as you will be able to discern if Satan is seeking to divide the group. You will also be able to help others see that they are fighting a spiritual battle and not other people or circumstances (Eph 6:12). Know that God wants to use you to help people get out of the bondage they are spiritually in. Your prayers are the best weapon. You have wonderful insights to help people especially as you point them to Scripture. You have been given this gift, not to judge others but so that you can pray effectively against the enemy's work in a person's life or ministry. This is a gift most counselors should have.

CHAPTER 7

The Service Gifts

W E NOW WANT TO look at the service gifts.

Service: I help many

There is a particular gift, without which, most of what happens in a church or Christian organizations would never be accomplished. It is a supernaturally empowered gift which ministers to the body of Christ as a whole and is one of the supporting structures. It is the gift of service *(diakonia)*. We derive our word "Deacon" from this word. In other words, a deacon is one who serves.

Definition: *The gift of service is the supernaturally empowered ability to identify and meet unmet needs to numerous believers to help accomplish God's work and enable other believers to grow and to make use of available resources to help accomplish the desired goals.*[31]

The gift of service is found in Romans 12:7. It has also been translated as the gift of ministry, which is the ability to minister to others. This gift differs from the gift of "helps," in that the primary use of this gift is not toward individuals per se, but toward groups of people or the church as a whole. As Peter Wagner states, "The gift of service is not a one-on-one, person-centered gift like the gifts of mercy and helps. It is more task-oriented. Service is usually directed more to an institution and its goals than to a particular person."[32] These are, in actuality, two separate types of ministries. This distinction can be seen in the example of bringing a meal to a mom who just recently had a newborn, or helping to prepare a potluck for an entire church. One helps the individual; the other helps a large number of believers.

Goal: To serve and help a group of people so that they can better use their gifts.

For example, improving the facilities or creating an environment so others can use their gifts in the lives of others: teaching, encouraging, leading, hospitality, etc. Other powerful ministries are conference teams that set up for meetings and seminars or church retreats and events. Even running sound and video systems is an expression of this gift. It enables a large group of believers to grow in their faith. In these cases it then enables others to use their gifts during that time.

The conference team of Cru (Campus Crusade for Christ International) is responsible for preparing the facilities for New Staff Orientation, Spring Break outreaches, and multitudes of conferences. Cru would not be as effective without this team enabling all the training it does. When I spoke to this team about spiritual gifts, I found that each staff person on the team loved what they did and all had the gift of service except the director. He had the spiritual gift of administration!

Biblical Examples

An excellent example of this gift is found in Acts 6:1–7. An issue arose over the fact that a certain type of widows was being overlooked in the serving of meals. The apostles were summoned to decide what should be done concerning the neglect of these individuals. They understood that the ministry of the Word and prayer must go on, and they themselves could not take time to minister to these widows. Therefore, they selected seven men to serve the widows. This is an example of how the service to these women helped the greater plan of spreading God's Word. The result of these men serving in this capacity is found in verse 7: "And the Word of God kept on spreading and the number of the disciples continued to increase greatly in Jerusalem, and a great many of the priests were becoming obedient to the faith!" Without those who have the gift of service, the spreading of the Word of God is thwarted. These individuals are absolutely essential in the ongoing ministry of the gospel in the local church!

This gift is often task-oriented. Today these people help the church grounds and the building look good. They help the teachers, work in the media ministry, do secretarial work, arrange transportation, set up chairs, work on the sound and light system, usher, provide nursery care, do cutouts for Vacation Bible School, help set up meals for all church potlucks, help clean up the kitchen after certain events, and other often unnoticed tasks which contribute to making the work of the ministry more effective. It is because of these people that all the other people in the church can grow effectively in their faith.

I encountered a wonderful example of this gift at work when I was ministering at a church in California. The leadership decided that one way we could make visitors stay around church longer and feel more welcome was to provide refreshments in the quad outside. We then needed to decide who would provide the refreshments. We decided that it would be best to assign to it to each adult Sunday school class to provide the refreshments for one month. Well, the reaction was very interesting. We found there were those that just were not excited at all about this. For them, it was a drudgery. As this ministry progressed, I saw that it was necessary to evaluate it and find out how those involved felt. I found that some of the men who were leaders in the classes or in the church really didn't enjoy this. However, I spoke to one woman, and she expressed to me how much she enjoyed setting up the tables, providing the refreshments, and especially working in the kitchen cleaning up all the dishes. I was amazed! This was the kind of thing which I dreaded the most, and here she was expressing that she "could stay all day working in the kitchen." It then dawned on me that she had the gift of service and was very motivated by it. She understood that her work behind the scenes accomplished a greater objective, which was to reach those who did not know the Lord.

What I discovered was that had we worked smarter, we would have looked for those who had the gift of service. They would have been more motivated than those with the speaking gifts.

Key Verses

"Therefore, my dear brothers and sisters, stand firm. Let nothing move you. Always give yourselves fully to the work of the Lord, because you know that your labor in the Lord is not in vain" (1 Cor. 15:58 NIV).

"So the Twelve gathered all the disciples together and said, 'It would not be right for us to neglect the ministry of the word of God in order to wait on tables. Brothers and sisters, choose seven men from

among you who are known to be full of the Spirit and
wisdom. We will turn this responsibility over to them
and will give our attention to prayer and the ministry
of the word'... So the word of God spread. The
number of disciples in Jerusalem increased rapidly,
and a large number of priests became obedient to the
faith" (Acts 6:2–4, 7 NIV).

"For God is not unjust so as to forget your work and
the love which you have shown toward His name,
in having ministered and in still ministering to the
saints" (Heb. 6:10).

"I know your works, your love and faith and service
and patient endurance, and that your latter works
exceed the first" (Rev. 2:19).

"For even the Son of Man came not to be served but
to serve others and to give his life as a ransom for
many" (Matt. 20:28 NLT).

"Never be lacking in zeal, but keep your spiritual
fervor, serving the Lord" (Rom. 12:11).

Development

Romans 12:7 says, **"If service, in his serving."** This explains how
a person who has the gift of service is to develop this gift. How
does a person learn to serve better? Simply by serving. If you
have the gift of service, get involved in serving. You will learn
what types of service better minister to people than other types.
Not everything that you think is service is going to minister or

work towards the larger goal of building up the kingdom of God. Busy work does not mean that the gift of service is being utilized to its utmost. You must become well defined in how your service can count most for the kingdom of God. The key is to get involved and serve, and then let the Holy Spirit teach you how your service can become most effective.

Note: The only differences between an elder and a deacon (1 Tim. 3, Tit. 1) is that elders must be able to teach which assumes they have the spiritual gift of teaching. Deacons and deaconesses are those who have the ability and gift to serve.

Motivation

Oftentimes what motivates a person who has the gift of service is that he or she is able to identify unmet needs. In other words, a person can look at the physical building, or the grounds or property, and come up with ideas that would make it look more attractive to the Lord. Other times, this person who has the gift of service can see certain things that are happening in the life of the church or organization and realize that there are certain things that could be done that would make the other ministries more effective. This person is motivated by the idea that what he or she contributes will help a larger and more visionary plan.

They are also motivated with the desire to see others succeed. They gain much delight in knowing that they have helped another person with a more "visible" ministry become more successful. These individuals are oftentimes self-sacrificing and Christ-like in their service. They often labor untiringly; when others are at rest, they are at work.

Charles Stanley points out in *God's Children Gifted for Ministry*,[33] these people often enjoy working most with others to get a certain task accomplished. Because this is true, it is important to be very careful not to let people who have the gift of service work alone frequently. They will tend to become discouraged and possibly even feel used. They work best when working together. There is something to the fact that Christ assigned the disciples to go out "two-by-two." It is easy for someone with the gift of service to burn out if he or she always has to be working alone.

These people are best motivated when they're continually reminded of how their work of service contributes to the larger body of Christ. They can never hear too often that their work is appreciated. It is best to always have them work with others and not alone.

Another way to keep those who have the gift of service motivated is to give short-term tasks. They gain much satisfaction by seeing a task completed. Charles Stanley points out, as well, that they are not motivated by being given a "five year task to accomplish."[34] He points out that they are far more motivated by having repeated short-term projects.

Service When Filled with the Holy Spirit

If you are a person who has the gift of service, what does it look like when you are filled with the Holy Spirit? You will see many of these characteristics in your life:

- You will enjoy working in the church or serving your organization.
- You will be alert to the needs of the church or organization.
- You will be available to help.
- You will be creative in meeting needs that are not currently being met.

- You will comprehend the big picture and find fulfillment is your service.
- You will have a sense of satisfaction at accomplishing even the most menial task.
- You will demonstrate Christ's likeness in a very profound way. Christ Himself said He did not come to be served, but to serve (Matt. 20:28).
- You will have a humble spirit.
- You will regularly read and study the Word of God for new strength every day.
- You will have a strong prayer life and pray for the needs of the body.

Service When Not Filled with the Holy Spirit

A person who has the gift of service needs to be sure that he or she is walking constantly in the Holy Spirit. If you are not, certain characteristics may begin to develop in your life:

- You may substitute service for personal devotion. A person needs to realize that their service is not in place of their personal devotions. You need to keep your relationship with God fresh and not let anything, including service, substitute for it.
- You may often feel resentful that no one appreciates you. This person needs to keep his eyes on the Lord and realize that they are working for Christ not for a church or ministry.
- When needs are not met, you may be tempted to become critical of others. In other words, you may become angry and upset that nobody else volunteers to meet needs.
- You may become critical of those who do not have the gift of service.

- You may easily burn out. It is essential to have the empowerment of the Holy Spirit when serving. Otherwise you will feel like you are the only one doing the Lord's work.
- You may stop being available, and then quit caring about the work of the Lord as a whole. At this point bitterness begins to creep in. The joy of serving the Lord is found by being filled with the Holy Spirit.

If Service Is Your Primary Spiritual Gift

Step out in confidence that God wants to use you to create an environment that helps others to grow in their faith or come to know Christ personally. Work with others and share your vision for how things can be more effective. Know that God is using you for a greater good. Don't be discouraged.

Helps: I help individuals

This word for the gift of helps (*Antilempsis*) is found only one time in the New Testament, 1 Corinthians 12:28. It is, however, found in the Septuagint where it often refers to God as our Helper. For example, "But You, O LORD, be not far off; O You my help, hasten to my assistance" (Ps. 22:19).

Definition: *The gift of helps is the supernaturally empowered ability God gives to certain members of the body of Christ to invest the talents and gifts they have in the life and ministry of other members of the body, thus enabling the person helped to increase the effectiveness of his or her spiritual gifts or ministry.*

Please note that in this definition, the purpose of helping another person is so the person helped will increase his or her effectiveness in the use of his own spiritual gifts. All of the spiritual gifts are to encourage other people to use their gifts. The gift of helps does likewise. The gift of helps is a one-on-one ministry. This gift differs from the gift of mercy in that mercy is given to those who are in deep need of compassion and are experiencing difficult times. The gift of helps comes to assist those who simply become bogged down in their situation in life. This is a very encouraging gift, as it helps others get back on their feet in serving God.

A person with the gift of helps is oftentimes viewed as God helping a person in a particular situation. These people are seen as being "sent" from God.

Most books I have examined have classified the gift of service and the gift of helps as one and the same gift. However, because they are not the same word in the Greek translation, that means they are two different gifts.

The distinction between the gift of service and the gift of helps is that the gift of service ministers to the body of Christ **at large**. The gift of helps, on the other hand, meets needs of **specific individuals**. The word in the Greek language for "helps" means "to provide helpful deeds or assistance."

Goal: By the leading of the Holy Spirit to ascertain who needs help and how to help that person so that he or she can better use their gifts to serve the Lord.

Characteristics

The gift of helps is a gift that will apply whatever possession or talent or skill a person has to help another person in need. It may be as simple as taking a meal to someone, helping a sick person clean his house, fixing something in his or her house or car, or simply helping that person perform a task. It is also helping someone else in their ministry. A person who has the gift of helps receives a great deal of joy in seeing that a person is greatly ministered to by things which he or she considers rather simple. This person does not mind giving his or her time or energies to help someone accomplish something, which they would not be able to do without assistance. I personally do not have the gift of helps, and I am constantly amazed at those who do. I have been helped by so many who have this gift, and I cannot express how encouraging that is to me. They do it with such joy, whereas I become frustrated or discouraged. They are able to solve the problem or help out in such a way that I notice it has to be from God. When I watch those who have the gift of helps, I definitely see the power of the Holy Spirit working in and through them. This person needs to understand that he or she is a tremendous encouragement to so many, and probably has no idea the ministry they have!

An example of an essential individual, who had the gift of helps, was Phoebe, in Romans 16:1–2. She was a servant in the church of Cenchrea, and, consequently, Paul says she was a major help to him. These individuals are motivated by helping another person to accomplish a greater goal.

Silas, Luke, Timothy, and others came alongside Paul to help him. God may use you to come alongside a leader to help him or her be successful. Leaders aways need assistance to help them accomplish their goals.

Development

If you have the gift of helps, simply learn of ways that you can help people.

I have a friend, Larry, who has the gift of helps in a very profound way. He has the ability to help other believers find jobs, connect with people who can help them with whatever issue they have, and solve money or personal problems. He also uses this with unbelievers to draw them to the Lord. He is always looking for ways to help people in their personal and professional lives.

Also, in developing this gift, be aware that not all "helping" helps people. Discern what is the best way to help someone. It is best to ask, "What would help you in your situation?" or "I have a suggestion, would doing _____ be helpful to you?" Because you have a supernatural gift, you may come up with ideas they had not thought of. This will most likely be warmly received.

In a church or organization, ask those in your leadership (including pastors or supervisors) what things you can do to help meet the goals of the team, organization, or church.

People need help with their finances, finding counseling, a place to live, finding a job. Perhaps there are many older people that need your help, or young moms or people who are sick. As you seek ways to help, you will learn discernment and what things greatly help other people. Remember to examine the fruit of your ministry to see if the people you have helped get back into using their own spiritual gifts for the Lord. Be careful about volunteering for everything just because there is a need! Be careful especially about volunteering for ministries in which you are not gifted. There will be times that you will need to fill in until the right gifted person comes, but set a time limit and trust that God will raise up the right person if this is a ministry that He wants to exist. Don't burn yourself out on ministries that God hasn't gifted you in!

Misunderstandings

It can become possible for those with the gift of helps to become discouraged and think they are the only ones helping out.

Oftentimes when an announcement is made from the pulpit that "We need help teaching fifth graders" or some other need, those with the spiritual gift of helps immediately feel a need to help out. The problem is that the help needed is more in the area of teaching or administration, and those with the gift of helps can find themselves volunteering for something that is beyond their giftedness.

Those with the gift of helps need to remember that they should pace themselves and do only what they are able to do. Remember that not everyone has the gift of helps. Those who have other gifts may be seen as not caring enough because they are doing things for the ministry as a whole and seem to not care for other people. If you have the gift of helps, you need to remember that your work is accomplishing the building of God's kingdom. The apostle Paul was constantly helped by Timothy, Luke, and others. Women provided meals and money for him and brought him his books and his cloak (2 Tim. 4:13). Women were tremendous helps with Christ and His ministry, especially in providing sustenance for the all disciples. Others may not appreciate or notice everything you do, but God always sees and will reward you for your labor. Remember, sometimes the best way to help a person may be to simply pray for that person.

Key Verses

> **"We urge you, brethren, admonish the unruly,**
> **encourage the fainthearted, help the weak, be patient**
> **with everyone" (1 Thess. 5:14).**

"I commend to you our sister Phoebe, who is a servant of the church which is at Cenchrea; that you receive her in the Lord in a manner worthy of the saints, and that you help her in whatever matter she may have need of you; for she herself has also been a helper of many, and of myself as well" (Rom. 16:1–2).

"Perhaps I will stay with you awhile, or even spend the winter, so that you can help me on my journey, wherever I go" (1 Cor. 16:6).

"As each one has received a special gift, employ it in serving one another as good stewards of the manifold grace of God. Whoever speaks, is to do so as one who is speaking the utterances of God; whoever serves is to do so as one who is serving by the strength which God supplies; so that in all things God may be glorified through Jesus Christ, to whom belongs the glory and dominion forever and ever. Amen" (1 Pet. 4:10).

Helps When Filled with the Holy Spirit

If you are a person who has the gift of helps and is filled with the Holy Spirit, you will:

- Be able to sense those who have need of help and will volunteer your assistance.
- Have a spirit of joy about you as you help others.
- Continue to help others, even when you do not feel appreciated.
- Sense people's thankfulness and spur others to likewise use their giftedness.

- You will enjoy working behind the scenes.
- Rejoice in other people's successes, knowing that you had a part.
- Keep a close, consistent walk with the Lord so as to discern which people God wants you to help.
- Be in the Word of God so you will keep yourself encouraged.

Helps When Not Filled with the Holy Spirit

If a person is carnal and not walking in the Spirit, he or she needs to be aware that certain characteristics will develop:

- They will become critical of others who do not have the gift of helps.
- They may think their gift is insignificant compared with other's giftedness.
- They will become bitter and resentful in having to help others. People will be seen as a burden and not a blessing.
- They will tend to forget the reason why they are helping others.
- They will begin to lose their joy and feel burned out.
- They will try to help others in ways they don't really need, and not help others when they truly do need help.
- They will become discouraged to the point of not using his or her gift of helps and then giving up on their walk with the Lord.
- They will begin avoiding people because they will become afraid that they will be asked to do something.
- They will have a poor prayer life and little or no study of God's Word.

If Helps Is Your Primary Spiritual Gift

Know that God will lead you to individuals who are stuck in life or overburdened and need help getting back on track with God and trusting Him. Be sure and set boundaries. You cannot help everyone, but you can help those whom God leads you to. Learn what does help others and what does not. Not everything offered is helpful. Seek the Holy Spirit to show you the real need of a person. Know that you are a "gift from God to that person." Be aware that the Holy Spirit may send non-Christians to you to help and by that lead them to the Lord.

Mercy: I care

Definition: *The gift of mercy is the supernaturally empowered ability to feel genuine empathy and compassion for individuals, both Christian and non-Christian, who suffer distressing physical, mental, or emotional problems, and to turn that caring into cheerful actions that reflect Christ's love and alleviates the suffering so that a person is drawn closer to the Lord.*

Of all the gifts, there are only two which are direct characteristics of the very nature of God. The first is **encouragement** (comfort). The second is **mercy**. The person with this gift will be able to demonstrate, in a supernatural way, the very character of God every time he or she uses this gift. It is a significant gift because it reflects the very heart of God. God is a God of mercy. He has chosen to show mercy on those who do not deserve it. Mercy is an act of compassion on those who are in total need and cannot help themselves. This describes precisely our state in life. We are in bondage to sin and we are totally helpless to save ourselves. Apart from the mercy of God, we cannot be saved. We are totally unable to rise above our sinfulness. For this reason, we need mercy.

The gift of mercy *(eleos)* (Rom. 12:8), is not simply a feeling of pity. It is an act of compassion. Whenever Jesus Christ had mercy on someone, He did something! As an act of mercy, He healed a man with a withered hand (Mark 3:5). Throughout His ministry, people's lives and future lives were changed by His acts of mercy. He had compassion on the crowds so He fed them. His ultimate act of mercy is saving people. Christ knows that the ultimate act of physical, emotional, and spiritual healing will take place when a person who is saved enters into eternity.

There is a goal to the gift of mercy. It is found in 2 Corinthians 4:1. The apostle Paul states, "Therefore, since we have this ministry, as we received mercy, we do not lose heart." The purpose of exercising the gift of mercy is so that the one who receives mercy does not "lose heart." The act of mercy rejuvenates and encourages a person to continue on in the Lord!

Goal: To meet whatever need is necessary to help a person become restored so that they can be productive for the kingdom of God.

Characteristics

What is exciting about the characteristic of the gift of mercy is that it is a gift which involves action. It is the ability to deeply feel emotions and empathy for a person's plight in life. However, many people feel pity, but few actually do something to alleviate the situation of the person for whom they feel pity. Many people feel powerless. This is why the gift of mercy is so necessary, because God empowers those with this gift to do something about those who are in need. People seek out those who need help and begin to work with them to make their life better. The gift of mercy is different from the gift of exhortation. The gift of exhortation will provide <u>words</u> of comfort; the person with the gift of mercy will provide <u>works</u> of comfort.

Those with the gift of mercy often express this gift in a one-to-one relationship. They have a keen ability to discern that a person is in need or hurting whether it is a physical need or an emotional need or even a spiritual need. They have a heart-felt desire to help this person without any expectation of repayment. These individuals tend to become angry at the callousness of society and angry at the callousness of others towards those in need. They want to do something. When they see a person hurting, they want to alleviate the pain. They feel deep concern and want to do something for those who have experienced loss, the prisoners, the blind, the poor, the aged, the physically handicapped, the shut-ins, the mentally ill, and those who are simply down on their fortunes in life. It is also an act of showing compassion on someone who does not deserve it. Although this gift is primarily for the body of Christ, people with the gift of mercy still direct their gift to unbelievers as well as with the intent of communicating the love of Christ. Their acts of kindness come naturally. They enjoy the fact that they cannot be repaid for their acts of kindness.

Every Christian is expected to demonstrate mercy towards others. This is part of the fruit of the Holy Spirit, which are deeds of gentleness, kindness, and goodness. Those who have the gift of mercy are used by God to demonstrate to all believers how to be kind, gentle, and good. It is well for the body of Christ to pay close attention to those who have this gift, to learn how to be more Christ-like.

People with this gift don't just say to the sick or bedridden or those who are in a difficult time in their life, "Call me if there's anything I can do for you." These are the ones who will say, "Do you mind if I bring a meal to your house tonight and arrange for others to provide for the other days?" Or, "Do you mind if I arrange for someone to come help clean your house?" Or "How about if I help arrange to have your children taken to all their after school functions while you are recovering?" These people get personally involved. They are the ones who will also help provide facilities for the physically handicapped in church. They are the ones who may try to start a deaf ministry or a ministry to single moms or to the mentally challenged. They will try to provide for the shut-ins. They seek to provide tapes or relationships with the elderly in the congregation. Without these individuals, a church would often become cold or callous. Those with the gift of mercy have an invaluable place in the body of Christ.

The gift of mercy is not simply ministering to those who are in deep need. These people like to show acts of compassion. For example, when my wife's father died, and we had to leave suddenly, someone with the gift of mercy asked if it would be all right to come and clean our house as a ministry to us while we were gone. Our lives were pretty much in disarray at that point, and I couldn't express how encouraging that was to me. It was definitely an act of kindness. Another person came by the house and gave us a fifty-dollar bill for the trip. What a blessing and encouragement.

One of the outstanding characteristics of the person, who has the gift of mercy, is that he or she does these acts "with cheerfulness." They can walk into a hospital room to visit someone and cheer him or her up. They are not glum and somber. Although they feel deep compassion, they do not express that empathy with depression. They have the ability to come in and encourage someone who is hospitalized. They are so cheerful because they see God at work in the situation!

I used to think that because I felt a great deal of compassion and pity for people, that I had the gift of mercy. Even though I had these feelings, I did not have the power to do anything for these people. I then realized that this was not my gift. So many times I simply felt helpless. Now I have discovered that even though I do not have this gift, I can help people by using my other gifts. Those with the gift of mercy experience God's supernatural enablement to actually do something for people who have a need.

Jesus Christ is the perfect example of not only feeling compassion but also exercising compassion of individuals and crowds.

Misunderstandings

Many cautions must be given and misunderstandings clarified relative to the gift of mercy.

- The avoidance of firmness may appear to be a weakness for the person with the gift of mercy. These people sometimes are unwilling to be decisive or allow a person who has brought something upon themselves to experience the consequences. People with the gift of mercy need to be cautious so as to not interfere with the plan of God. Suffering is much a part of the Christian life. Although those with the gift of mercy want to alleviate other's suffering, they need to understand that at times this is the hand of God at work to accomplish His purpose and they need to be sure not to interfere with that plan. It takes discernment on their part to understand when to become involved and when not to. They need to be careful not to alleviate the consequences of sin. This gift is primarily for use on those who have been dealt a blow simply because of the unfairness of life.

- They may appear to be guided more by emotions than logic.
- They need to be extremely cautious about dealing with those of the opposite sex. For example, a woman with the gift of mercy trying to help a man who has been down and out, or involved in drugs or some other predicament in life, may find that she becomes emotionally attached to this individual as he becomes very emotionally attached to her. In the same case, a man who has the gift of mercy and uses it on a woman who is experiencing difficulties in life, be it her marriage or whatever situation, may find himself so emotionally attached, that his good intentions end up in sexual involvement. People with the gift of mercy begin with the purest motives and agape love for another person. This does not protect them, however, from emotional attachment that ends up in sin. The best way for a person who has the gift of mercy to deal with a person of the opposite sex is to never help that person by themselves. Always involve someone else. The best case would be to deal with this person only once, and then direct them to someone of the same sex who can help them without any emotional baggage involved.
- They can easily be taken advantage of. What I have found in many cases is that if someone with the gift of mercy works in the church, they always tend to help those who come asking the church for help without asking any serious questions. In my experience, many of those outside of church requesting some kind of financial help are not genuinely honest. There are those in deep need who

need to be helped; however, churches, because of their desire to be compassionate, are easy targets. In one of the churches I served, we finally were able to resolve the situation by passing on those who had needs to those who had the gift of discernment. What we found in the majority of cases, unfortunately, was that the people were not being honest with us in terms of the need that they had. They simply saw the church as an easy way to gain money to continue their lifestyle. There is much joy when we discover those who do have a genuine need and we are able to help them.

- They tend to attract the hurting, the down-and-outers, and the very needy in a congregation. Because of this, they need to learn to pace themselves and involve others with their gifts to help so they do not become overwhelmed.
- They have a tendency to be attracted to those with the spiritual gift of exhortation. This is good, because it helps balance deeds of mercy with words of exhortation from the Scriptures.

Development

There are several ways to develop the gift of mercy.

- Develop cheerfulness. As the apostle Paul states, **"He who shows mercy, with cheerfulness"** (Rom. 12:8). Learn to use this gift with cheerfulness, not with a spirit of despondency or discouragement. Cheerfulness will add volumes to your ability to help others.
- Develop it in such a way that a person's suffering isn't just alleviated, but that he or she is strengthened and directed to better service with the Lord (2 Cor. 4:1).
- Discover what truly helps a person in the long run. It is one thing to give a person a fish; it is another thing to teach a person how to fish.

- Study the Scriptures to learn about God's mercy, especially the life of Christ, to learn about how genuine mercy is demonstrated.
- Realize that the best gift of mercy expressed to a non-Christian is to bring them to the Great Problem Solver, the Lord Jesus Christ.
- In helping a believer, make sure that he or she learns to depend upon God and His Word rather than just people or you.
- Develop a strong prayer life so as to be able to help them, not just physically or emotionally, but spiritually.

Key Verses

"The LORD is compassionate and merciful, slow to get angry and filled with unfailing love" (Ps. 103:8 NLT).

"He feels pity for the weak and the needy, and He will rescue them" (Ps. 72:13 NLT).

"When three of Job's friends heard of the tragedy he had suffered, they got together and traveled from their homes to comfort and console him.... Then they sat on the ground with him for seven days and nights. No one said a word to Job, for they saw that his suffering was too great for words" (Job 2:11, 13 NLT).

"This is what the LORD of Heaven's Armies says: Judge fairly and show mercy and kindness to one another" (Zech. 7:9 NLT).

"Blessed are the merciful, for they shall receive mercy" (Matt. 5:7).

"When he saw the crowds, he had compassion for them, because they were harassed and helpless, like sheep without a shepherd" (Matt. 9:36 NIV).

"Then Jesus called his disciples to him and said, "I have compassion on the crowd because they have been with me now three days and have nothing to eat. And I am unwilling to send them away hungry, lest they faint on the way" (Matt. 15:32 NIV).

"Blessed be the God and Father of our Lord Jesus Christ, the Father of mercies and God of all comfort, who comforts us in all our affliction, so that we may be able to comfort those who are in any affliction, with the comfort with which we ourselves are comforted by God" (2 Cor. 1:3–4).

"But the wisdom from above is first of all pure. It is also peace loving, gentle at all times, and willing to yield to others. It is full of mercy and good deeds. It shows no favoritism and is always sincere" (James 3:17 NLT).

Mercy When Filled with the Holy Spirit

A person who has the gift of mercy and is walking in the Spirit they will express many of the following characteristics:

- Cheerfulness. This is the joy of the Holy Spirit as you serve the Lord.

- Discernment. You will be able to discern who needs genuine help and how to best help them.
- You will help turn a person's eyes to the Lord, not just yourself.
- Discipline. You will live a disciplined life so as to not become overwhelmed by all the needs in the church and in the world.
- You will be able to be firm when necessary. You will need to be able to confront sin if sin is involved in a person's suffering.
- Impartiality. You will not be partial in who is helped. The Lord Jesus Christ was not partial.
- Your decisions will be based on the Word of God, not emotions. You will be strongly controlled by the Holy Spirit.
- You will have a strong devotion life. Because this tends to be an emotional gift, your life needs to be governed by the stability of the Word of God and by staying in constant contact with the Lord through prayer.

Mercy When Not Filled with the Holy Spirit

It is very important that a person with the gift of mercy be aware if they are not walking in the Spirit. The reasons are as follows:

- An inability to be decisive when necessary.
- Taking up the offenses of the one who is hurt. This is a violation of Scripture as we are not permitted to take up another person's offense. A person who is offended must follow Matthew 18 in dealing with his or her offense.
- Basing decisions on emotions rather than the Word of God.
- Improper affections for a person of the opposite sex. If a person is not walking in the Holy Spirit, they may use

this gift to develop relationships with a person of the opposite sex, which will ultimately lead them into sin.

- Partiality. They will tend to select those whom they want to help and not others.
- Sympathizing with those who are violating God's standards. Christ did not show mercy to the Pharisees or Sadducees who were living in direct disobedience to God's Word. A person with the gift of mercy must discern not to use this gift with those who want little or nothing to do with God and His ways.
- Establishing possessive friendships with others.
- No desire to study the Bible or have a significant prayer life.

If Mercy Is Your Primary Spiritual Gift

You have a wonderful gift to communicate the love of God in a substantial way that draws people closer to Him. You will be considered a "God-send" to the people you help. You have the ability to meet people's needs in a way that others struggle with. Be discerning as to those you help. When it is no longer "cheerfully done" then you may either need to reconsider those you are helping or get away with the Lord so that He can have mercy on you and rejuvenate your spirit. God can use your gift to turn many non-Christians to Christ and encourage the rejected Christians to the love of their Savior.

Giving: I inspire, equip, and provide

Definition: *The gift of giving is the supernaturally empowered ability to contribute financial and material resources to the work of the Lord with liberality and cheerfulness in such a way that it encourages, inspires, and blesses others.*

As with all the gifts, the purpose is to give a visual or demonstrative example of what God wants us to be doing as a regular part of our lives. This is the purpose of the gift of giving. The goal of one who has the gift of giving is to teach all those who do not, how to loosen their attachment to the material things of this world. Praise God for the incredible ministry of those who have the gift of giving.

The gift of giving *(metadidomi)* (Rom. 12:8) is made up of two words (meta-didomi). The two words are "to give" with the additional word "with" or "over." Meaning to "give over" or to impart what one person has to another. This word is used five times in the New Testament. In Luke 3:11, John the Baptist says, "Let the man who has two tunics <u>share</u> with him who has none and let him who has food do likewise" (emphasis mine). In Romans 1:11, the apostle Paul says, "For I long to see you in order that I may <u>impart</u> some spiritual gift to you, that you may be established" (emphasis mine). The apostle Paul wanted to share what giftedness he had, so that others would be more firmly established in their faith. In Ephesians 4:28 the thief is told to steal no more, but to get a job in order that he may "<u>share</u> with him who has need" (emphasis mine). In Romans 12:8 it states that he who gives is to do it with cheerfulness.

Every Christian not only has the responsibility, but the privilege to give. Most people, by nature, find it very difficult to give liberally. We all need to be taught the joys of giving, and then to experience the blessings of giving to the Lord on a regular basis. Because God understands that it is difficult for us to hold loosely to the things of this world, He has not only exhorted us in His Word to give, but He has also given us living examples of what a joyful, freeing, liberating life is enjoyed by those with the gift of giving. Although the whole concept of giving is very sensitive to many people, for a person to be truly freed up in life, this needs to be tackled head on. Satan knows well that the more he can convince us to hang on tightly to our earthly possessions, the more bondage we will be in. For that reason, he has made giving such a "taboo" subject. God, however, knows that for us to experience the abundant life, we need to give. Had He not given the ultimate gift, which was His Son, and His life and death for us, we would not be able to experience the gift of heaven.

Even though everyone is admonished to give, there are certain people who are supernaturally empowered to give above and beyond any human logic. These individuals have the gift of giving.

Goal: To give in such a way that it encourages the hearts of others to give in faith to God and further the advancement of the kingdom of God.

Characteristics

There are many refreshing characteristics about the person who has the gift of giving. A misunderstanding needs to be cleared up at this point though. A person with the gift of giving does not necessarily have large amounts of money. The gift of giving does not depend on how much a person has. It is his or her heart. Often a person who has the gift of giving is blessed financially so that they can have more to give. This is all part of their ministry. Another key point is that giving does not just mean financially. It means giving of anything they have. A good example of this is found in Acts 4, where even though many did not have something to give financially, they still gave of their belongings to help others in need. Those with the gift of giving love to give of their money and of their possessions. They would be glad to give the shirt off their backs if there was a need. Finances have little to do with this gift.

The person with the gift of giving will demonstrate many of these following characteristics:

- They live lives of thankfulness. Their entire motivation is out of thankfulness to God for what He has done for him or her. They are ever conscious of the greatness of God giving to them. Because of this reason, they are very humble and thankful.

- They love to give. They live to give. They will do whatever they can so they will have something to give. I have a friend named Christopher who has the gift of giving. He was so frustrated when he was in transition in his job, because he did not have money to give. He could not wait to get a job so he could begin giving again.

- An ability to invest wisely in order to have more money available to give away. God seems to bless these people in their ability to multiply their investments. Christ said, "He who is faithful in little will be faithful in much" (Luke 1:10). God will continue to bless a person who invests wisely in order to give.

- Is more motivated to give as a result of the Lord's promptings, not as a result of appeals. Although they will give when an appeal is made, they are far more interested in giving when an appeal is not made. When they see a need, they like to meet it.

- Does not keep a tally of what percentage they have given to the Lord. If you ask a person with the gift of giving how much he or she has given to the Lord that year, chances are they will have no idea. They do not give in order to have a tax write-off.

- They tithe on a regular basis. Those who have the gift of giving usually give at least 10% of their income but do not find their main satisfaction as giving in this capacity. They long to give more.
- They hold loosely to the things of this world. Those who have the gift of giving do not seem materialistic at all. The type of house they live in, whether it is exquisite or simple, has very little relevance to them.
- Experiences greater satisfaction giving to large projects or large needs rather than to a general budget. Although these people see the need to keep open the doors of a church, and keep all the ministries functioning, their heart responds to a greater capacity when a large need is requested. For example, a need arose in our church when a woman who was in job transition suddenly came down with pneumonia. Her case was severe, and she had to be hospitalized. This couple had no money to pay their hospital bills. This need was made known to our church body from the pulpit. They needed $7,000 for their expenses. Everybody was wondering if it was possible to scrape up enough money to help out. Amazingly, one person with the gift of giving wrote a check for the entire $7,000! This couple never knew who that person was. Later I found out by accident who it was and was amazed to realize that this person did not have $7,000 lying around. He truly gave sacrificially. (I found out later that this was a fourth of his yearly salary.)
- A desire to give secretly. These people are not motivated at all by receiving praise for their giving. They are more highly motivated by seeing others praise God for the gift. Christ said in Matthew 6:3-4, "But when you give alms, do not let your left hand know what your right hand is doing that your alms may be in secret and your Father

who sees in secret will repay you." Alms giving is not giving directly to the Lord. All giving to the Lord in the Old and New Testament was public. Alms giving is giving specifically to people. When a person receives a gift in secret, he has no one to thank but the Lord.

- A tendency to practice personal frugality with their own finances. These people live a disciplined life when it comes to their budget. They have a supernatural ability to be content with the basic necessities of life. I also believe that a person who has the ministry of "voluntary poverty" (1 Cor. 13:3) has either the gift of giving or the gift of faith, or both. They are more content giving away what they have than acquiring things. My friend that I mentioned earlier, Christopher, told me the story of the time he was in a restaurant with some people when a girl expressed that she did not have a car to get home or go to work the next day because her's was in the shop. Even though Christopher did not have the money to help her out, he simply said, "Why don't you take my car?" This girl was not even a Christian and was totally shocked that he would say this. She said, "How will you get home or get to work?" And he said, "Oh, I'll figure out a way." The girl took him up on his offer, and this was a key instrument in being a testimony to the Lord. This is the nature of those with the gift of giving. They want to give, and they have little regard for their own personal convenience.

- An ability to see financial needs which tend to be overlooked by others. Those with the gift of giving are constantly looking for ways to minister to others. Another example of this was when someone found out that a member of the church did not have a heater for his apartment and went out and bought one without the other person knowing who gave it. What was interesting is that he enclosed the receipt just in case the person didn't like the brand and wanted to go back and pick out something else.

- A desire to give gifts which are of high quality. This is very significant. I saw this at work at my church in California. There was an incident where the wildfires in the mountains of San Bernardino burned down many houses. One couple in our church had their beautiful home and all their belongings burned up in this fire. As he was sharing this experience with a small group of us, he said that he learned something that could be passed on to help others learn how to give. He had a very prominent position in his job. All of his dress clothes for work were burned up. He stated that they received many boxes of clothes after the fire. He said as his family opened the boxes they saw that many of them were simply castoffs or used and outdated clothing that were not very attractive. He understood the heart of the many people who gave, but it was not what his family needed. There were some people, however, who understood their situation they took them down to buy brand new clothes for himself and all his children. There were others who gave money, directly, for them to buy a new wardrobe. His comment was that it greatly ministered to him and his family that there were those who understood what their true need was in terms of their loss. It was those who had the gift of giving that gave the high quality gifts to this family. They had to box up many of these other "gifts" and send them on. Those with the gift of giving do not give "junk" for Jesus. They want the excellence of their gift to reflect on the excellence of their Lord.

- A desire to use giving as a way to motivate others to give. It is very important to those with the gift of giving that they allow themselves to be used by God to motivate others to give. They need to understand that their primary ministry is not giving to meet needs, but to encourage and demonstrate to others the joys of giving and giving liberally.

Misunderstandings

There are several misunderstandings and frustrations associated with a person with this gift:

- They are often frustrated because they don't have more to give. There is a wonderful older lady in our church who has the gift of giving. She lives on a fixed income and cannot give financially; however, she is a wonderful canner. She cans all types of fruits and vegetables and gives them away. My family and I have been very blessed by her giving. She is constantly running around saying, "The Lord wants us to give, and He wants us to give what we can, and this is what I can give." She says this with a big smile on her face. What a tremendous testimony she is.

- Because people with the gift of giving sometimes give very large sums, this can be misunderstood as a desire to control the ministry. This is not the case. They are simply glad to give, and they hope that what they give is used very effectively.

- Their encouragement to others to give may not be very well received. They may be misunderstood as using a high pressure tactic. Again, this is not the case. They simply understand how blessed a person is when he gives and he gives liberally.

- Sometimes these people are approached to give and do not always give. This could be misunderstood as a lack of generosity or interest in the ministry. Again, this is not the case. They simply need to give as they feel led by the Lord. They tend to give according to what motivates them. They are often irritated and frustrated by constant pressures or appeals to give. They sometimes are taken advantage of because of their generosity. In many cases, they simply wish that those who have not given much could give more. *A major frustration occurs when a person with the gift of giving marries someone without it.* This is always humorous in the sense that the husband may come home and say, "Honey, where was that money we were saving for the new stereo?" And his wife may say, "Well, there was this couple in our neighborhood who had a deep need, and I just felt it was more important to give to them."

- There may be incidences when the savings account is depleted unbeknownst to the other. It is very important for this type of couple to learn to give so that both feel comfortable. Spouses who do not have the gift of giving will be very blessed if he or she will learn how to be less attached to the things of the world. The one with the gift of giving will have to learn to be a little more planned and less spontaneous in his or her giving. *He or she, by all means, needs to learn to include their spouse.* It is easy for them to become irritated or misunderstood because of the feelings they have when they don't see others giving as freely. They get very discouraged at the materialism in the local church today.

Key Verses

"Besides, in my devotion to the temple of my God I now give my personal treasures of gold and silver for

the temple of my God, over and above everything I
have provided for this holy temple" (1 Chron. 29:3
NIV).

"But King David said to Ornan, 'No, but I will surely
buy it for the full price; for I will not take what is
yours for the LORD, or offer a burnt offering which
costs me nothing'" (1 Chron. 21:24).

"Honor the LORD from your wealth and from the
first of all your produce; So your barns will be filled
with plenty and your vats will overflow with new
wine" (Prov. 3:9).

"Give to the one who asks you, and do not turn away
from the one who wants to borrow from you" (Matt.
5:42).

"Give freely and become more wealthy; be stingy and
lose everything. The generous will prosper; those who
refresh others will themselves be refreshed" (Prov.
11:24 NLT).

"The point is this: whoever sows sparingly will
also reap sparingly, and whoever sows bountifully
will also reap bountifully. Each one must give as
he has made up his mind, not reluctantly or under
compulsion, for God loves a cheerful giver. And
God is able to make all grace abound to you, so that
having all sufficiency in all things at all times, you
may abound in every good work" (2 Cor. 9:6 ESV).

"Teach those who are rich in this world not to be proud and not to trust in their money, which is so unreliable. Their trust should be in God, who richly gives us all we need for our enjoyment. Tell them to use their money to do good. They should be rich in good works and generous to those in need, always being ready to share with others. By doing this they will be storing up their treasure as a good foundation for the future so that they may experience true life" (1 Tim. 6:17 NLT).

Development

The apostle Paul says in Romans 12:8, "He who gives with liberality." The word "liberality" literally means "without folds" (*haplotēs*). In other words, the idea is as a piece of cloth or parchment could be folded and have several sides, the rendering here means to give with only one intent, not many intents. Or a better way to put it would be to give with singleness of mind without pretense. It also has the idea of giving with liberality (2 Cor. 8:2). The intent of this admonition is for the person who has the gift of giving to learn to give without attachments and to also give freely and abundantly. This is necessary because of how it helps others to simply give unto the Lord without expecting in return.

- If you have this gift, use it as frequently as possible. Learn to give freely and once you give, learn to let it go. Not everyone who receives your gift will use it for the best. What you give may not always be accepted in the purest way. Don't worry about that — let God bless you for giving.
- Also learn to give strategically. If you have the gift of giving, often you may be the person who "primes the pump."

Sometimes the need seems so great that your gift of giving may be what spurs others to meet this need.

- Follow the leading of the Holy Spirit. He knows the needs, and He knows who needs to be ministered to the most. As you learn to walk in the Holy Spirit, you will sense when to give and when not to give. Feel free to not give to everything. There are far more needs to be met than you are able to meet. If you cannot meet that need with a clear conscience and total freedom in the Lord, then God has raised up somebody else to meet that need if He wants it met. It does not all depend on you. Study 2 Corinthians 8 and 9 for more insights on giving.

Special Note

Often times, I am asked about what a person should do in the area of giving when their spouse is not a Christian. This can be very difficult, especially if the spouse does not want any of their money to be tithed. Many women find themselves in this position who have non-Christian husbands. They truly have a desire to give to the Lord, but their husband is not open to it. Here are some suggestions that might help:

1. Talk openly with your husband or wife about how this means a great deal to you.
2. See if the two of you can come to a compromise. For example, if you work, would your spouse be agreeable to you tithing off your income? If you do not work outside the home, then would there be any amount that they would be willing to allow to be tithed?
3. Explain to your spouse that God will give back, in many different ways, what you give to Him.

4. If your spouse is simply hostile to giving any money whatsoever, then do not push it. Remember, your ultimate goal is to win your spouse to the Lord. Your submission to the wishes of your spouse, especially in an area he or she knows means a great deal to you, may do wonders in leading them to the Lord.

5. At this point, simply ask the Lord for ways that you can be a giving person in other areas other than finances. Perhaps you can make things for others, work on their car or house for them, or simply give of your time. All of these are ways to give.

Giving When Filled with the Holy Spirit

A person with the gift of giving who walks in the Spirit will experience many of these characteristics:

- Joyfulness. You will truly enjoy giving.
- Contentment. You will live a very content life because you have such loose attachments to this world. Like the apostle Paul, you will learn to be content in whatever circumstance you are in (Phil. 4:11).
- A disciplined life. Your financial house will be in order. Perhaps other areas of your life may not, but this is one area that you enjoy giving attention to because you want to be able to give more.
- Discernment. You will be able to discern when you should or should not give.
- A "heavenly mind." You will be more inclined to live your life with your eyes on **"the things above not on the things that are on the earth"** (Col. 3:1–2).
- A tremendous compassion for the needs and misfortunes of others.

- Self-control. You will be able to control how you spend your money.
- A need to be industrious. You will be resourceful in knowing how to get the most out of what you have.
- Thankfulness. You will live a very grateful, thankful life.
- A strong student of God's Word. Because you are so thankful for what God has done for you, you will want to learn more of what God has to say and all that He has for you. For that reason, you will enjoy studying God's Word.
- A strong prayer life. You realize that you cannot meet all the needs, so you realize that God wants to be the One who will meet their needs.
- Humility. You will not be so concerned about who receives the credit. You will be happy if the Lord alone receives the credit. Like John the Baptist, **"He must increase, I must decrease"** (John 3:30), is the way you feel. You are not out for your own glory, but for Christ's.

Giving When Not Filled with the Holy Spirit

What happens when a person with the gift of giving does not keep walking in the Spirit? Many of these characteristics become true in his or her life:

- Misery. They simply begin to lose the desire to give or feel that nothing is good enough for them to give to.
- Possessive. They begin to see their money and possessions as their own and not the Lord's.
- Partiality. They begin to be selective in an unhealthy way to whom they will give and to whom they will not give.
- Critical. They become critical of others who don't give, or they become critical of their church and how the finances are used within the church.

- Callous. They become hardened to all the needs of the world and people. They think the needs of the world are so great that they give up and become apathetic.
- Little interest for the Word of God because they think they will be convicted because of their lifestyle.
- Poor prayer life. Their heart becomes hardened towards the needs of others, and they quit praying for them.
- Unthankful. They lose that wonderful spirit of thankfulness which made their lives so refreshing.

If Giving Is Your Primary Spiritual Gift

Your job will be to help discern who to help and what churches or organizations are most strategic to give to. Your example of giving without limitations will be an example to others. You will be able to help your church and other ministries give in a way that is most helpful to the growing of the kingdom. Your giving to non-Christians will also help lead others to Christ. You have an extremely strategic gift.

CHAPTER 8

Manifestation Gifts, God, the Supernatural, and the Sign Gifts

The Gifts of Healings, Miracles, Tongues, and Interpretation

ALL SPIRITUAL GIFTS ARE supernatural. None are more supernatural than others as they all depend on the power of the Holy Spirit.

1 Corinthians 12:7 says, "To each one is given the **manifestation** of the Spirit...." The manifestation spoken of here is the Holy Spirit's supernatural power. It is the same manifestation of the supernatural power of God at work whether He is using Moses to part the Red Sea, or a person with the gift of evangelism opening the eyes for someone to see spiritually. All the gifts require a dependence on the supernatural power of God. The gift of healings required the same dependence upon the Spirit of God as the gift of service or helps.

It has been my experience within the circles of Christianity that there are two views concerning spiritual gifts. Most Christians lean towards one or the other. *The first view is that all the gifts are in existence today to the same manner and degree which they were in the first century. The second view holds that not all the gifts are in effect today to the same degree which they were in the first century.* Those who hold the latter view also hold that several gifts have ceased and are no longer in existence. Both of these views have difficulties in terms of remaining consistent with the teachings of Scripture. My desire and goal is to help bring clarification and a healthy understanding of the plan and working of the Holy Spirit. Regardless of which of these two views we hold, we must be consistent in our interpretation of Scripture. We cannot change our method of interpreting the Scriptures simply to justify our position.

In his book, *Surprised by the Power of the Spirit,*[35] Jack Deere makes a very good case for why all the gifts are in effect today. I recommend the reading of this book to anyone. However, what I have seen in his book, and in others, is that because people see God's Holy Spirit at work in a supernatural manner, they then interpret that as being the result of spiritual gifts: in particular, the gift of miracles and the gift of healings. I personally do not believe this is an accurate way to interpret God's supernatural work today. How then, do we make sense out of the "sign gifts" in the Bible? I think there is a way.

I want to give you my view of God, the supernatural, and the sign gifts. This view is based on seeking a consistent interpretation of Scripture and my research. With this view, I have been at peace biblically as to what God's Spirit has been performing at this time in history. I think as well, I will be able to clear up some confusion that surrounds these gifts today.

My view is that the power for God to perform the supernatural, the miraculous, and the ability to heal is as completely available today as it has been for all the ages. I do not believe that God has limited His works of the supernatural and miraculous to simply a few gifted individuals. He has opened His entire miracle producing power to all believers. Because every Christian has the Holy Spirit, we are able to perform the same works of Jesus Christ because we have the same Holy Spirit within us. This ability to perform works of the supernatural does not depend on a person's giftedness. I do believe though, God's methodology has changed for how He operates today. Instead of limiting the ability to heal and perform miracles to a few select individuals, He has now opened it up to all of His children through the power of the Holy Spirit. His power is available to every sincere believer!

Having said that, I still hold firmly that the gifts of miracles, healings, tongues, and interpretations of tongues are not manifested today in the same manner in which they were manifested in the first century. I believe the confusion which Christians have today is based on their interpretation of Hebrews 13:8 which states, "Jesus Christ is the same yesterday and today, yes and forever." This emphatically states that Jesus Christ does not change. This, however, does not state that God's methodology in working throughout the ages does not change. It obviously has changed throughout history. God's method of dealing with Adam and Eve was different from the way He dealt with Abraham or how God dealt with the nation of Israel through Moses. He does not deal with us as Christians today in the same manner. He dealt with the nation of Israel differently in the times of Elijah and Elisha. His method of dealing with His children after the institution of the church and the New Testament being completed is different than the methodology which He used before the New Testament was completed. It had to be. His purpose and His plan has never changed, which is to bring glory to Himself and to the Lord Jesus Christ. His power is still available today. Anyone who calls on the name of the Lord (Yahweh) experiences God's saving power and grace in his or her life. Whoever calls on the name of the Lord Jesus Christ has available to him or her all the power of the universe. Just because you do not have the gift of miracles or the gift of healings does not mean that God cannot use you to perform miracles and healings!

How is it explained that people today are performing healings and miracles? It is not because they have been given a spiritual gift. It is because God has chosen to heal and perform miracles through them. I do not have the gift of miracles nor the gift of healings. However, I have been privileged to be used by God to see Him heal people simply as a result of my praying and calling on the all powerful, almighty Name of the Lord Jesus Christ to perform a work of healing or a miracle in that person's life. This happened with my close friend Glenn who was terminal with a dying liver because of hepatitis. After praying with him on the phone for his healing, he told me he sensed something just happened in his liver. He went to the doctor, and the doctor could not find anything wrong with his liver. He was then taken off the liver transplant list! *It has nothing to do with my giftedness; it has everything to do with the power of Jesus Christ.* The good news is that this should encourage every Christian. It should encourage you to pray more and expect God to use you more to perform the supernatural.

How can I say that these particular gifts are not in effect today? As I have spoken with many people of the charismatic persuasion, every one has agreed that, yes, something has changed.

If they are honest with themselves, they will admit that the exact nature of the New Testament giftedness is not being manifested today. This is especially true in the case of tongues. The manifestation of tongues as appears in Acts 2 (where every person who spoke in a tongue spoke in a common existing language) is not a common experience in the life of every church. I wish however, that it were! For example: When we moved into our first church building in Boise, Idaho, World Relief had its office in the basement. They were bringing in immigrants all the time. They constantly needed interpreters to not only help translate, but to share the gospel. Churches are replete with those who have the gift of service. However, it would have been wonderful to find just one with the tongue that could speak Bosnian. What a ministry we could have! However, for some reason, God has chosen not to have the Acts 2 manifestation of the gifts of tongues like the other gifts. There are many foreigners visiting our churches every Sunday. It would be wonderful if they could hear the gospel supernaturally in their own tongue as a common occurrence!

Does the Acts 2 gift of tongues exist today? From my study and observation, not as it was in the first century. I wish it was. It would not affect my theology or belief system. However, can the Holy Spirit supernaturally manifest Himself through another person so that they speak a foreign language in a tongue of another person? Absolutely! I believe that He can and has done this in the same manner that He has manifested Himself through Christians to perform other works in which they were not gifted. What I mean by this is that **the Holy Spirit is free to manifest Himself in any capacity through any believer for any reason at any time!**

Just because you do not have the gift of exhortation does not mean that the Holy Spirit might not choose to use you to exhort another believer as if He were speaking to that person through you. Just because the Holy Spirit uses you in this capacity in a particular instance, does not mean that you have suddenly been given the gift of exhortation. A person through whom the Holy Spirit chooses to heal has not automatically been given the gift of healing. The Holy Spirit may choose to manifest Himself through you by speaking in the foreign language of the person He desires to reach for Christ. A person whom the Holy Spirit chooses to use in this way does not necessarily have the gift of tongues. A gift means we are free to use it whenever we want and as frequently as we want to. *Otherwise it is not a gift!* This is true with the gift of healings and miracles. A person was free to use that gift whenever they felt there was a need to use it.

The point of all this is that the Holy Spirit is free to manifest Himself in any way He chooses as He has throughout history. This does not mean that His methodology is the same; it simply means that His power is still the same. My personal challenge to each person is to not miss out on the supernatural power which is available to you by calling on the name of the Lord Jesus Christ to perform the supernatural. The ability to work miracles does not reside in ourselves, but only in the God of the universe.

Acts 10:38 states, "You know of Jesus of Nazareth, how God anointed Him with the Holy Spirit and with power, and how He went about doing good, and healing all who were oppressed by the devil for God was with Him."

The key here is that "God was with Him." Another interesting verse is found in Luke 5:17: "And it came about one day that He was teaching and there were some Pharisees and teachers of the law sitting there, who had come from every village of Galilee and Judea and from Jerusalem and the power of the Lord was present for Him to perform healing."

Again the key here is that "the power of the Lord was present to perform healing." I believe that it is because Jesus Christ is inside a believer that this power is available to each one of us. The key is utilizing the power of Jesus Christ by faith and expecting Him to answer your prayers!

May He be pleased to use you and me more to glorify His name through the manifestations of His Holy Spirit and power!

Key Understanding

For us to gain a better understanding of the gift of miracles and the gift of healings, a very important passage needs to be examined. Hebrews 2:3–4 states, "How shall we escape if we neglect so great a salvation? After it was at first spoken through the Lord, it was confirmed to us by those who heard, God also bearing witness with them, both by **signs** and **wonders** and by **various miracles** and by **gifts of the Holy Spirit** according to His own will" (NASB emphasis mine).

We need to understand why God used signs, wonders, various miracles, and the manifestations of the Holy Spirit in the first century. According to verse 3, it states that these were used to confirm the great salvation God has made available to mankind. Notice that the past tense is used when it states, **"it was confirmed to us."** The confirming is in the *past*. The **"bearing witness"** in verse 4 is in the *present tense*. This does say that God may continue, if He so chooses, to bear witness of the confirmation that was in the past of the salvation which He has secured for all mankind by using signs, wonders, various miracles, and gifts of the Holy Spirit. Part of the confusion is the translation of the phrase **"gifts of the Holy Spirit."** In actuality, the word **"gifts"** is not in the Greek language. It would be very significant if it were, but it is not. The word "gift" used here in Greek is the word *merismos* (not *charisma*) which means "distributions of the Holy Spirit." According to *The Complete Biblical Library*, this means *"distinct manifestations of the Spirit's power by which God confirmed the preaching of the gospel."*[36] It is not the gifts of the Holy Spirit which confirm the gospel, but His manifestations or distributions of His power. This to me indicates that the Holy Spirit is still free to exercise whatever He deems necessary to bring glory to Jesus Christ.

The three other key words are of great significance. The word **"signs"** is *semeion* in Greek. *"The word indicates that the event is not an empty ostentation of power, but it is significant in that it points beyond itself to the reality of the mighty hand of God in operation."*[37]

The significance of a sign is that it points back to God. In the Old Testament, Genesis 4:15, the sun and the moon are signs which point to God. The rainbow was a sign that pointed back to God. God enabled His servants to perform signs (Exod. 4:17, 28, 30) with the result and intent that the people might turn to God. This is the reason God would perform any sign today, to direct people not to the one who performs it, but to the One who provides the power for it, meaning Jesus Christ Himself.

The next word is **"wonders,"** or *teras* which means basically to "do that which is beyond the ordinary." It would cause astonishment in those who beheld these wonders. Its purpose also was to bring a sense of awe to people in worship to God (Acts 2:43). The phrase **"various miracles"** is the word for power or *dunamis* where we receive our word dynamite. Rogers states, "The word emphasizes the dynamic character of the event with particular regard to its outcome or effect."[38] This is God's manifestation of His power in reversing the course of nature.

A word of caution needs to be stated at this point: all three of these can be replicated and imitated by Satan himself (2 Thess. 2:9). This is why it is important to utilize those with the gift of discernment and determine whether or not any sign, wonder, or act of power is of God or of Satan. I am afraid too many churches today, because they are seeing signs and wonders, are being misled by the enemy. Signs and wonders do not mean that God is present. Satan is able to imitate and replicate any of the spiritual gifts. He does this to mislead the people. This will become more evident the closer we get to Christ's return (see the book of Revelation). In her book, *The Beautiful Side of Evil*, Johanna Michaelsen records her experiences in South America seeing healings take place first hand. It became clear to her that these healings, although supernatural, were not from God but demonic. The people who were healed did not remain healed and became worse or died. The result was people not turning to Jesus Christ but away from Him.

What Hebrews 2:3–4 does allow is the availability today of the Holy Spirit's manifestation for His power to be used through any believer! It is this supernatural power of Jesus Christ we want to tap into and experience in our everyday lives.

Healings: I help recover

Definition: *The gift of healings is the supernaturally empowered ability God gave to certain members of the body of Christ to serve as His agents to cure every form of illness and restore spiritual,* *physical, emotional, and mental health apart from the use of natural means.*

The gift of healings is found in 1 Corinthians 12:9, 28, 30. The root word *'iama* means to cure. It is the power to heal, **the ability to cause people to be well again.**

In each of these references, it is in the plural form (*'iamaton*). It is important to understand why it is in the <u>plural</u> and not the <u>singular</u>. The gift of healings means that a person was able to heal in many different ways and capacities. It also means that there were different types of healings which took place. Just as there are different kinds of illnesses, so there are different kinds of healings. This was a very important gift, especially in the time of Christ, so the people could understand that Jesus Christ is the total and complete Healer. He can heal emotionally, He can heal physically, and He can heal spiritually. No matter what the problem is, He can heal it.

Goal: To be used by God to bring emotional, spiritual, or physical healing to a person so that they may bring glory to God and enthusiastically serve Him more effectively.

Biblical Examples

Jesus Christ

To fully understand what is meant by the gift of healings, the best place to look is the life of Christ. He performed various types of healings:

- He healed the brokenhearted (Luke 4:18). Because this is the first mention of Christ's ability to heal, it may be the primary use of His healing power.
- He was able to heal any disease (Luke 6:17).

- He was able to heal a deaf person (Mark 7:31–37).
- He was able to restore sight (Mark 8:22–26).
- He was able to heal a crippled woman (Luke 13:10–17).
- He was able to restore a severed appendage (Luke 22:49–51).
- He was able to heal spiritually and mentally when He rebuked the unclean spirit (Luke 9:42).

In all of these cases Christ demonstrates that He has the ability to perform whatever it takes to heal a person. Some people may need to be healed physically, some emotionally or mentally, or some need to be healed from the ravages of Satan in their lives, and He is able to heal them all. Likewise, a person with the gift of healings had the same ability as Christ did to heal others.

The Apostles, Paul and Peter

Other examples, from the life of Peter and Paul, demonstrate the uniqueness of this gift. The question needs to be asked, "If the gift of healings is in effect today, why is it not being manifested as commonly as the gift of teaching or the gift of helps? Why is not the manifestation of this gift as common in the same way today as it was then?" As I have studied this gift, I have realized that there are some differences between the healings that take place today, and the healings that took place in the New Testament. The same power is at work today, just a different methodology.

Peter was able to heal a lame man (Acts 3:11). It seemed that even Peter's shadow was able to heal people (Acts 5:15). The apostle Paul himself was able to perform healings as well as *his handkerchief* (Acts 19:12)!

Characteristics

The following characteristics are evident in the gift of healings:

- This person is able to perform all types of healings. Whatever the person's main need is, whether emotional, physical, or freedom from demonic power, the gift of healings is able to heal that person.

- This gift was used as prominently among non-Christians as it was Christians (Acts 3:6), as evidenced by Paul's handkerchief.

- In most cases, it was instantaneous, though not always (Luke 17:11–19). The ten lepers were not healed until they turned and went on their way.

- It is not dependent on the faith of the one being healed (Acts 3:6). If this was the same gift, then a person with the gift of healings would, in many cases, be able to heal every person they pray for. Although some people feel that this is an unfair example, when you consider that Paul's handkerchief healed everyone it touched, surely someone with the gift of healings and praying in the name and power of the Lord Jesus Christ would honor the Lord by healing as many people as possible. Christ would often do this when He entered town after town.

- The gift of healings does have its limitation. Even after having just spoken about the power of the one with the gift of healings, Christ Himself was not able to perform healings because of the spiritual dynamics that were taking place. This was very clear when He returned to His own town of Nazareth (Matt. 13:58).

- Not every illness is healed by the gift of healings (2 Tim. 4:20).

- God may choose to heal apart from the gift of healings (1 Tim. 5:23). Many people use these last two passages as proof that the gift of healings eventually ceased. This may be so, but it does not mean that the power to heal no longer exists. God is still in control of when a person is healed and when he or she is not.

Misunderstandings

The misunderstandings that center on God's ability to heal is what needs to be addressed. Many people become discouraged because they have prayed continually to be healed and have not experienced God's healing power. As you study the healing examples throughout the Bible, you will come to understand that there is *not* a definite pattern.

- Sometimes a person is healed based on his or her own faith (Matt. 9:22).
- Sometimes a person is healed based on the faith of the one performing the healing (Acts 3:4–7).
- Sometimes God simply heals because someone asks to be healed (Luke 18:38–42).
- Sometimes God heals whether or not a person asks (Acts 19:11–12).
- Sometimes God heals non-Christians, and sometimes they give Him the glory and sometimes they don't (2 Kgs. 5:1–14).

God heals some Christians and not others. All of this to say that God cannot be manipulated nor instructed. God is sovereign. He will not heal in every case. If that were the situation, then there would be no purpose to suffering. The whole book of 1 Peter deals with how to handle suffering in life. If the way to handle suffering were simply to find someone with the gift of healings and heal us, then there would be no point in writing many of the books and passages about suffering. The apostle Paul, although he had the gift of healings, did not experience healing in at least one area of his life (2 Cor. 12:9–12). Whether God heals miracu-lously or by using conventional means, all healing is His healing. God still wants to be glorified through our suffering or glorified through our healing. I was healed of cancer myself. Even though I prayed to be healed instantaneously, went to healing services, had hands laid on me, God in His sovereignty and gracious-ness chose for me to go through a three-year process of chemo, diet, prayers, etc., before I was healed. (There was a lot in my character He needed to work on before I was healed.) I still feel my healing was miraculous and of Him! All the prayers of my friends and family were answered.

We are still admonished to pray about everything (Phil. 4:6). We are not to give up praying (Luke 18:1). Just because God may have said "no" to a person being healed, does not mean He does not want that person to continue to pray. God's will is always manifested through our praying. Remember in Hebrews 2:4 it is "according to **His** own will."

Key Verses

> "But He was pierced for our transgressions, He was crushed for our iniquities; the punishment that brought us peace was upon Him, and by His wounds we are healed" (Isa. 53:5).

> "Heal me, O LORD, and I shall be healed; save me, and I shall be saved, for You are my praise" (Jer. 17:14).

> "The news about Him spread throughout all Syria; and they brought to Him all who were ill, those suffering with various diseases and pains, demoniacs,

epileptics, paralytics; and He healed them" (Matt. 4:24 emphasis mine).

"Crowds gathered also from the towns around Jerusalem, bringing their sick and those tormented by evil spirits, and all of them were healed" (Acts 5:16 NIV).

"For unclean spirits, crying out with a loud voice, came out of many who had them, and many who were paralyzed or lame were healed" (Acts 8:7 ESV).

"It happened that the father of Publius lay sick with fever and dysentery. And Paul visited him and prayed, and putting his hands on him healed him" (Acts 28:8).

The Ministry of Healing When Filled with the Holy Spirit

A person who is filled with the Holy Spirit and has the gift of healings can:

- Heal anybody he or she chooses as the Lord directs.
- Heal people spiritually, emotionally, or physically.
- Have the ability to discern what type of healing a person is in need of.
- Be sensitive as to when God wants to perform a work of healing.
- Be able to heal non-Christians as well as Christians.
- Find that when a person is healed, they become a Christian or a more committed Christian.
- Has a very strong and powerful prayer life.
- Knows God's Word well enough to claim His promises for healings.

The Ministry of Healing When Not Filled with the Holy Spirit

The person who is not walking in the power of the Holy Spirit will see the following:

- An immediate loss in the ability to heal and loss of power in his or her life.
- Will excuse sin in his or her own life because of all the good they think they are doing by praying for the healing of others.
- Will use the healings to bring glory to themselves, not to Jesus Christ, or will become arrogant and prideful.
- Will desire to heal people so that they might become prominent and important, rather than Jesus Christ.
- Will stop relying on prayer and having a personal prayer time.
- Will have less regard for the Bible.
- Will begin to become involved with spiritism and heresy.

Development

The following is written so that you might see God use you more in terms of healing others. The two key areas here are faith and prayer. Whenever I encountered a spiritual inventory test, which showed someone had the gift of healings or miracles, I found an interesting statistic. Everyone who scored high on the gift of healings or miracles also scored high in the areas of intercession or faith. It seems there is a direct correlation between a person's prayer life or faith and his or her seeing healings and miracles performed. In either case, develop your prayer life and faith. Step out in boldness. Do not hesitate to pray for the healing of others. Lay hands on people and call on the name of the Lord Jesus Christ to heal them. Invoke the use of your elders. James

5:13–15 has authorized the elders in the local church to minister in the area of healing.

Look for things that may block healing. For example, unconfessed sin (James 5:15), lack of faith, or demonic oppression. Learn to seek the Holy Spirit on how to pray. Often when I pray for those who are in need of healing I ask the Holy Spirit to show me how to pray for that person. Sometimes He will show me to pray against the demonic activity in the person's life, pray toward his or her own lack of faith, or pray for physical problems. He may also confirm within me that God is choosing not to heal that person at that point or only will heal them when they get home to glory. In any case, seek the guidance of the Holy Spirit on how to pray.

Miracles: I can change circumstances

Definition: *The gift of miracles is the supernaturally empowered ability that God gave to certain believers to serve as human intermediaries to perform powerful acts that were perceived by observers to have altered the ordinary course of nature and respond in glorifying God.*

The gift of miracles (1 Cor. 12:10, 28) is literally "**working of power.**" The word for miracles is *dunamis* where we receive our word "dynamite." This ability to perform works of power is available to every Christian (Mark 9:23) but was given to certain individuals in the New Testament in order to speed up the spread of the gospel of Christ. This gift is different than the gift of healings, in that it goes beyond simply healing someone of a disease. It is the ability to alter the ordinary course of nature for the glory of God. Part of the purpose of this gift was to not only demonstrate the reality of God and help people place their faith in Christ, but also was to encourage Christians to understand the power of God which was available to them. Like any gift, it was a means to demonstrate what is to be a normal part of the Christian life. As you read all the miracles in the Old and New Testament, remember that this power is still available to you today. God is as much today the God of miracles as He has been in the past and will be in the future. It is my firm conviction that the only reason more of God's power is not seen among Christians today is the lack of faith, lack of boldness and courage to rely on His power, and an inability to understand the ministry of the Holy Spirit in a person's life, especially in terms of the supernatural. Remember that Christ said in Acts 1:8, "But you shall receive power [*dunamis*] when the Holy Spirit has come upon you and you shall be My witnesses both in Jerusalem, and in all Judea and Samaria, and even to the remotest part of the earth." This power to perform miracles is the exact same power that accompanies a person when they receive the Holy Spirit. The purpose of accomplishing the supernatural is for the furthering and spreading of the gospel of Christ. Its primary usage is to be a witness of Jesus Christ and His Lordship over nature, earth, the spiritual realm, and the universe.

There is confusion today because people hear reports of someone raising a person from the dead, healing someone, or reversing the course of nature. They use this to demonstrate that the gift of miracles is at work today. Again, I think this is a misunderstanding. God is still able, today, to raise the dead and reverse the course of nature. I do not doubt many of these stories. I have heard many of them myself. I simply believe that this is a power that is available to all believers, not only to a few. Simply because God uses a person in one instance to raise a person from the dead does not mean that person has that ability from that point on to exercise that whenever he or she desires. It is simply that God chose to manifest His power for a specific reason at that given point in time. This should encourage everyone to understand that God can use them to perform the supernatural.

Goal: To be used of God to alter the normal course of events concerning people or nature, so that God is glorified and others will surrender to the Lord and serve Him more fully.

Characteristics

A person with the gift of miracles is able to change the ordinary course of nature. He or she is able to call on the power of God to change a circumstance.

The Gift of Miracles in the Life of Christ

Jesus Christ performed many miracles. He demonstrated:

- The ability to turn water into wine (John 2:1–11).
- The power to remove demons from another person (Matt. 8:28–34).
- The ability to raise the dead (Matt. 9:18–19; John 11:17–44).
- The power to multiply food, as in the feeding of the 5,000 (Matt. 4:14–21).
- The power to walk on water (Matt. 14:24–33).
- The power to manifest a curse (Matt. 21:18–19).
- The power to still a storm (Mark 4:35–41).

New Testament Believers

To a certain degree, many of the New Testament apostles and disciples were able to perform similar acts of power. Not every miracle, which Christ performed, was replicated by the disciples. However, many acts of power were demonstrated:

- **The ability to raise the dead.** This was seen both in Peter and Paul (Acts 9:38–42 and Acts 20:9–12). In this incidence, Paul was able to raise a young man who had fallen from an upper window and had died.
- **The ability to curse a person by causing them to be blind (Acts 13:11–12).** In this amazing case, the apostle Paul was able to use the power of God to make a person blind as a consequence of his sin. It was not a permanent blindness, but it was simply to teach a person of his need to give God glory.
- **The ability to cast out demons** and demonstrate power over demonic forces (Acts 8:7).
- **Other signs and wonders.** There were many other signs and wonders performed which we do not have record of. This ability was not limited to simply the apostles. Stephen had this ability (Acts 6:8) as well as apostles other than the original twelve (2 Cor. 12:12). It is interesting to note that all the apostles had the ability to perform signs and wonders (Rom. 15:18–19 & Heb. 2:3–4). This gift was more prominent among apostles than other members of the body of Christ.

I believe that God, in His wisdom, has chosen not so much to manifest His works of miracles through a few gifted individuals, but through the body of Christ at large. With Satan's ability to deceive and replicate many of the miracles, it would become too easy for a person with this ability to be sought after and possibly even worshiped. This was the problem Paul ran into in Acts 14 and 17. God manifests His power now in a much more selected fashion by the use of faith and prayer.

Misunderstandings

Some of the misunderstandings associated with the power of miracles is that God's power needs to flow through a person when he performs the miracle. This is not so. His power is manifested through prayer more than anything else. An excellent example of this is when Peter was freed from prison as a result of the prayers of the other Christians (Acts 12:5–11).

Paul and Silas experienced this same type of miracle when they were bound and chained and were suddenly released (Acts 16:25–26). *It seems that today God is choosing to use the power of prayer more than a gifted individual to accomplish His miracles.*

There is also a strong correlation between the faith of a person and the ability to experience the supernatural power. Even Christ Himself knew that His ability to perform miracles was limited by the lack of people's faith (Matt. 13:58).

A person whom God uses to perform miracles can be easily misunderstood as trying to receive glory for himself or herself. Often this is not the case for the Spirit-filled person. He or she simply wants to see God glorified. However, as in any case of using one's giftedness, it can easily be turned into self-glorification.

Development

How can you see God's power more at work in your life? It takes maturity and development in certain areas.

- It involves being filled with the Holy Spirit (Acts 1:8, Eph. 5:18).
- It involves unwavering faith (Mark 9:14, 23).
- It involves boldness in prayer. Call on the name of the Lord Jesus Christ of Nazareth who rose from the dead. There is supernatural power in the name of God. His

power is manifested through the name above all names which is the Lord Jesus Christ (John 15:16).

- Understand that the main purpose of God's power is to lead a person to Christ. **The ultimate and most profound demonstration of God's power is the ability to save a soul from the clutches of hell and to change a person's life** (Rom. 1:16–17). In this Paul says, "**It is the power [dunamis] of God for salvation to everyone who believes, to the Jew first and also to the Greek**" (**emphasis mine**). Remember that a person will be ultimately and permanently healed when he or she goes into the presence of Christ. It is actually of little consequence that a person suffers 40 to 70 years physically or mentally when for all eternity they will be completely healed and made whole.

- If you want to see more of God's power, be involved in evangelism.

- Step out in boldness. Expect God to do the supernatural through you.

- Persevere. Simply because you do not see answers to prayer or manifestations of God's power, do not give up. Continue to expect God to use you as you pray for others.

The Ministry of Miracles When Filled with the Holy Spirit

If God is leading you to have a greater ministry in this area, you will need to understand the characteristics of being filled with the Spirit. A person with this ministry will evidence the following:

- A positive attitude. This person believes greatly in all the promises of God.

- An extraordinary faith. This person thinks nothing of believing that mountains can be moved.

- A very powerful prayer life. This person is undaunted in for what he or she prays. They will continue to pray until they see the answers.
- Will give any and all glory to God.
- A humbleness. They are very humble because they realize this is completely of God and has nothing to do with themselves.
- A thankful heart. They are very thankful that they have been saved and have the privilege of being used by God.
- They are not afraid to pray about anything or feel that any request is too big or too small. They expect all kinds of miracles.
- A very powerful knowledge of the Word of God. This person spends great amounts of time studying the Scriptures so he or she can learn more about God and His power.
- The ability to discern the leading of the Holy Spirit. The Holy Spirit does not want miracles performed in every situation. A person must have the ability to discern when it is or is not time for a miracle to be performed.

The Ministry of Miracles When Not Filled with the Holy Spirit

Those who are being used by God in this capacity and yet fail to walk in the Holy Spirit will evidence many of the following characteristics:

- Pride. They will begin to think that there is something special about themselves. Remember pride comes before a fall.
- Inflict guilt. When a person does not see answers to his or her prayers, or any miracles take place, they will blame the other person as having sin in his or her life or a lack

of faith. They make the other person feel responsible for the lack of miracle.

- They have faith in themselves, not in God.
- Rationalizes sin in their own lives. This person thinks that because God's power is on him or her and God is using them, that the sin that is in their lives is compensated by the good they do for others.
- Poor prayer life. They do not continually walk in the power of the Spirit and keep close contact with the Lord.
- Poor devotional life. They begin to live their lives by emotions, not on their regular intake of the Word of God.
- The ability to lead people astray. They begin to have people follow them, not the Lord Jesus Christ.

Application

Trust that God wants to use you to heal others and perform supernatural acts for His glory. For example: praying for God to stop the rain at an outdoor Christian concert or crusade, protecting people, blinding the eyes of those who hunt down Christians to persecute, etc. There is power in the name of the Lord Jesus Christ!

Tongues: I glorify

Perhaps one of the most profound and remarkable gifts of the New Testament is the gift of tongues. The word in Greek for this gift, found in 1 Corinthians 12:10, 28, is the word *glossa*. This is where we derive our word "glossary." No gift, however, has caused as much confusion as this one. My goal is not so much to deal with whether or not this gift is in effect today, as it is to communicate the purpose of this gift and the Scriptural parameters within which this gift is to be used.

Definition: *The gift of tongues is the supernaturally empowered ability to speak in a language one has never learned, which gives praise and glory to God to those who hear it.*

The Purpose of Tongues

The gift of tongues expresses, as no other, the heart of God. This manifestation of God's Spirit is designed to speak the love of God to the very heart of a non-believer. The purpose of tongues is found in 1 Corinthians 14:21–22: "In the law it is written, 'By men of strange tongues and by the lips of strangers I will speak to this people, and even so they will not listen to Me,' says the Lord. So then tongues are for a sign, not to those who believe, but to unbelievers...." This purpose points out that the manifestation of the ability to speak in a foreign language is primarily to reach the lost. This becomes very evident when the history of tongues is traced beginning in Acts 2.

Goal: To proclaim praises to God and give evidence of His presence and love in the midst of unbelievers and believers so that they also may praise and glorify God.

What Is the Gift of Tongues?

Tongues is first mentioned in Mark 16:17: "And these signs will accompany those who have believed: in My name they will cast out demons, they will speak with new tongues." Everyone who spoke Greek in that day knew what *glossa* meant. It always referred to a language, dialect, or speech. It could mean a physical tongue, or something "tongue-shaped." However, they understood in this context that it meant a language.

The second mention of tongues is found in Acts 2:4–13. When the Holy Spirit came upon all the New Testament believers, they began to speak with "other tongues, as the Spirit was giving them utterance" (Acts 2:4).

> "Now there were staying in Jerusalem God-fearing
> Jews from every nation under heaven. When
> they heard this sound, a crowd came together in
> bewilderment, because each one heard their own
> language being spoken. Utterly amazed, they asked:
> 'Aren't all these who are speaking Galileans? Then
> how is it that each of us hears them in our native
> language? Parthians, Medes and Elamites; residents
> of Mesopotamia, Judea and Cappadocia, Pontus and
> Asia, Phrygia and Pamphylia, Egypt and the parts of
> Libya near Cyrene; visitors from Rome (both Jews
> and converts to Judaism); Cretans and Arabs—we
> hear them declaring the wonders of God in our own
> tongues!'" (Acts 2:5–11 NIV).

Please note that these languages which were being spoken were distinct languages. They were the Egyptian, Turkish, Italian, Greek, Arabic, Hebrew, and Libyan languages. All of these languages exist today. Why did this happen? It happened because God was trying to communicate that He is a God, not of Jews only, but of the entire world. The people of these languages must have been totally overwhelmed that the God of the universe was communicating to them so personally and specifically. Notice in verse 8 that they were spoken to in their "native language." God, in the depth of His love and tenderness, reached down and spoke to the very heart of these people. What they heard in their own unique language were the "wonders of God" (v. 11). They could not refute the very power and love of God toward them.

The other occurrence is found in Acts 10:46. This is where the Gentiles, having become believers, spoke with tongues. What people were amazed at was that non-Jews had received the Holy Spirit and manifested this by speaking in tongues. Some believe that although Acts 17 does not state that the Samaritans spoke in tongues, it may have occurred because they were saved and received the Holy Spirit at that point. If you traced the baptism of the Holy Spirit, it came first upon the Jews when they believed, then the Samaritans, then to the Gentiles. It is obvious that the Spirit of God was moving throughout the world as was predicted in Acts 1:8.

The last occurrence in the book of Acts is Acts 19:6, when Paul ventures into Europe and Asia Minor and they begin to speak with tongues.

It is obvious from the book of Acts that speaking in tongues is a known, earthly occurence. A person with the gift of tongues has the ability to speak in an unknown language of another nation.

Unknown Language

There are those who also state that the gift of tongues is not only a known language, but is also the unknown language of angels. This is derived from 1 Corinthians 13:1. Paul, in this verse, is not stating that the gift of tongues is the language of angels. His point in this passage is simply that if he had the ability to speak every known language in the universe, but didn't have love, it would profit him nothing.

Others state that this is a prayer language. This is derived from 1 Corinthians 14:14: **"For if I pray in a tongue, my spirit prays, but my mind is unfruitful."** To remain consistent in interpreting this text, it does seem that there is the ability to pray in an unknown language. The gift of tongues may then well be the ability to speak in a known foreign language or an unknown heavenly language. On the other hand, it may be that there are gifts of tongues to which the Bible is referring.

It has been interesting as I have had conversation with those who believe fervently that the gift of tongues is for today, that every one of them admits that the manifestation of the gift of tongues found in Acts 2 is not as prevalent in the church today. If this gift were prevalent, we would find those who had the gift of tongues and spoke Russian, and send them off to Russia. The doors are wide open today. To have the gift of tongues with the Russian dialect would mean that this person never studied Russian in his or her life; they simply had the ability to speak it. We would also find those who had the ability to speak in the tongue of the Chinese, because that is another door that is open, though quickly closing. Those who are intellectually honest have stated that this ability to speak Egyptian, Libyan, Turkish, Italian, or any other language is not manifested in the local church today in as common a way as the other gifts. They have stated to me that, "Yes, there does seem to be a change in the gift of tongues." Has God lost His love for the nations that do not know the Lord Jesus Christ? Absolutely not! Why then is the gift of tongues as found in Acts 2 not being manifested today? I think this is a serious question that scholars need to answer. As I mentioned earlier, it would have been wonderful to have those in our church with this gift to minister to all the Bosnians who came through World Relief which had its offices in our church.

What about the ability to pray in an unknown language as expressed in 1 Corinthians 14? That has to be responded to in terms of the characteristic of tongues.

Characteristics

Some say that all speaking of tongues is of God, some say it is humanly and psychologically induced, and others say it is an imitation created by the evil one. There is no question in my own mind that legitimate (not humanly induced) "tongues" is a supernatural phenomenon. I have been in services where people have spoken in tongues and sung in tongues. It was an unusual event to hear everyone in the congregation singing the same tone and murmur. That, I know was not humanly induced. I must say that my spirit was not at peace during this event.

Test for the True Gift of Tongues

Can tongues be counterfeited? Absolutely. Satan is able to manifest the speaking of tongues as well as all the other spiritual gifts, but he does it for a different reason: he does it to glorify himself or to distract a person from a simple devotion to Christ. "But I am afraid that, as the serpent deceived Eve by his craftiness, your minds will be led astray from the simplicity and purity of devotion to Christ" (2 Cor. 11:3).

It has been shown also, throughout history, that a person does not need to be a Christian to speak in tongues. Muslims, Mormons, cults, and tribes in Africa also have demonstrated the ability to speak in tongues. In the song "Can't Get Enough" by the New Radicals, he speaks (sings) in tongues, and this is not a Christian song. How then do we determine what the true gift of tongues is and what is the counterfeit? Fortunately, Scripture assumes that there will be a need to test whether a spirit or a tongue is of God or not. It has given several specific ways to determine if it is or not:

1. Tongues from God is a known language. Whether it's an earthly or a heavenly language, it is a language.

2. Because it is a language, it has linguistic characteristics. It must follow the patterns of a known language. Remember, God did not just create the language of angels. He also created the languages of the earth which follow the patterns of angelic language.

3. It is not gibberish. No language on earth follows the pattern of gibberish.

4. It is not a language of repetition. A tongue which continually repeats the same phrase is not a tongue which is from God. Acts 2:11 states that they were **"speaking of the mighty deeds of God."** That is not repetitious phrases. That is clear cut articulation.

5. The gift of tongues was received <u>immediately</u> at conversion. As we studied earlier, every spiritual gift is received at the moment of conversion. **"In Him, you are made complete..."** (Col. 2:10). Study every passage in the book of Acts. When did a person begin to speak in tongues? It was the moment they were converted. Any post-conversion ability to speak in tongues is not the gift of tongues from God.

6. Speaking in tongues is not a sign of salvation. The apostle Paul makes this perfectly clear in 1 Corinthians 12:30 when he states, **"All do not speak with tongues do they?"**

7. The true gift of tongues will pass the test of the spirits (1 John 4:2). This is the passage God has given to us because He knew that there would be false spirits trying to enter into the church. If any one of these characteristics is not true, then the gift of tongues is not legitimate. It is either self-induced or demonic.

How to Test the Gift of Tongues

It is absolutely crucial that if a person speaks in a tongue, that he or she have it tested. How is it tested? 1 John 4:1–3 spells out exactly how to test any spirit, including the spirit of a tongue: "Beloved, do not believe every spirit, but test the spirits to see whether they are from God because many false prophets have gone out into the world. By this you know the Spirit of God: every spirit that confesses that Jesus Christ has come in the flesh is from God. And every spirit that does not confess Jesus is not from God and this is the spirit of the antichrist, of which you have heard that it is coming, and now it is already in the world."

To "confess that Jesus Christ has come in the flesh" is to acknowledge that God Himself has come into the world in the person of Jesus Christ.

The test of the spirit is to ask the spirit of the tongue if Jesus Christ has come in the flesh. When the spirit of the tongue is asked this question and remains silent or says no, you can know assuredly that it is a false tongue from the pit. If the spirit responds with a resounding "yes!" or in praises to God Almighty and the Lord Jesus Christ (in English), then it is of God.

How Do You Test the Spirit of the Tongue?

1. Have the person speak in the tongue.

2. While the person is speaking in the tongue, ask Jesus Christ to reveal if it is a true tongue or not.

3. Then ask the spirit of the tongue (out loud) if Jesus Christ of Nazareth has come in the flesh.

4. If there is no response or a verbal "no," then you know it is a false tongue and needs to be rebuked. If you want to ask for an interpretation, do so. You do this by commanding the spirit (in the Name of the Lord Jesus Christ of Nazareth) to speak to the mind of the person and give the interpretation. Just have the person repeat what they hear without any editing.

5. If the spirit of the tongue responds with a "yes," then ask for an interpretation.

Note: A person can test their own tongue by speaking out loud in tongues and then testing their tongue spirit by asking it out loud if Jesus Christ has come in the flesh. They can then command it to give them the interpretation of the tongue they just spoke in. They will hear the interpretation in their mind. If it is true, praise God! They will hear a resounding "yes" in their mind and the praises to God. If not, they will hear the lies from the demon of the false tongue.

In most instances, when I have been part of testing the spirit of a tongue, it has proven to be false. It was a demon praising himself, Satan, or evil. He was using a believer to accomplish this. Think of the subtlety of Satan. He is so cunning and evil that he has deceived Christians into thinking they are praising God, when they are, in actuality, praising themselves or Satan or evil.

In one example, we asked a young lady who spoke in tongues to begin speaking in that tongue. As she spoke, we noticed that there was repetition of phrases. While she was speaking, she was asked the question, "Spirit of the tongue, has Jesus Christ come in the flesh?" At that point, the spirit of the tongue just continued speaking its gibberish and ignored the question. When the spirit of the tongue was then asked to translate what it had been saying, this was its interpretation. *"All hail all power of evilness, come sit well within. Presence stay and work thy might toward kingdom come array."* The spirit was then asked when it entered into the person, and it was revealed that it was during a time when the person had been sexually molested.

In another example when a tongue was tested, the interpretation showed that it was a demon praising himself, magic, and evil. When this woman was asked when she received her tongue, she replied that it came at a Christian camp when a number of her Christian friends laid hands on her so that she could receive the tongue. She was very shocked to realize that it was not a tongue from God.

In another instance, when we tested another person's tongue, it was with much resistance that we received the interpretation. This person had made friends with a Native American spirit. The tongue sounded like a Native American tongue. The spirit of the tongue was commanded to interpret what it had been saying. When the spirit finally gave its interpretation, a deep sadness came over the woman when she realized what she had been saying. All these years she thought she had been praising God. The demon gave its interpretation: *"God is not real."* He then stopped and had to be commanded to continue. *"He's a liar, a thief, Father of lies, He's unholy, Thief of all liars. He doesn't care about anyone. He has no mercy. God is dead! He never existed. He's the thief of all liars."* The demon was then asked, "Didn't you personalize this for her?" "Yes." "What did you say?" *"I am her god, always have been, always will be."*

No wonder this woman struggled with her faith in God, His love for her, and her personal self-image! She was delivered of this tongue (as were all the others) and has grown leaps and bounds in her walk with God. All tongues are not from God!

I am sorry to say that many well-meaning Christians are being used by demons to give praise, honor, and glory to Satan and evil.

Some people ask, "How can this be, because when I speak in tongues, I have such a good, warm feeling." Of course Satan or demons would give "warm feelings" along with speaking in tongues. He wants himself and his works to be praised. Feelings have absolutely nothing to do with the legitimacy of tongues. Satan's ability to deceive runs deep.

Another example of this is when a woman had her husband test the spirit of her tongue. I asked her what the spirit of the tongue said when it was asked if Jesus had come in the flesh. She said, "Oh, it didn't say anything, but this warm feeling came over my husband and me so we knew it was of God." The Scriptures do not say, "If you receive a warm, good feeling, that it is of God." It is very clear that there must be a verbal, public declaration of "Yes, He has come in the flesh." This is another example of Satan's deception by using feelings not Scripture.

Others may be saying, "How is it that a Christian can have a demon speaking through him or her?" Satan is using the physical instrument of the person's body for his own glory. This is the same way that a Christian can commit adultery or use his hands to commit a crime. The instruments of our body must be presented not as instruments of unrighteousness, but of righteousness to God (Rom. 6:13).

In every case of a false tongue that I have personally witnessed, the Christian had received the ability to speak in a tongue after conversion. Often it was even by other Christians laying hands on the person. Regardless of the intentions, Satan has a way of penetrating people's lives.

Have I ever experienced a person who spoke in a tongue pass the test? Yes, the Spirit acknowledged Jesus as having come in the flesh and began glorifying and praising God. When asked to interpret the tongue, the Spirit translated the tongue into praises to Jesus Christ and God Almighty. The Bible says not to refuse the speaking of tongues (1 Cor. 14:39), but it also states that a person who speaks in a tongue is to have it tested.

Special Note

Some people become very alarmed at the thought that an evil spirit would be speaking through them. This in reality is no different than how James warns us about the tongue in James 3:8–10: "But no one can tame the tongue, it is a restless evil and full of deadly poison. With it we <u>bless</u> our Lord and Father and with it we <u>curse</u> men, who have been made in the likeness of God; from the same mouth come both blessing and cursing. My brethren, these things ought not to be this way" (emphasis mine).

We can choose to glorify God or curse Him with our tongue. Even though we do it in English, it still could be demonically initiated. (Have you ever wondered where those swear words come from that pop into your mind?) This may even be worse than speaking in a false tongue because *everyone* can understand it!

What if we hear someone speaking in a tongue? Should we say something about it? Only if you feel led by the Holy Spirit. We are not to judge.

It is always a time to reflect about how much victory we have over our own tongue.

How to Handle a False Tongue

If you find that you speak in a tongue, have it tested. If it does not verbally and audibly state that Jesus Christ has come in the flesh, then the tongue needs to be rebuked and cast out. Resist the temptation to speak or sing in this tongue. Do not allow your physical tongue to be used as an instrument, unbeknownst to you, to praise Satan, a demon, and evil or to curse God. You can test it yourself. A girl who came to me about her tongues tested herself and found out that a demon was praising himself and evil and condemning her.

What about True Manifestations Today?

Is the ability to speak in a tongue, as in Acts 2, manifested today? I have heard numerous testimonies of people who have spoken in a foreign language to a person of another country and were used of God to witness to that person. For example, one woman in our church told our class of a story of a friend of hers who was sitting in a church when the girl next to her began to speak in Chinese. As it turned out, the girl sitting next to her friend was Chinese and was visiting the church and knew no English. She heard God speak to her through Chinese. She began to weep and gave her life to the Lord. I asked the question at that point, "Was there a Jew present in the midst?" She responded, "As a matter of fact, the pastor was half Jewish!"

Does this mean that the gift of tongues was being manifest-ed? I do not think so. I do believe that the Holy Spirit can, and will, whenever He determines, manifest Himself by giving a person the ability to speak in a foreign language. Just as He is able to perform a miracle through others, does not necessarily mean that this person automatically has this gift. God can use any Christian, any time, to speak through him or her using a for-eign language. It simply does not constitute the gift of tongues. It is a manifestation of the Spirit, but not as a person so desires. I praise God for those times when the Holy Spirit has manifest-ed Himself to unbelievers by the hearing of their own language. What a remarkable touch of God's love to that person.

Guidelines for the Use of Tongues

Any church who desires to permit the gift of tongues, must fol-low the following guidelines that are derived from 1 Corinthians 14:

1. No more than two or three should speak in a tongue (v. 27).
2. Only one person is to speak at a time (v. 27). Services where the entire congregation is muttering in tongues is a violation of this passage.
3. If there is no interpreter, there is to be no speaking of tongues (v. 28).
4. Women are asked not to speak in tongues out loud in a church service (v. 34).
5. Everything is to be done properly and in an orderly man-ner. Chaos and disorder are not of God (v. 40).

These are the guidelines that God has set down for His church, and they should not be violated. These guidelines are for the protection of God's church and His people.

What about Baptism of the Holy Spirit?

There is a prevalent teaching today that Christians need to be baptized in the Holy Spirit, especially to receive the "fullness of the Spirit" which includes all of His power. This teaching also states that the "Baptism of the Holy Spirit" is accompanied by the speaking in tongues. This is addressed in the addendum on page 307.

Speaking in Tongues When Filled with the Holy Spirit

This is very important because, if you recall, the book of 1 Corinthians was written to the believers in Corinth because they were definitely not controlled and directed by the Holy Spirit (1 Cor. 2–3). Many of them were practicing speaking in tongues and yet they were carnal (living like non-Christians). Exercising a gift can be done whether or not we are walking in the Holy Spirit. It has nothing to do with our spirituality. Paul had to rebuke the Corinthians for this reason.

The person who speaks in tongues and walks in the Spirit will demonstrate the following characteristics:

- Humility. This person will not feel that it is because he or she is special that they have this ability.
- Will seek to use this gift to reach as many non-Christians as possible. **"So then, tongues are for a sign, not to those who believe, but to unbelievers..." (1 Cor. 14:22).**
- They will control the tongue, not allow the tongue to control them. The people in the book of Acts spoke in tongues because they wanted to.

- They will not try to induce others to speak in tongues. They understand that it is the Holy Spirit who distributes as He wills (1 Cor. 12:11).
- They will not flaunt this gift.
- They will have a deep and personal prayer life.
- Their lives will be governed by the Word of God, not by emotions. They will have deep study of the Word of God.

Speaking in Tongues When Not Filled with the Holy Spirit

Obviously, the Corinthians were not walking in the Spirit, as they had so many factions and divisions among them. Speaking in tongues has nothing to do with determining one's spirituality. A person who is not walking in the Spirit will begin to manifest some of the following characteristics:

- Pridefulness. They will think they are more spiritually mature than others because they have this gift.
- False spirituality. They will think that they have insights into the spirit world that others do not.
- Very emotional. They will tend to govern their lives based on emotions rather than the Word of God.
- Overemphasis on the role of the Holy Spirit in his or her life. Remember that the Holy Spirit came to glorify Christ, not Himself (John 16:14).
- An inconsistent walk with the Lord.
- Hypocrisy. A person will rationalize sin in his or her life because they feel they have an unusual ability to commune with God.
- A poor prayer life. They will substitute speaking in tongues for direct intercession on behalf of others in their own language.

- A poor study of the Word of God. They will be apathetic toward the Word of God, thinking it is enough to be led by the Holy Spirit.
- An adaptation of false doctrine. They will begin to adopt a view that there is a different or additional baptism than the one baptism of Ephesians 4:5: **"There is one Lord, one faith, one baptism."** They will begin to teach other Christians that they need a second blessing in their lives. They may even mislead non-Christians into thinking that they need to be baptized in the Spirit as well as receiving the Lord Jesus Christ. In either case, false doctrine has crept into this person's life.

Interpretation: I can explain

Definition: *The gift of interpretation is the supernaturally empowered ability to make known in the common day language the message of the one who speaks in a tongue and its explanation.*

The gift of interpretation (*hermeneia*) is a gift which must follow the gift of tongues. Obviously, since tongues are a supernatural manifestation of the Holy Spirit, there needs to be a way to explain what a person who speaks in tongues is saying, in order that the entire body of Christ may be edified and built up. What is most unusual about this gift is that this is the only gift of which we have no Biblical example of its use except for the admonition to use it in 1 Cor. 14. There is a great deal taught about it, however there's no example of it being used in the book of Acts or in the Gospels. Because of this, we must try to determine how it is and was used.

What else is interesting is that two Greek words are actually used to translate this gift. In 1 Corinthians 12:10 it states, "To another various kinds of tongues, and to another the interpretation of tongues." The word for "interpretation" in this verse is the word *hermeneia*. This is the word from which we derive our English word "hermeneutics." Hermeneutics is the science of interpreting the Bible. In this case, the word means more "to translate" as well as to interpret. The gift of interpretation is to translate or explain what someone has said in a tongue.

The other use for the gift of interpretation is found in 1 Corinthians 12:30 which states, "All do not speak with tongues, do they? All do not interpret, do they?" The Greek word used here is *diermeneuo*. It has basically the meaning "to explain, interpret or translate." It is used eight times in the New Testament, and is used especially in Luke 24:27 which states, "And beginning with Moses and all the prophets, He explained to them all the things concerning Him and all the Scriptures" (emphasis mine). It has the idea not only to translate, but to expound upon or explain something. It would seem that the person with the gift of interpretation would not only be able to translate what another person says, but in some cases to explain the meaning of it. (Although this gift might mean to exegete and interpret Scripture, the tie in to tongues makes it difficult to separate it from tongues and place it as a gift totally unrelated to it.)

Goal: To make known, or explain the words of God which were spoken by someone with the gift of tongues so that others are drawn to Christ for salvation or are encouraged to further serve God enthusiastically.

Characteristics

We fortunately have teaching regarding speaking in tongues and interpreting the tongues. There are several characteristics and guidelines that accompany the gift of interpretation.

1. The purpose of the gift is **"so that the church may receive edifying"** (1 Cor. 14:5). Don't miss the significance of this. It is not for everybody to sit around and marvel that something supernatural has happened in their midst. It is so that the people in the church may grow to maturity in Christ. The emphasis is not on the person speaking, but on the actions of the people being spoken to.

2. People with the gift of tongues were dependent upon those with the gift of interpretation (1 Cor. 14:6–11). Speaking in tongues will only sound like babble if what is spoken is not made known. This does not negate someone who knows this foreign language (i.e. Egyptian, Chinese, etc.) from giving the translation. Anyone who is familiar with this language can do the interpreting.

3. The ability to interpret one's own speaking in tongues does not necessitate that the person has that gift. 1 Corinthians 14:13 states, **"Therefore let one who speaks in a tongue pray that he may interpret."** This verse needs some explaining. Some may see this verse as exhorting the person who speaks in tongues to ask for the gift of interpretation. This is not a proper understanding of this verse. He is not saying, "Therefore let the one who speaks in a tongue pray that he may receive the gift of interpretation." It is simply for that person to ask God

that he may interpret what he has said. This does not mean that he or she now has the gift of interpretation to interpret somebody else's speaking in tongues. This is the equivalent of somebody asking God to heal another person, and because God answers that prayer, does not mean that person has the gift of healing. It is also the same as a person who is placed in a position where he needs to teach, and he asks God for the ability to teach on a particular occasion and God answers that prayer. As I have stated before, God is able to give all the manifestations of the Holy Spirit to any person at any given time or place. This does not mean that a person has that gift indefinitely.

4. This gift is very similar to the gift of prophecy and teaching as it will help edify, exhort, and console a congregation (1 Cor. 14:5–6).

5. The person who has the gift of interpretation must also be tested as to its authenticity (1 John 4:1–3). This is very important, because Satan, who is able to counterfeit all of these gifts, can also bring false interpretations. The person with the gift of interpretation must ask that spirit whether or not Jesus Christ has come in the flesh. Any silence, or no response, indicates that it is a false spirit.

6. Every interpretation must not contradict any portion of the Bible whatsoever. If a person gives an interpretation that is not 100% accurate with Scripture, it is a false and deceiving spirit and interpretation! The interpretation must be rejected and the spirit rebuked.

Misunderstandings

There have been some tragedies, as Satan has been able to destroy some people's lives through a misunderstanding of some of these manifestation gifts. For example, a young lady, who's a friend of mine, received an interpretation on prophecy during a gathering of Christians where she was told that she was to develop a relationship with a particular man. She took this as being from the Lord. As it turned out, the man was not even a Christian, and was even an alcoholic. She continued to develop a relationship with him, ending up moving in his house, becoming pregnant, and marrying him. Unfortunately, her life became miserable as a result. She, in the process had given up a relationship with a very godly, Christian man based on this particular event. Christians need to beware!

Another major misunderstanding is that people will often tend to seek somebody else to speak to them through a tongue with an interpretation rather than reading the Bible themselves for God's own direction.

Development

A person who claims he or she has the gift of interpretation must be a thorough student of the Word of God. This person must also learn to walk in the power of the Holy Spirit so as to discern the Spirit using him or her rather than a false spirit. This person must also learn to be a thorough exegete of Scripture. In other words, they must know the Bible inside and out and be a good student in terms of using commentaries and other means like those who have the gift of knowledge to explain Scripture. This person must also be willing to have his or her ability constantly tested as to its authenticity. Remember that a person could take an interpretation as being God communicating to him directly. They must never be off!

Interpretation When Filled with the Holy Spirit

A person having the gift of interpretation and is filled with the Holy Spirit will characterize the following:

- When hearing another person speaking in a tongue will be able to understand it as their own language.
- Every time they interpret it will be 100% accurate with the Bible and will edify, comfort, and exhort.
- Is very humble and does not seek their own glory.
- Is very sensitive to where another person is in terms of his or her own spiritual growth.
- Will never be disruptive or disorderly in a church service.
- Will have a very strong personal, devotional life.
- Will have a very powerful prayer life.
- Will be a thorough student of God's Word and will always trust the authority of God's Word over their own gift.

Interpretation When Not Filled with the Holy Spirit

The person who claims to have this gift and does not walk in the Spirit will manifest these characteristics:

- Will push to have their own way in a church service.
- Will interrupt and disrupt a service or someone who is speaking.
- Will not be patient and wait to give their interpretation.
- Will begin to tell other people how to live their own lives.
- Will begin to say that God is speaking when He is not.
- Will give interpretations that contradict the Word of God or are very confusing.
- Has a very shallow knowledge of the Word of God and poor Bible study disciplines.

- Will seek to glorify themselves or draw attention to themselves.

CHAPTER 9

The Marital Status Gifts

W E NOW ENTER INTO the area of two special gifts which people have not always understood as being spiritual gifts. The gift of singleness and the gift of marriage.

Singleness: I am undivided/undistracted

Definition: *The gift of singleness is the supernaturally empowered ability to be more effective building up the body by being single than being married, to enjoy being single, and to have greater self-control over the sexual area of one's life so as to serve the Lord without distraction.*

Confusion surrounds these two because even non-Christians are either single or married. However, please understand that the spiritual gift of singleness and marriage is still a *charisma* gift in the same way that the gift of eternal life is a charisma gift. The gift of eternal life is always a supernatural work of God. In the same way, singleness and marriage were originally designed as a supernatural work of God. The creation of man to serve God, and the creation of a couple to serve God has always been the Lord's intent with our state of life. A person has the ability to reject the gift of eternal life and live for themselves. So also a person has the ability to be single and live for himself or herself, or be married and choose to live for themselves, not for God.

What we discover with the gift of singleness and marriage is that whatever state we are in, it is a means to capitalize on God's supernatural ability to serve Him and to build up the body of Christ.

The gift of singleness is found in 1 Corinthians 7:7: "I wish that all of you were as I am. But each of you has your own gift from God; one has this gift, another has that." He is referring to two gifts here. The gift of singleness or the gift of marriage. The NLT (2nd ed.) translates this verse: "But I wish everyone were single, just as I am. But God gives to some the gift of marriage, and to others the gift of singleness." Paul is so excited about his own gift of singleness and sees the importance of it in terms of serving the Lord, that he would be delighted to have as many in his state as possible, because he knows how enjoyable it is and effective it is in serving the Lord. What a contrast to the view of the world today.

The entire purpose of the gift of "singleness" is to be able to serve the Lord more effectively, and that a person would be a greater blessing to the body of Christ and more able to build up the church being single than if he or she were married.

Goal: To use my singleness to further the kingdom of God more so than if I were married.

Characteristics

Fortunately, we do have teaching from Christ concerning being single. Matthew 19:12 says, "Some are born as eunuchs [celebate], some have been made eunuchs by others, and some choose not to marry for the sake of the Kingdom of Heaven. Let anyone accept this who can" (NLT).

Christ is stating that there are three categories of those who are celibate.

1. Those who are born that way. This may mean they have no sexual desire or are physically unable to respond sexually. Or, these may be people whom God has set apart for Himself to devote themselves completely to their relationship with Him. They simply desire to devote themselves fully to the Lord rather than add a spouse to their lives. This was the case with the apostle Paul. He thoroughly enjoyed his relationship with Christ and felt no need for a spouse.

2. There are those who are celibate because it is demanded of them. These individuals do not necessarily have the spiritual gift of singleness; they are forced into this situation. One particular church is finding a struggle with this, in that they are demanding everyone who serves in an official position be celibate. They have found that those who are placed in this official duty do not necessarily have the gift of singleness. As a result, the individuals who are celibate do not have the supernaturally empowered ability to exercise self-control in the sexual area. Consequently, it does cause problems. It is not wrong to require the gift of singleness to serve God in a particular area; however, you must make sure that a person has that spiritual gift from God and not force it upon him or her.

3. Those who are celibate for the sake of the kingdom of God. These people have the gift of singleness and choose

to use it to be more effective in serving the Lord. Even Paul states in 1 Timothy 4:1–5 that singleness is not to be required.

Other characteristics about the person with the gift of singleness are found in 1 Corinthians 7:32–35.

> "I want you to be free from the concerns of this life. An unmarried man can spend his time doing the Lord's work and thinking how to please Him. But a married man has to think about his earthly responsibilities and how to please his wife. His interests are divided. In the same way, a woman who is no longer married or has never been married can be devoted to the Lord and holy in body and in spirit. But a married woman has to think about her earthly responsibilities and how to please her husband. I am saying this for your benefit, not to place restrictions on you. I want you to do whatever will help you serve the Lord best, with as few distractions as possible" (NLT).

Notice what this passage points out about the single life:

1. This life is less encumbered.
2. A person who is single is able to concentrate more on the Lord than one who is married.
3. Does not have divided interests.
4. Is far more effective serving God single than if he or she were married.
5. Is in a privileged position.

As you study the Bible, you will find that many of the individuals used greatly by God were never married. It is truly a blessed state. Nehemiah was never married. Daniel was never married. We have no record that Ezra was ever married. There are many others throughout the Old Testament who were never married. In the New Testament, obviously the apostle Paul was not married, Christ Himself was not married, and we have no record that many of the disciples were ever married. We know some were, but we don't know that all were.

We do find in the Old Testament that those who were married were not more blessed than those who weren't. As a matter of fact, in most cases, those who were married, Moses, Job, David, Solomon, etc., had an even more difficult time being more fully devoted to the Lord than those who were single. If God has called you to have the gift of singleness, plan on being used greatly by Him for His kingdom!

Misunderstandings

This gift has a great deal of misunderstandings accompanying it. Not only that, but unfortunately the body of Christ does not necessarily promote very highly the gift of singleness.

- **Life is on hold:** Unfortunately, the church today, and possibly outside the church, communicates that a person's life is on hold until he or she is married. They communicate that it is as if a person is in a jet flying around waiting to land. This is not a biblical picture at all! People also often communicate that something "is wrong with you" if you don't get married. Scripture teaches the contrary, that you are much freer to serve God and to be more effective than if you were married. Marriage can be more of a hindrance than it is a blessing to serving God.

- **A person is not complete if he or she is not married:** Scripture communicates over and over that **"in Him you**

have been made complete" (Col. 2:10). You do not need to be married to be complete.

- **You do not need to have children to be complete**: As much as children can be a blessing from God, they can also be a heartache. A person's effectiveness in serving the Lord is irrelevant to whether or not he or she has children.

- **Having the gift of singleness does not make a person lesser of a man or a woman.** You may still have yearnings for a physical relationship with a person, however it is not an overwhelming drive in your life. When these times come, if you ask God to give you grace, He will give you the strength to make it through without falling into temptation.

- **A strong desire to serve the Lord:** A person has such a deep relationship with the Lord and enjoys intimacy with Him, that he or she is fearful of losing that intimacy by bringing another person into his or her life in such a close capacity. They prefer the freedom to serving the Lord in this capacity and don't want to lose that freedom. This was how the apostle Paul felt.

Development

This gift can be developed in very significant ways. If you have the gift of singleness, seek to develop it. You can do this in many ways.

- Get involved in serving the Lord. You have a gift given to you that is designed to build up the body of Christ. Seek greater ways to serve the Lord and put it to use. For example, I know one man, whether or not he has the gift of singleness, is still using his singleness as an opportunity to serve the Lord. He chose to help out another fellow whose wife had left him with the children. He temporarily moved out of his apartment into my friend's house to help him get the kids ready for school and make it through this difficult time in his life. What an encouragement he is!

- Concentrate on your own walk with the Lord. You have much time to yourself. Use it to become a master of the Bible. Begin to study it inside and out.
- Seek avenues to teach or pass on biblical knowledge you have learned.
- Volunteer to help in other ministries within the church.
- Help promote the prayer ministry within a church. You have time available to you which most married couples do not have, and any pastor would be greatly blessed to have those who use their singleness to develop a very powerful and strong prayer ministry within the church.
- Use your singleness as an opportunity for holiness.
- You can use your singleness to minister spiritually to the children of your married friends.
- Use your imagination. The sky's the limit in terms of your ability to serve the Lord. You are freer to go on mission trips than anyone else! Take advantage of those opportunities!

Singleness When Filled with the Holy Spirit

A person who has the gift of singleness and is walking in the Spirit will develop the following characteristics:

- Will have an inner joy and contentment about being single.
- Will have an ability to exercise self-control in the physical area of one's life.
- Will be a blessing to other people, especially to those who are married.

- Will be used greatly by the Lord.
- Has a strong devotion to the Lord. This person is an example to others in terms of commitment to the Lord.
- Lives a holy and pure life.
- Is able to devote him or herself often to prayer.
- Has a strong knowledge of the Word of God.

Singleness When Not Filled with the Holy Spirit

The person who has this gift, but does not walk in the Spirit needs to be very careful. He or she could demonstrate some of the following characteristics.

- A bitterness and resentment at being single.
- Not interested in helping other people.
- Allows themselves to become distracted by other things of the world.
- Will seek ungodly pursuits rather than Godly pursuits.
- Begins to live an unholy and impure life.
- Shows little interest for the things of the Lord.
- Does not take advantage of his or her free time to study the Word of God and pray.

If you are single right now, know that God is using you to reach those whom you most likely would not be able to reach were you to be married. Also, know that He cherishes having your undivided attention and wants to bless you for this.

Marriage: We are united to serve the Lord

Definition: *The spiritual gift of marriage is the supernaturally empowered ability to be more effective serving Christ married than unmarried, to live for the building of the kingdom of God, and to be more effective for Christ married than single.*

It follows that if the gift of singleness is a spiritual gift, then the gift of marriage is a spiritual gift also. Please understand that the reason God created marriage is so that a couple may *serve Him, not each other.* The world has missed out on the very purpose of marriage. They think marriage is a means to fulfill some need in their own lives. This has never been the case. Although it fills an "aloneness" need, the purpose of marriage is to serve God together as a couple. Because marriage is a spiritual gift, by definition, the purpose of a couple being married is that they might live to "build up the body of Christ." Any marriage that is not building up the body of Christ is not a marriage blessed by God. It is missing out on the very reason God created marriage.

In Genesis 1 and 2, the purpose for God creating man and woman is that together they would exemplify the very nature of God Himself. The two of them are to manifest to the world the relationship between God the Father and God the Son and God the Holy Spirit. The characteristic of God was not fully manifested in the male or the female. The nature of God was manifested in both man and woman together. **Therefore, the purpose of marriage is also that the world may see what God is like as a couple lives for Jesus Christ.**

Because it is a spiritual gift, it contains the promise of God to provide the supernatural ability to have a Godly marriage and to fulfill the purpose for which He created it. If you are married, He will give you the supernatural power to live for Him as a couple and to fulfill His plan for marriage. This will ensure a rich, rewarding, and fulfilling marriage beyond anyone's imagination or dreams. To be married for any other reason than to live for God and His kingdom only opens the door wide for a disillusioned and discouraged marriage relationship.

Goal: To use my gift of marriage to work together with my husband or wife to encourage and build up other Christians and further the kingdom of God.

Characteristics

The characteristics of the spiritual gift of marriage are as follows:

- As a couple you "seek first His kingdom and His righteousness" (Matt. 6:33). The overriding desire of the one with the gift of marriage is that he or she sees marriage as a more effective means of seeking the kingdom of God than being single.
- The couple with the gift of marriage will be an example of a good marriage to the body of Christ at large.
- They will serve God together more effectively than serving Him separately even though married. It is very important that a couple seek to serve God together than simply trying to serve Him individually even though married. This does not mean that you won't do separate things in terms of using your gift, but it does mean that you view your marriage as a blessing to the body of Christ and will seek to be seen together more than apart.
- Each person will be more concerned about the interest of the other rather than themselves. This is agape love.
- Is more concerned about meeting the other person's sexual needs than their own. 1 Corinthians 7:3–5 says that neither the husband or wife should deprive one another in the physical area except for set times of prayer: "Let the husband fulfill his duty to his wife, and likewise also the wife to her husband. The wife does not have authority over her own body, but the husband does and likewise also the husband does not have authority over his own body, but the wife does. Stop depriving one another, except by agreement for a time that you may devote

yourselves to prayer, and come together again lest Satan tempt you because of your lack of self-control."

- It is very important, especially for the man, to seek to fulfill his wife's needs sexually with the same desire he has to have his own physical needs met. It is also very important for the wife to *not* withhold sexual intimacy with her husband. It will only serve to give Satan a stronghold and build a wedge between the the two.

- A person with the gift of marriage sees his or her partner as an asset to serving God, not a liability. Hebrews 13:20–21 states, "Now, may the God of peace ... equip you in every good thing to do His will, working in us that which is pleasing in His sight through Jesus Christ, to whom be the glory forever and ever. Amen." He or she views their spouse as God's equipping him or her to better serve the Lord. If your desire is to have a spouse for any other reason than equipping you to better serve God, then it is better not to marry. You will only be disappointed.

- You will seek to have a ministry as a couple.

- You will sense an incompleteness in terms of serving God if your spouse is not with you than when he or she is with you.

Misunderstandings

The misunderstandings that come with this are many.

- A person views marriage as God's gift to them rather than as their gift to God. As a result, it is easy for a couple or a person to begin to live a self-centered life. God never created marriage for what we could get out of it, but for what we could give.

- People think that because marriage is a gift of God, that they should not have difficulties. Difficulties are a part of marriage. Marriage is also a refining process in our lives.

It is a means to learn to become less self-centered rather than more self-centered. Selfishness should never be a part of any marriage.

- Marriage is often misunderstood by thinking that a couple is to live for themselves or to meet the other person's needs. Although meeting the other person's needs is Biblical, it is not the purpose for marriage. The purpose of marriage is to meet the needs of the body of Christ and God's kingdom over our own needs. In this situation, you will have a far more fulfilling marriage.
- Marriage is not so much marrying the right person as it is becoming the right person.
- Two people being married become one to serve God together. There is a growing closer together and to the Lord, not growing separate.

Development

If you desire to be married and are not, begin seeking to become the right person rather than concentrating more on finding the right person. Develop your commitment to the Lord. As Jan, my wife, says, "If you are not content being single, you will not be content being married." Contentment comes from the Lord, not from another person or from another situation in life. Learn to become content now, and you will have a wonderful marriage because you will not be looking for the other person to meet your needs, but to God who always meets your needs.

If you are married, seek, as a couple, how you can better serve the Lord together. Seek to have devotions together and a prayer life which prays about everything.

For the husband, he needs to develop his skills as a spiritual leader by leading his wife in prayer, going to church, Bible study and being the spiritual leader of the children. He needs to learn to be the example of one who follows the Lord so his wife can follow.

For the wife, she needs to learn how to be the kind of wife God wants her to be. Study Ephesians 5 and 1 Peter 3.

The husband must also learn to love his wife as Christ loved the church. The wife must learn how to respect and build up her husband, not tear him down (Eph. 5).

The purpose of children is to have "more arrows" to penetrate for the kingdom of God. Children are not to be seen as a means of meeting some longing or need in our own life, but children are to be a means to further build up the kingdom of God.

To develop the spiritual gift of marriage, read as many books on marriage as you possibly can. Learn how to romance your spouse and keep the flame afire. Continue to pray for each other. Claim Scripture for the other spouse to God.

As much as possible, seek to serve the Lord together. You are one flesh; you come as a package to the body of Christ. Do everything together when it comes to ministering if at all possible.

Marriage When Filled with the Holy Spirit

It is not difficult at all to determine if a couple is Spirit-filled. As a matter of fact, the whole teaching on the Spirit-filled life in Ephesians 5 is in the context of marriage. If there is any place that we need to be filled with the Spirit the most, it is in our marriages. The following characteristics are of those couples who are Spirit-filled:

- They demonstrate a godly love, patience, and acceptance for each other as found in 1 Corinthians 13.

- They have an overriding desire as a couple to be used by God.
- They are actively involved in ministry in their church.
- They have their priorities straight in life in putting God first, themselves second, their children third, and their jobs fourth.
- They see children as a means to further the kingdom of God.
- They have a joy about them in being married.
- They have a strong sexual life together.
- The husband loves and romances his wife. The wife respects and cherishes her husband.
- They are constantly building each other up, not tearing each other down.
- They have a strong prayer life where they pray about all their concerns together as well as for each other.
- The peace of Christ rules the majority of time in the home.
- They both will have a strong devotion time with the Lord. They will, at least, each have their own personal study time in the Word of God, and may occasionally have it together.
- The children see their parents as living for Christ, not themselves, each other, or even for the children. There is a strong feeling of security in the children's lives.

Marriage When Not Filled with the Holy Spirit

Any marriage that is not filled with the Holy Spirit is in danger of failing. The warning signs are the following characteristics:

- Little interest in serving God and His kingdom together.
- An independence from each other.
- Constant belittling and tearing each other down.
- Very little forgiveness or acceptance of each other.

- Wife's unwillingness to submit to the leadership of her husband, and the husband's unwillingness to romance and unconditionally love his wife.
- Little interest in going to church together as a couple or a family.
- A reversal of roles where the wife takes on the spiritual leadership of the family and the husband neglects his duty.
- No interest in building up the marriage or making it stronger.
- A loss of one's "first love." This is often the case in most marriages, and Scripture admonishes us to go back to doing the things that you did to attract and win your spouse in the first place. My wife, Jan, tells each couple, "If you want to renew the spark, go have an affair with each other!"
- Loss of priorities. A couple is more interested in the things they can accumulate rather than the things they can do for the kingdom of God.
- Are more concerned about what the other person can do for them rather than what they can do for the other person.
- A selfishness in the sexual area, or simply withholding from the other person. Remember, sex is a barometer to determine the condition of one's marriage as well as one's condition with the Lord.
- No prayer life or study of the Word of God.
- No ministry together.

CHAPTER 10

Discovering Your Primary Gift

Y OU MAY NOT HAVE realized this, but you have a primary spiritual gift. Although you may have many spiritual gifts, there is one gift that stands out above and beyond all the rest. The primary gift is the one God has given to you which is supported by all of your other gifts. In other words, your main success and motivation in serving God is based upon your primary spiritual gift. You can be most effective when you use this particular gift. *Once you discover your primary spiritual gift you will know your job description. You will know God's will for your life. You will know how He wants to use you the rest of your life!*

Where does the teaching come from that a person has one, and only one, primary gift? It is derived from 1 Peter 4:10, which states, **"As each one has received a special <u>gift</u>, employ it in serving one another, as good stewards of the manifold grace of God"** (emphasis mine).

Notice that Peter does not say, "as each one has received many gifts, employ them in serving one another." He uses the singular gift. What is evident from Scripture is that it is possible to have more than one spiritual gift. For example, the apostle Paul obviously had more than the gift of apostle. He had the gift of healings, miracles, preaching (prophecy) and teaching. Did he have a primary gift? The answer is yes. It is the gift of apostle. All his other gifts supported and enhanced his gift of apostle.

Chances are, you already now what your primary gift is. First Peter 4:11 states that it is either a serving or a speaking gift. You simply need to determine which of the speaking or serving gifts you have and you will understand what your primary gift is.

How to Determine Your Primary Gift

How can you discover what your primary gift is? You simply need to review all your spiritual gifts and look for the one that ignites your heart the most. Ask yourself the question, "If I could only have one gift and had to get rid of all the others, which one would I keep?" The one you would keep is most likely your primary gift. It is the one that is truly you.

Some of you may say, "Well I scored a fifteen, or I was equally high in all my gifts. Do I still have a primary gift?" The answer is still yes. You may score equally high on other gifts, but there is still one that is your primary gift. It may also be that your primary gift was not necessarily the one in which you scored the highest. *It is the one that allows you to be the most effective and motivates you the most and is the most "you."*

You will also need to discern which gift is enhancing which gift. For example, one woman I spoke to mentioned that she felt that her two strongest gifts were the gift of encouragement and the gift of serving. I asked her, "Do you serve in order to encourage someone, or do you encourage someone by serving them?" This is a very significant distinction. She was able to discern that her primary gift was the gift of service, and she used the gift of service to encourage others. If on the other hand, she had the gift of encouragement, and saw service as a means to encourage someone, then encouragement would be the primary gift.

I know beyond a shadow of a doubt that my primary gift is the gift of encouragement. I love to encourage people. This is the one gift I could not do without. *I know what my job description is every day. It is to encourage others.* Even though I am equally gifted in the area of preaching, teaching, leadership, and knowledge, I use my gift of preaching to encourage people. I teach with the purpose of encouraging others. My whole style in leadership is a leadership style based on encouragement, exhortation, and consolation of others. If I use a gift, and a person has not been personally built up and encouraged, then I have failed in using my primary gift.

Other Examples

To give you some further illustrations as to how a person's primary gift works, let me use some examples. A person's primary gift may be the gift of faith. But that person also has the gift of wisdom and knowledge. His wisdom and his knowledge is used to enhance his faith. On the other hand, if a person's primary gift is wisdom, but he has the gift of faith and knowledge as well, he would seek to use his gift of faith and knowledge to convey wisdom to another person. If a person's primary gift is teaching, but he has the gift of leadership and administration, he would find that his leadership and his administration is based upon helping people come to a better understanding of what Scripture has to say.

Another example would be a person with the gift of helps, giving, and teaching. If his primary gift is the gift of helps, he would want to help people through his giving or teaching. If, however, his primary gift was the gift of giving, the primary way that he would help would be financially as opposed to giving being a way to help. He would use giving as a means of teaching as well.

A person may have the gift of evangelism, exhortation, and service. If his primary gift is evangelist, he would use his gift of exhortation to exhort and encourage others to become a Christian, and his service would be service primarily to lead someone to Christ.

The illustrations could go on. Examine your own gifts and determine which one is the foremost of your gifts. If you are not able to discern that yet, simply continue to serve the Lord. Of all that you do, watch which one you think is most helpful to people and motivates you the most. This most likely is your primary gift. You then have your life-long job description from God!

Summary

This is the most important truth you can discover about spiritual gifts! Once you understand your primary spiritual gift, you're ready to serve God in the most effective manner. You will experience more of His supernatural power and grace manifested in your life as you concentrate on using your primary gift. All of your ministry can be organized and directed by the use of your primary gift. Discover your primary gift and use it! You will then begin to see God use you beyond your imagination. Do not be content until you fully understand what your primary spiritual gift is, how to use it, how to develop it, and how to be most effective with it! *Every time you minister with your primary spiritual gift, it will be life-giving to you!*

CHAPTER 11

Your Ministry Gift

A T THIS POINT YOU may be wondering whether or not there are some gifts that have been omitted. This is the chapter where these gifts will be explained. As mentioned in the beginning of this book, according to 1 Corinthians 12:4–7, we are given various gifts, various ministries, and various results.

This chapter deals with you and your ministry. God has given you a spiritual gift so that you can have a ministry. A ministry is defined as **the sphere in which your gifts are used to be the most effective**.

Your ministry will involve a particular type of people in a particular setting. For example, just because a person has the gift of teaching, his or her ministry is not simply in one sphere. Every person does not have the same sphere or aspect of ministry. One person who has the gift of teaching may have a ministry in the area of young children, youth, or adults. The means in which they use this gift may be teaching, or music, or perhaps using puppets with children. Some people may want to use multi-media to utilize their gift of teaching. The means and ministry, as the Bible says, are multi-varied.

The same is true with the serving gifts. The person who has the gift of service or helps may enjoy serving older people more than he or she does younger. They may enjoy serving with a mission organization rather than a local church. The things they do to help or to serve may be different than other ways. For example, a person's ministry may be to bring food to the shut-ins as his main means of service, as opposed to those who would enjoy working on the grounds of a church. They may prefer preparing the sanctuary for worship or overseeing a church cookout. Again, the sky is the limit as to how we serve God.

Biblical Ministries

You may have heard people talk about the gift of missionary, hospitality, exorcism, music, craftsmanship, creative communication, etc. As we have noted, these are gifts, but not spiritual gifts. A ministry is still a gift from God, but is a *dorea* gift, not a *charisma* gift. As we saw in Ephesians 4, Paul considered his ministry of missionary as a *dorea* gift, not a *charisma* gift. His gifts were used as he traveled the world planting and establishing churches.

I would define a ministry gift as *a sphere of exhortations given in the Bible.* There are other ministries not mentioned in the Bible, but are ministries none the less. For the purpose of helping to gain an understanding of what a person's gift or ministry is, I will limit it to a few examples derived from the Bible.

Examples of Biblical Ministries

A Biblical ministry is defined as the fulfillment of a particular command or exhortation given in the Bible. A ministry would seek to be an organized way to fulfill one of these admonitions. For example, here are several admonitions given to us which are also ministries.

1. Prayer
2. Hospitality
3. Music
4. Craftsmanship
5. Exorcism
6. Missionary
7. Voluntary poverty
8. Martyrdom

A person who is given the gift ministry of <u>prayer</u> would seek to use whatever gifts he or she may have to have a ministry of <u>prayer</u>. For example, this person may have the gift of faith, administration, discernment, or leadership and use these gifts to develop a prayer ministry. <u>Music</u> is also a ministry by which a person could use his gift of encouragement, teaching, exhortation, or mercy. <u>Hospitality</u> is also a gift ministry. A person may want to discern what gifts he or she has that he or she wants to use in terms of being hospitable. For example, the gift of mercy, service, helps, wisdom, marriage, and singleness are all gifts which lend well to the ministry of hospitality.

Chances are that the person with the ministry of <u>craftsmanship</u>, which is mentioned in the Old Testament (Exod. 30:22–35 & 31:3–11), has the gift of service. However, not everyone who has the gift of service has the ministry of craftsmanship.

<u>Exorcism</u> is also a ministry. This ministry is mentioned as a responsibility of the disciples to carry out. The person with the gift of exorcism would definitely need the gift of faith, discernment, and possibly wisdom and knowledge. (My friend who tested the spirit of someone's tongue has this ministry.) This ministry comes from Mark 3:14–15: "And He appointed twelve,

so that they would be with Him and that He could send them out to preach, and to have authority to cast out the demons."

Missionary, which is mentioned in Ephesians 4, could be used by a person with the gift of leadership, administration, knowledge, teaching, or wisdom. He may even have a serving gift. Mercy, helps, or service could be used in another culture.

Ministry of voluntary poverty explains why some people will travel about exhorting others to sell all their belongings, give them to the poor and follow the Lord. This in actuality is their ministry. It is not the ministry of everyone else. These people most likely have the gift of faith and/or the gift of giving. They may even have the gift of evangelism. But it is their ministry, not necessarily everyone else's.

Martyrdom has also been called a spiritual gift, but it is simply a ministry gift which is also mentioned in 1 Corinthians 13:1–3. This would most likely use the spiritual gift of faith.

The list of other gifts of ministry can continue. There are obviously more. As you read through the Bible, you may find some areas which appeal to you in terms of admonition. For example, as you read through 1 Thessalonians 2 and see how Paul nourished and nurtured the church, you may find your heart ignited to do likewise. Simply ask God to show you what your ministry should be as you study the Scriptures.

As I stated earlier, the ministry God has for you may not necessarily be mentioned in the Bible. Chances are that it is, but you may discover a ministry that is not in the Bible. For example, your ministry may be utilizing the internet for the greater growth of the kingdom of God. Just be sure that you are utilizing your primary gift by using the computer if this is your situation.

Characteristics of a Biblical Ministry

Remember that a God-given ministry has with it the same supernatural enablement of one's spiritual gift. This is so that God still receives the glory. He gives us the tools and sphere in which to minister. He also gives us the fruit. This is so that in every aspect of our lives, He is glorified. We can claim nothing as coming from ourselves. The strength and privilege of serving God comes from Him.

The Test for Biblical Ministries

Because many of these ministries have been treated as spiritual gifts, there are ways to discern whether or not these may or may not be your particular ministry. If after reading these explanations, you perceive that this is an area where you score highly, you can be assured that this is one area of ministry God wants you to be involved in.

Ministry Gift of Hospitality: I make others feel welcomed

How do you know whether or not God has given you the ministry gift of hospitality? I owe much to Dr. Peter Wagner for his illustration. He states that if when you have people over, you clean the house, bring out the best silverware, cook a fancy meal, and do everything you can to help them feel welcome when they arrive, but heave a big sigh of relief when they leave, *you do not have the ministry gift of hospitality.*

If on the other hand, someone comes over, you don't worry about how the house looks or what meal you have prepared, and people state they feel at home with you, *you have the ministry gift of hospitality.*

This ministry is highly effective in making people feel welcomed at church, in the office, etc.

Definition: *The ministry gift of hospitality is the supernaturally empowered ability to use their gifts to provide open house and warm welcome for those in need of food, lodging, or use of their possessions.*

Ministry Gift of Prayer/Intercession: I help move God

This is a very important ministry, as it will help out your pastor and other people in the church. Most pastors' main ministry is not prayer. Statistically, it is reported that pastors do not spend an extremely long amount of time in prayer. This may sound shocking, but it is not their primary ministry, or they would not be a pastor-teacher. A pastor must utilize the prayers of others for the success of his ministry. If you respond very strongly in this area, please let your pastor or leader know so they may be able to utilize you in the church. If you pray for ten minutes and it seems like an hour, this is not your ministry. However, if you pray for an hour and it seems like ten minutes, then God has something special for you!

Definition: *The ministry gift of prayer/intercession is the supernaturally empowered ability to pray for extended periods of time on a regular basis and see frequent and specific answers to prayers, to a degree much greater than that which is expected of the average Christian.*

Ministry Gift of Music/Vocal: I promote worship

This ministry will utilize many of your other gifts and help build up the body of Christ.

Definition: *The ministry gift of music is the supernaturally empowered ability to use one's other spiritual gifts by singing lyrics and praises to the Lord, playing a musical instrument, or writing songs by which others are benefited and brought closer to the Lord.*

This was a wonderful ministry of King David which he gave to believers.

Ministry Gift of Craftsmanship/Creative Communication: I can create for God

This ministry gift is broken down into two areas of manual and artistic. You may find that these are your expressions of using your other gifts. Some churches use a spiritual gifts test that includes "Creative Communication." I believe this is a part of this ministry gift.

Definition: *The ministry gift of craftsmanship is the supernaturally empowered ability to use their other spiritual gifts, skills, abilities and mind to further the kingdom of God through artistic, and other creative means to communicate. This ministry gift may also be used in the areas of maintenance, care, and upkeep for the benefit and beautification of God's kingdom here on earth.*

Ministry Gift of Missionary: I penetrate other cultures with the gospel

This is a very important ministry for one to discern, because you will understand whether or not God is calling you to minister to another culture. This does not necessarily mean that you leave the country; it simply means that you minister outside your own homogeneous and cultural environment. You may have this ministry calling, and God wants you to minister to a particular cultural group within the U.S., or your city, or He may want to lead you to another country.

Definition: *The ministry gift of missionary is the supernaturally empowered ability to use their other spiritual gifts to minister in a second culture.*

This is very similar to the spiritual gift of Apostleship, and it may be the main means by which to use that particular spiritual gift.

Ministry Gift of Exorcism: I destroy strongholds

A new battle-front has surfaced which is doing "hand to hand" combat with and against the enemy. God is raising up people in the area of deliverance to destroy Satan's strongholds in people's lives.

Definition: *The ministry gift of exorcism is the supernaturally empowered ability to use their other spiritual gifts to destroy demonic strongholds in the lives of other believers.*

Summary

Tests could be derived for other forms of ministries. This may be a ministry that you would even enjoy, by coming up with various tests for other ministries to help other Christians. I encourage much more work to be done in this area.

There may be a rising question as to what happens when other Christians call ministries spiritual gifts. It personally does not bother me. I understand what a person means. I will ask what a person's spiritual gifts are, and I will also ask them if they have the gift of hospitality or missionary. Many people may not be able to discern that there is difference between a spiritual gift and a ministry gift, but in either case they are all from God. I make the distinction because I want to be as biblically accurate as possible, and I encourage others to do so as well.

My prayer for you is that you will quickly discover, if you have not already, the sphere of ministry where God wants you to serve. We are all called to serve. Because of this, we all have a ministry. Every single person has a ministry given to him or her by God. Each of us has a job to do! I pray also that you continue to experience God's supernatural power in an even greater way in your life so you will be able to serve Him more effectively.

Conclusion

CONGRATULATIONS ON FINISHING THIS book! My prayer for you and the promise which I claim for you is Ephesians 3:20–21, **"Now to Him who is able to do far more abundantly beyond all we ask or think, according to the <u>power</u> that works within us, to Him be the glory in the church and in Christ Jesus to all generations forever and ever. Amen."**

God's supernatural power is available to you every day, every minute of your life. He wants to do far more than you are even able to ask in prayer or to think of. He can do this because His supernatural power is limitless. He gives His power, though, only to those who want to see Jesus Christ glorified. If this is your desire, then you have the unlimited resources of God's power. Expect Him to use you to perform miracles!

My admonition to you for the rest of your life is to know your primary gift and use it. Develop all your spiritual gifts, and use them. Understand what areas of ministry or ministries God wants you to be in, and go for it with all your heart. Rely on His strength every day to accomplish His will. You will find over the years that living by your spiritual gifts, you will enjoy serving the Lord and it will always be life-giving to you.

May God richly bless you as you seek to serve Him through His supernatural gifts and power!

Addendum

Questions Pertaining to Specific Topics

Can we not receive a gift by the laying on of hands?

This question arises from 1 Timothy 4:14 which shows Paul speaking to Timothy, "Do not neglect your gift, which was given you through a prophetic message when the body of elders laid their hands on you" (NIV). The appearance here is that Timothy received a gift when the elders laid hands on him and prophesied over him. The difficulty we have with this passage, is we do not know what the gift is. It appears, by the writing of 1 & 2 Timothy, that the gift Paul is referring to is the gift of his position as pastor-teacher over the church of Ephesus. The whole essence of 1 & 2 Timothy is to encourage Timothy to do what God has called him to as a pastor, which is to take leadership of the church. It seems that Timothy was shy about using his giftedness. Paul needed to remind him of this in 2 Timothy 1:7: **"For God has not given us a spirit of timidity, but of power and love and discipline."** Timothy needed the reminder of his position.

The question then is, when did Timothy receive this gift or office? We do not know if this verse refers to when Timothy became a Christian and hands were laid upon him, or later when he was commissioned as head over the church of Ephesus. It could have been a confirming by the elders as Timothy was commissioned to be the pastor of the church in this important city. It may be, though, that this was a special circumstance by which Timothy was given the gift of the office of pastor-teacher (or apostle) of this very important church. Even if this was the case, it needs to be taken in context of the entire New Testament. This is the only incident we have of a person receiving a gift by the laying on of hands and prophecy by elders. In our church we do similar laying on of hands as we commission people to the mission field, when they become an elder, or when someone begins a new ministry. Prophecy is not just foretelling; it is also forth-telling or declaring the Word of God. These elders declared to Timothy that he was the pastor-teacher or whatever gift he had that was significant for his ministry. For a person to be in the same situation as Timothy, he would have to be chosen by elders for a particular position. The elders would then have to lay on hands and declare according to the Word of God what office or ministry this person is fulfilling. To have other Christians who are not elders laying hands on people to pass on a gift is not only unbiblical but is very dangerous. It leaves that person open to foreign spirits that are not of God.

Do not miss the point of this passage. It is not to emphasize **when** Timothy received the gift, but that he is not to **neglect** the gift that is in him. The same is true for all of us — we need to be sure not to neglect the gift which God has already given to us as believers.

Can spiritual gifts be imparted?

This is like the previous question but it stems from Romans 1:11: "For I long to see you in order that I may <u>impart</u> some spiritual gift to you, that you may be established" (emphasis mine). The question is, what does Paul mean by this? Does it mean that he is going to give them a spiritual gift they don't have? How do you give a spiritual gift to a church versus a person? The answer is found in the meaning of the word "impart." In Greek, the word is *metadidomi* which means to "impart, share, give." Paul is stating that he wants to visit them for the purpose of establishing (strengthening) them by *sharing his giftedness* in whatever capacity will help them. This is captured by another translation: "For I am longing to see you so that I may <u>share</u> with you some spiritual gift to <u>strengthen</u> you" (Rom. 1:11 NRV emphasis mine). This word is also used in 1 Thessalonians 2:8: "So we cared for you. Because we loved you so much, we were delighted to <u>share with you</u> not only the gospel of God but our lives as well" (NIV emphasis mine). This is consistent with the purpose of spiritual gifts. We have guest speakers in our church to share their spiritual gifts to strengthen us in ways different than usual. This is also the purpose of having outside help for other spiritual ministries (i.e. small groups, etc.). The bottom line is that the body is strengthened and further established in its faith.

Is there a correlation between speaking in tongues and the baptism of the Holy Spirit?

As mentioned in the gift of tongues, the confusion of tongues and the baptism of the Holy Spirit will be addressed here. The following is from a track that I received from a church.[39]

It teaches that a Christian must receive a second baptism and speak in tongues:

When we are "Born Again," we receive the Spirit (a breath - John 20:22).

When we are Baptized with the Holy Spirit, we are filled with the Spirit (a mighty rushing wind - Acts 2:2, 4).

The Baptism of the Holy Spirit is for Today

The Promise of the Father, known as the Baptism in the Holy Spirit, was **promised to all future generations of Christians** (Acts 2:38–39). Certainly, we in the 20th Century need all that Christ provided for the 1st Century Church....

The **Baptism in the Holy Spirit** is **accompanied by evidence of speaking in tongues.** "...the promise of the Holy Spirit, He poured out this, which you now see and hear" (Acts 2:33).

Who in the Bible encouraged speaking in tongues?

- **Jesus told** His disciples that **believers** would be able to **speak in tongues** (Mark 16:17).
- **Paul encouraged** believers to speak in **tongues** (1 Cor. 14:5,18, 26, 39).

Who can understand tongues?

- **God can** understand tongues (1 Cor. 14:2).
- **No man can** understand tongues (1 Cor. 14:2).
- **How should we use tongues?**
- **Pray and sing** in tongues (1 Cor. 14:14–15).

> *What do tongues do for us?*
> - *Gives us a special communication with God (Rom. 8:26).*
> - *Builds up our faith (Jude 20).*
> - *We should ask, seek, and knock to receive the Holy Spirit who will come and teach us to pray (Luke 11:13, 19 & Rom.* 8:26 emphasis theirs).

Commentary

This line of teaching not only misuses and misinterprets Scripture but is false and dangerous.

There are many reasons why this teaching is erroneous and false:

1. There is no command whatsoever to be "baptized in or with the Holy Spirit."

There are only four references to the baptism of the Holy Spirit, and none of them are a command.

- Mark 1:8: "I baptized you with water but He will baptize you with the Holy Spirit." (Also repeated by Matthew and Luke in their gospels [Matt. 3:11 & Luke 3:16]).
- John 1:33: "I did not recognize Him, but He who sent me to baptize in water said to me, 'He upon whom you see the Spirit descending and remaining upon Him, this is the One who baptizes in the Holy Spirit.'"
- Acts 1:5: "...for John baptized with water, but you shall be baptized with the Holy Spirit not many days from now."
- Acts 11:16: "And I remembered the word of the Lord, how He used to say, 'John baptized with water, but you shall be baptized with the Holy Spirit.'"

Please notice that all of these are references are to show the distinction between John's ministry and Christ's. None of these are commands given to us as believers. This is a promise that Christ is going to bring the Holy Spirit with Him and give the Holy Spirit to believers.

Nowhere in the epistles are we commanded to be baptized in the Holy Spirit. We are commanded to be "**filled with the Spirit**" (Eph. 5:18) and "**to walk in the Spirit**" and to "**live by the Spirit**" (Gal. 5:16, 24) but never to be "baptized in the Spirit." One would think that a major doctrine such as being baptized in the Spirit would have ample commands to be so. However, there is not one in the Bible!

Of the 81 references to baptism in the New testament, only nine include a reference to the Holy Spirit. The emphasis of baptism is not the Holy Spirit but Jesus Christ.

2. In all the references this tract uses to justify the doctrine of "baptism in the Holy Spirit" not one even uses the phrase "baptism in the Spirit." The references are to being **"filled"** with the Spirit.

3. The Bible clearly teaches that there is only one baptism, not two or more.

> **Ephesians 4:4–5: "There is one body and one Spirit, just as also you were called in one hope of your calling one Lord, one faith, one baptism."**

There are no more two baptisms for believers any more than there are two bodies, two Lords, or two faiths! There was the baptism of John, which was before Christ's ministry, but there was no baptism of John after Christ's death and resurrection. No one is baptized into John's baptism today and then baptized into Christ. John's baptism was of repentance (Matt. 3:11) (it was a heart preparation for the coming of the Messiah). Christ's baptism was an indication of salvation and to publicly acknowledge that one was a follower of Christ.

4. We are commanded to be baptized in the "Name of the Father and the Son and the Holy Spirit." We are not commanded to have three different baptisms. One for the Father, one for the Son, and one for the Holy Spirit.

5. The power of the Holy Spirit comes from being "filled" with the Holy Spirit. The confusion of this teaching is that a believer must have a one-time experience of being baptized in the Spirit to receive the power of the Holy Spirit. This is just plain false. If it were so, why then would a Christian ever struggle again with his or her flesh? Do they need to be re-baptized? Obviously not. They do however, need to be refilled. This is why we are commanded to be continually filled with the Holy Spirit. "And do not get drunk with wine, for that is dissipation, but be filled with the Spirit" (Eph. 5:18).

It would be wonderful to have a one-time experience and then no longer have to struggle with sin and always experience joy and power, but this is not so. We must live by faith and choose to let the Holy Spirit lead and empower us on a daily basis.

6. Tongues are not for every believer. I am so sorry to hear and see this being taught by some today. Not only did I address this earlier, but also again, if it was God's intention for every believer to speak in tongues, then surely it would be commanded somewhere in Scripture. No where is there a command for a believer to speak in tongues!

The proof text used to support that tongues is for every believer is 1 Corinthians 14:5. Paul states: "Now <u>I wish</u> that you all spoke in tongues, but even more that you would prophesy and greater is one who prophesies than one who speaks in tongues, unless he interprets, so that the church may receive edifying" (emphasis mine).

This is not a command but a wish or desire on Paul's part. If one holds that this is an indication that every believer is and should speak in a tongue, then **they must also hold** that every believer is to be single because Paul uses the exact phrase in Greek in 1 Corinthians 7:7: "Yet *I wish* that all men were even as I myself am. However, each man has his own gift from God, one in this manner, and another in that" (emphasis mine). Paul was single and was encouraging singleness here but not commanding it. Paul uses the Greek word *thelo* in both verses. This word means to "wish, want, or desire". It is not a command. If it was meant to be a command, Paul would have used a different Greek construction. A person must be as vehement about teaching that every believer must be single as he or she is about speaking in tongues if they are going to be consistent with Scripture!

7. Speaking in tongues has nothing to do with a "special communication with God." The proof texts, Romans 8:26 and Jude 20, do <u>not</u> even mention tongues. This is one of the ministries of the Holy Spirit to pray for us and to help us pray. One does not need the gift of tongues to have the Holy Spirit pray for them.

8. To say that "no man can understand tongues" denies the gift of interpretation. Again, this is false teaching in complete violation of Scripture. How is that in Acts 2, they all heard their own language being spoken?

Unfortunately, this kind of teaching confuses and misleads Christians. It also, unintentionally, encourages opening up a believer to demonic spirits.

Perspective

One thing Christians need to come to grip with is whether or not, when they receive Jesus Christ into their lives as Lord and Savior, they are given all they need to live the Christian life in a victorious manner. I believe unequivocally that the Bible does teach this. Ephesians 1:3 states that God "has blessed us with <u>every</u> spiritual blessing in the heavenly places in Christ" (emphasis mine). In other words, there is no blessing God has for a believer that doesn't come with Jesus Christ. Notice it says that He has blessed us with **<u>every</u>** spiritual blessing. There is no more for Him to give!

Colossians 2:10 states that "...in Him you have been made complete." Again, here the point is that God has given us everything we need to live a life pleasing to Him and a victorious life. We simply need to appropriate the power and fullness He has given to us. There is **<u>nothing</u>** more God needs to give to us to make us complete. We are fully complete in Christ. To teach that Jesus Christ alone is not sufficient and that a Christian needs more, simply flies in the face of what God has already provided in Christ. He is **all** we need.

If you have been taught that you need to be baptized in the Spirit, my encouragement to you is to not look back to a past experience (other than your conversion), but to look to the Lord and let Him draw you closer to Him than you ever have before. Let Christ show you the depth of His love that is available to you every moment. You don't need another experience; you simply need to fellowship with Him and enjoy what He has for you right now. Let Him show you how fully compete you are in Him and let Him show you that you don't need anything more than Him.

Endnotes

1   I am so grateful to Bill Gothard for his original idea of this illustration from his manual in "Basic Life Principles." I have taken the liberty to refine it and add more spiritual gifts to it.

2   *Spiritul Gifts app by Mark Stewart.*

3   John McArthur, Jr., *the Church-the Body of Christ* (Grand Rapids: Zondervan Publ. House, 1973), 136.

4   Leslie B. Flynn, *Nineteen Gifts of the Spirit,* (Victor Books: Wheaton, Ill., 1974), 12.

5   David Hubbard, *Unwrapping Your Spiritual Gifts,* (Word Book: Waco, Texas, 1985), 13.

6   W. E. Vines, *Expository Dictionary of New Testament Words*, (Old Tappen, New Jersey: Flemming H. Revell, 1966).

7   Motivational Gifts, 36.

8   Peter Wagner, *Your Spiritual Gifts Can Help Your Church Grow* (Ventura, Ca.: Regal Books, 1985), Chapter 4.

9   W. E. Vines, *Expository Dictionary of New Testament Words*, (Old Tappen, New Jersey: Flemming H. Revell, 1966).

10 "Spiritual Gift of Apostleship," Spiritual Gifts Test, accessed June 30, 2022, https://spiritualgiftstest.com/spiritual-gift-apostleship/.

[11] William McRae, 139.

[12] W. E. Vines, *Expository Dictionary of New Testament Words*, (Old Tappen, New Jersey: Flemming H. Revell, 1966), 302.

[13] Paul Hamar, 158.

[14] Peter Wagner, 159.

[15] W. E. Vines, *Expository Dictionary of New Testament Words*, (Old Tappen, New Jersey: Flemming H. Revell, 1966), 302.

[16] Paul Hamar, 158.

[17] Peter Wagner, 159.

[18] Leslie B. Flynn, *Nineteen Gifts of the Spirit*, (Victor Books: Wheaton, Ill., 1974), 82.

[19] Dr. John C. Wex, "Spiritual Gifts, a Model to Mobilize the Members," (Gift of Exhortation) handout, n.d.

[20] Peter Wagner, *Your Spiritual Gifts Can Help Your Church Grow* (Ventura, Ca.: Regal Books, 1985), 154.

[21] The *Complete Biblical Library, The New Testament Study Bible: Romans- Corinthians*, (Springfield, Mi.: World Library Press: 1991), 415.

[22] William McRae, *The Dynamics of the Spiritual Gifts*, (Grand Rapids: Zondervan, 1980), 67.

[23] Peter Wagner, *Your Spiritual Gifts Can Help Your Church Grow* (Ventura, Ca.: Regal Books, 1985), 158.

[24] McRae, ibid., 68.

[25] Leslie B. Flynn, *Nineteen Gifts of the Spirit*, (Victor Books: Wheaton, Ill., 1974), 143.

[26] The *Complete Biblical Library Dictionary: The New Testament Greek-English Dictionary* "Pi-Rho" (Springfield, Mo.: The Complete Biblical Library Press, 1991), 303.

[27] William E. Yaeger, *Who's Holding the Umbrella?* (Cambridge, Ontario: Thomas Nelson, Inc. 1982) 30.

28 Yaeger, ibid, 15.

29 Yaeger, ibid, 13.

30 Peter Wagner, *Your Spiritual Gifts Can Help Your Church Grow* (Ventura, Ca.: Regal Books, 1985), 162.

31 *The Complete Biblical Library Dictionary: The New Testament Greek-English Dictionary* "Sigma-Omega" (Springfield, Mo.: The Complete Biblical Library Press, 1991), 99.

32 Robert Lee, *By Christ Compelled*, (Grand Rapids, MI: Zondervan, 1969), 45.

33 *The Complete Biblical Library Dictionary: The New Testament Greek-English Dictionary* "Delta-Epsilon" (Springfield, Mo.: The Complete Biblical Library Press, 1991), 83.

34 This definition is very similar to Peter Wagner's definition (Ibid., 226). When something is done well and needs very little improvement, I don't want to change things just to be novel. Most of the definitions by the different authors are, fortunately, very much the same. Dr. Wagner and myself see the distinction between the gift of helps and the gift of service. My only addition to Dr. Wagner's definition is the emphasis on the supernaturally empowered aspect which we need to be reminded at every opportunity.

35 Peter Wagner, *Your Spiritual Gifts Can Help Your Church Grow* (Ventura, Ca.: Regal Books, 1985), 226.

36 Charles F. Stanley, In Touch Ministries Tape Cassette, "The Motivational Gift of Serving," 1982.

37 Ibid.

38 Jack Deere, *Surprised by the Power of the Spirit*, (Grand Rapids: Zondervan Publishing House, 1993), 247.

39 *The Complete Biblical Library: Greek-English Dictionary*, (Springfield, Missouri, 1991), s.v., #3183, 155.

[40] Cleon Rogers, *Linguistic Key to the Greek New Testament*, (Grand Rapids: Zondervan, 1980), 667.

[41] Rogers, Ibid., 667.

[42] Francis Anfuso, *The Baptism in the Holy Spirit*, (South Lake Tahoe, Ca.: Christian Equippers International, 1981) pgs 9, 15, 19.

Scripture Index

Chapter 1

Chapter 2

Chapter 3

1 Corinthians 12
1 Peter 4:10–11
Romans 12:6–8
1 Corinthians 12:1–31
Ephesians 4:11
1 Corinthians 7:7
1 Corinthians 12:5
Ephesians 3:7
Matthew 25

Chapter 4

1 Corinthians 12:1
Colossians 1:18
1 Corinthians 2:16
1 Corinthians 12
1 Peter 4:10
1 Corinthians 12:7
Genesis 39:4
1 Peter 4:11
1 Timothy 3
Matthew 25:14–30
Ephesians 4:11–16
1 Corinthians 12–14
Romans 11:29
1 Corinthians 12:31
Romans 12

Chapter 5

John 20:21
Luke 10:2
Matthew 28:19
Acts 2:17
2 Timothy 4:2
Deuteronomy 6:6–7

James 5:15
Matthew 10:8
Matthew 21:22
John 14:12
Colossians 3
1 Corinthians 7
Ephesians 5

Chapter 6

Ephesians 2:19–20
Acts 1:25
Mark 3:13–15
Matthew 28:19–20
Romans 15:20
John 3:30
Matthew 10
Acts 6:4
Ephesians 2:20
Isaiah 40:1
Romans 12:1–2
1 Corinthains 14:3
1 Thessalonains 2:11–12
Romans 15:4
1 Timothy 4:13
1 Corinthians 14:3
Acts 15:32
Luke 3:18
Romans 12:7
1 Corinthians 12:28–29
Ephesians 4:11
Acts 13:1
Colossians 3:16
Acts 2:42
2 Timothy 2:2
Ezra 7:10
Luke 1:1–4

Proverbs 13:14
Matthew 7:28–29
Acts 5:42
Acts 15:35
Acts 18:11
2 Timothy 2:15
Romans 12:7
Ephesians 4:15
John 1:14
Ephesians 4:15
1 Corinthians 12:8
Job 36:4
Proverbs 1:7
1 Chronicles 12:32
Isaiah 33:6
Romans 11:33
Ephesians 1:17
Colossians 2:3
1 Corinthians 15:33
Matthew 18:15
Galatians 6:1
1 Chronicles 12:32
2 Chronicles 1:10
Daniel 1:4
Philippians 1:9
2 Peter 3:17–18
Ezra 7:10
John 13:17
Proverbs 1:7
1 Corinthians 8:1
1 Corinthians 12:8
Ephesians 4:15
1 Corinthians 1:30
1 Chronicles 12:32
Deuteronomy 34:9
2 Chronicles 1:10
Psalms 49:3

Luke 2:52
Isaiah 33:6
Colossians 2:3
Matthew 11:19
Proverbs 9:10
Jeremiah 9:23–24
1 Corinithians 1:30
Jeremiah 9:23
Romans 12:8
2 Corinthians 1:3–4
1 Thessalonians 5:11
2 Timothy 4:2
Ephesians 4:1
1 Thessalonians 2:11–12
John 14:16
1 John 2:1
Hebrews 10:25
Colossians 1:28–29
1 Samuel 23:16–17
Acts 14:22
Acts 16:40
Acts 15:31–32
1 Peter 5:1–2
Hebrews 13:22
Acts 1:23
Acts 4:36
Acts 9:27
Acts 15:39
Romans 12:8
John 8
Matthew 23
1 Thessalonians 5:14
Romans 12:8
Deuteronomy 3:28
1 Samuel 23:16
2 Chronicles 30:22
Isaiah 35:3

1 Timothy 4:12
Hebrews 11:33–34
Romans 12:8
1 Corinthians 12
1 Maccabees 5:19
1 Thessolonians 5:12
1 Timothy 3:4–5, 12
1 Timothy 5:17
Titus 3:8
Acts 17:11
Romans 12:8
2 Peter 1:10
1 Corinthians 12:28
Proverbs 1:5
Acts 27:11
Exodus 18:13–26
Acts 6:1–7
2 Samuel 8:15
Proverbs 11:14
Proverbs 24:6
1 Corinthians 14:33
1 Corinthians 14:40
Ephesians 4:11
2 Timothy 4:5
Ephesians 4:11–12
2 Corinthians 5:14
Acts 21:8
Acts 8:26–40
Romans 9:3
Mark 1:14–15
Mark 1:38
Mark 6:12
Acts 5:42
Acts 8:4
Acts 8:35
2 Corinthians 5:14–15
2 Corinthians 15:3–6

Chapter 7

1 Corinthians 16:6
1 Peter 4:10
Romans 12:8
Mark 3:5
2 Corinthians 4:1
Romans 12:8
2 Corinthians 4:1
Psalms 103:8
Psalms 72:13
Job 2:11,13
Zechariah 7:9
Matthew 5:7
Matthew 9:36
Matthew 15:32
2 Corinthians 1:3–4
James 3:17
Matthew 18
Romans 12:8
Luke 3:11
Romans 1:11
Ephesians 4:28
Acts 4
Luke 1:10
Matthew 6:3–4
1 Corinthians 13:3
1 Chronicles 29:3
1 Chronicles 21:24
Proverbs 3:9
Matthew 5:16
Matthew 5:42
Proverbs 11:24
2 Corinthians 9:6
1 Timothy 6:17
Romans 12:8
2 Corinthians 8:2
2 Corinthians 8–9
Philippians 4:11

Isaiah 53:5
Jeremiah 17:14
Matthew 4:24
Acts 5:16
Acts 8:7
Acts 28:8
James 5:13–15
1 Corinthians 12:10,28
Mark 9:23
Acts 1:8
John 2:1–11
Matthew 8:28–34
Matthew 9:18–19
John 11:17–44
Matthew 4:14–21
Matthew 14:24–33
Matthew 21:18–19
Mark 4:35–41
Acts 9:38–42
Acts 20:9–12
Acts 13:11–12
Acts 8:7
Acts 6:8
2 Corinthians 12:12
Romans 15:18–19
Hebrews 2:3–4
Acts 14 & 17
Acts 12:5–11
Acts 16:25–26
Matthew 13:58
Acts 1:8
Ephesians 5:18
Mark 9:14,23
John 15:16
Romans 1:16–17
1 Corinthians 12:10,28
1 Corinthians 14:21–22

Chapter 9

1 Corinthians 7:7
Matthew 19:12
1 Timothy 4:1–5
1 Corinthians 7:32–35
Colossians 2:10
Genesis 1–2
Matthew 6:33
1 Corinthians 7:3–5
Hebrews 13:20–21
Ephesians 5
1 Peter 5
1 Corinthians 13

Chapter 10

1 Peter 4:10
1 Peter 4:11

Chapter 11

1 Corinthians 12:4–7
Ephesians 4
Exodus 30:22–35 & 31:3–11
Mark 3:14–15
Ephesians 4
1 Corinthians 13:1–3
1 Thessalonians 2

Conclusion

Ephesians 3:20–21

Addendum

1 Timothy 4:14
2 Timothy 1:7
Romans 1:11

If you enjoyed this book, will you help me spread the word?

T HERE ARE SEVERAL WAYS you can help me get the word out about the message of this book:

1. Post a 5-Star review on Amazon.
2. Share the book on your Blog, Facebook, Twitter, Instagram, LinkedIn—any social media you regularly use!
3. Recommend the book to friends—word-of-mouth is still the most effective form of advertising.
4. Purchase additional copies to give away as gifts.